Jesus: The Una

JESUS

THE **UNAUTHORIZED** BIOGRAPHY

Martyn Whittock & Esther Whittock

LION

Published by
Lion Hudson Limited
Wilkinson House, Jordan Hill Business Park
Banbury Road, Oxford OX2 8DR, England
www.lionhudson.com

ISBN 978 0 7459 8094 2
e-ISBN 978 0 7459 8095 9

First edition 2021

Acknowledgments
Scripture quotations are taken from the New Revised Standard Version Bible: Anglicized Edition, copyright © 1989, 1995 National Council of the Churches of Christ in the United States of America. Used by permission. All rights reserved worldwide.

A catalogue record for this book is available from the British Library

Printed and bound in the United Kingdom, April 2021, LH26

In memory of **Colin Smith** (1941–2017), whose quiet but unwavering faith in God will remain an inspiration to us and to all who knew him. His kindness to everyone he met was amazing and his humble, selfless character was a true witness to the Christ he followed. This dedication is a small token of our gratitude for having this man in our lives. One could not have wished for a better role model.

And to **Dr Andrew Chester**, whose vast knowledge of Christology, great humour, and patience made lectures and seminars so enjoyable. His humble kindness knows no bounds and his care for his students was, and continues to be, greatly appreciated. A legend!

Contents

Acknowledgments

We are grateful to a number of people who have assisted us in the writing of this book. These include tutors and lecturers at the University of Cambridge, who contributed to Esther's theological understanding, and family and friends, whose insights and support are greatly valued and much appreciated. We also wish to thank our agent Robert Dudley, as well as Jon Oliver, Josh Wells, Lyn Roberts, Katie Carter, and the rest of the team at Lion Hudson for all of their advice, encouragement, and support.

All errors, of course, are our own.

Preface

This book explores the evidence for Jesus: his life, teachings, actions, and significance. Starting from the accounts in the New Testament, we will carefully explore and analyze these, in order to explain how and why they present Jesus as they do, and what we can learn from their accounts. This involves addressing complications and difficult issues, in order to understand the life and times of Jesus, his context, and his impact on those around him. We will also critically examine the evidence of archaeology regarding the society in which he lived; and the early written sources outside of the New Testament which refer to him. Our objective throughout is to discover something of the reality of this extraordinary person and why such astonishing and controversial claims were, and are, made about him.

CHAPTER 1

A conversation of many "voices"

To write a biography of a man who did not commit a single word to paper (for paper read papyrus), never wrote down his thoughts, never published his manifesto or programme, might seem to pose a bit of a problem. After all, how can we know what this man really thought or what his motivations were? A biography which cannot reference a single word or reflection set down by its subject might appear a little unusual. When one reflects for a moment on the life of Jesus, one has to admit that this is, indeed, the state of affairs. It may come as a surprise because we are not used to thinking of him in this way but it is the undeniable reality. Confucius may not actually have written the so-called *Five Classics*, but traditionally many Chinese people thought he had. Julius Caesar wrote his *Gallic Wars* as a self-promoting combat dispatch that could be put up around the forum in Rome to get his version of events into the public domain. St Augustine wrote his *Confessions* as an autobiography which would set out the development of his inner life as he moved from Roman paganism to Christianity. Alfred the Great wrote his *Preface to The Pastoral Care* so everyone could see his vision for rebuilding Wessex after the Viking Wars. William Bradford wrote *Of Plymouth Plantation*, so those who came afterward would understand why the Pilgrims sailed to North America. We could go on. And today, when biographies are written, they are often as reliant on access to the subject's personal papers and documents, as they are on the thoughts and conclusions of others. Often that is, but not always. For there are, of course, also what are termed "unauthorized biographies"; those where the writer(s) cannot access the private archives of the person about whom they are writing.

For would-be biographers, in these cases, that is not an insurmountable problem, if we have the evidence of those who knew the person, listened to them, set down what they thought. In such cases we are in with a chance. Such evidence might be at one-remove, but it is pretty close to the subject and many historians of the medieval, classical, and ancient world would be very pleased indeed to have sources which were, almost certainly, eyewitnesses (or connected to eyewitnesses) of the events they describe. As we shall shortly see, this is arguably the case when it comes to reconstructing the life, times, thought, and impact of Jesus. This is so, even if later commentators on these texts disagree over the extent to which these sources record the actual words and events of Jesus and his life; or debate whether or not these are the constructs of a community of believers in the generation following these momentous activities. We will return to that issue shortly, because we will need to establish something of the nature of these crucial pieces of written evidence. In addition, if we can cross-reference these sources to other corroborative pieces of evidence then our exploration can really begin to gain traction. And this is true whether these other "witnesses" specifically refer to the events we are exploring or simply corroborate the impression we are getting of the life, times, outlook, and teaching of Jesus.

The perspectives of the Gospels

The Christian "canonical" (officially accepted) Gospels abound in details concerning the life, movements, and experiences of Jesus and date from very close to his lifetime. This does not mean that they have to be accepted as accurate, but they certainly *claim* to be eyewitness reports, or at least closely associated with eyewitnesses and – whether they are accurate or not – the time-proximity of their compilation to the events described is striking. From a historian's point of view it is actually a great strength that there are four of them. This gives us different perspectives on events, and recognizes that all four share certain core beliefs about Jesus and his impact. It also means that we have a broad base of evidence; we are not just dependent on one definitive document which has been edited in order to create one official and acceptable version. What is sometimes claimed to be a weakness (four Gospels, which at times offer differing versions of events) is, in fact, a substantial strength. And the sheer number of surviving early manuscripts of the four canonical Gospels is remarkable; as is their high level of agreement with each other. One should also note the rapidity with which the four canonical Gospels were accepted as authoritative within the early Christian communities. Also, it should be remembered that this was a time before Christianity commanded state power to impose orthodoxy.

There is strong evidence, from the writings of early church leaders, that all four canonical Gospels were accepted across most church communities by about the year 180.[1] The so-called *Muratorian Fragment* suggests that the basic New Testament canon was in place by the year 200.[2] That is not, of course, the date of its writing but, rather, of the acceptance of a collection of long-established documents constituting what we now call the New Testament; and the exclusion of other documents which were regarded as lacking authoritative connections to the first generation of believers. With regard to actual manuscripts: there survive some 5,300 in Greek (with very high levels of textual agreement); and 10,000 manuscripts survive in Latin, Syriac, Coptic, etc.[3] Famously, the *John Rylands MS P52,* of the *Gospel of John* has been dated to as early as 100–150;[4] the *Chester Beatty MS* (containing many of the letters) dates from c. 200.[5] Almost all of the New Testament is present in surviving manuscripts compiled before the year 300. Soon after this date, complete parchment manuscripts survive (containing virtually the whole New Testament). And this is all prior to the church possessing coercive state power sufficient to enforce uniformity. This is remarkable, to put it mildly. What it basically means is that we can be extremely confident that, when we open the New Testament today, we have what was written; and footnotes in the best editions (and in commentaries) give us insights into the best attested variant readings where these occur in the surviving manuscript evidence. We will also argue that the outline of events they recount is broadly corroborated by other forms of evidence regarding religious beliefs, politics, and society.

This does not mean that what they say necessarily represents what actually happened. More-conservative and more-liberal scholars differ over this matter. The former would describe them as rooted in eyewitness accounts of those present at events or from communities with strong connections to those present. In short, they are rooted in historical information, albeit framed and composed in order to present a faith case. The latter would reject their historical credentials and, instead, describe them as products of the later Christian communities' confession statements of their proclaimed faith (even legends) which sought to present these as based on the original words and deeds of Jesus.[6] Non-believers and sceptics might argue that just because a person says something was said or occurred does not mean that it actually was or did. But, whatever the stance taken, it does mean that we have a range of different accounts regarding Jesus and his significance which *were compiled very close to the time of the "events" they describe.* And many experts would argue that these are rooted in the memories of eyewitnesses. This then leaves the matter to the individual of whether to believe them or not.

The authors of this book come down on the side of those who argue that we have in the Gospels a record that is rooted in eyewitness accounts, although accepting that they were compiled, framed, and redacted in the context of communities of believers who had strong beliefs regarding the significance of Jesus, and who wanted to present their case through the words and actions of the one they had come to believe had been sent by God. We will leave readers to decide whether they accept the authenticity of these claims and whether they concur with the original compilers concerning the supernatural agency, power, and significance of Jesus. The authors have their own beliefs and views regarding this, but will not be imposing those on readers. Readers must make up their own minds. What we have aimed to do is to analyze, explore, and explain what was presented and claimed about the life of this first-century Jewish preacher and teacher; and to set this in the context of the time, in as far as the evidence survives sufficient to achieve this.

The role of a modern biography

So, having said that we don't have any words written by Jesus, we now seem to have reached the point where we can conclude that people claiming to be eyewitnesses were writing down reports of his life, words, and actions within a generation of these occurring. So, in that case, who needs a modern biography? Surely we have four already? We call them the Gospels of Matthew, Mark, Luke, and John. Of these, Matthew, Mark, and Luke are often termed the "synoptic gospels" because they contain many of the same stories and teaching; often similarly arranged; using comparable or at times identical wording. The description is derived from a Greek word, meaning to broadly see things from the same point of view. All four Gospels were written in Greek, the international language of the eastern Mediterranean in the first century AD. Most of the authors probably spoke Aramaic at home, understood Hebrew in the synagogue, and used Greek to get the message out to the widest audience possible. Plus, by the time of compilation, the early Christian community was well on the way to becoming Greek-speaking and was no longer a sect within Judaism. This was a seismic shift for a Jewish group, believing in a Jewish messiah.

Many experts believe that the Gospel of Mark was the first Gospel to be written, probably around the year 70. The same general agreement would accept that the Gospel of Matthew and the Gospel of Luke were both composed sometime in the 80s.[7] These latter two seem to have been written independently of each other and used significant amounts of material peculiar to themselves. For example, the familiar events associated with the Christmas story are found only in Luke; on the other hand, the visit of the Magi is found only in Matthew and this Gospel contains none of the other well-known traditions concerning Jesus' birth. However, despite this, they seem to have used a version of the Gospel of Mark (possibly one slightly earlier than the version we have today), along with material that was not in Mark. This additional material may have been in the form of a collection of Jesus' sayings.[8]

This hypothetical collection of sayings is often referred to as the *Synoptic Sayings Source* or, more usually, "*Q*" (from the German word *quelle*, meaning "source"). *Q* may have been compiled very early indeed; maybe as early as the 40s or 50s. What is called *Q* no longer exists as such, but many experts believe it can be traced through the common material found in Matthew and Luke and so can broadly be reconstructed from this usage. It is even possible that Matthew used a slightly different version of *Q* to that used by Luke. Or it may be that Luke followed the order of *Q* more closely.[9] But that is getting more complex than we can attempt to explore in this overview. Some experts think it is possible to deconstruct the synoptic gospels in order to identify a number of, once-independent, written collections of traditions associated with Jesus: collections of miracle stories, collections of sayings revealing heavenly wisdom, passion accounts, and so on. These once-independent sources, it is argued, were originally collated by particular church communities, in order to support their specific theological interests, liturgies, and teaching needs. The Gospel-compilers then incorporated them into their writings. How convincingly the identification of these original sources can be done varies between different scholars proposing this approach and there is no one agreed view on this.

Early church tradition, from as far back as Papias of Hierapolis (died: c. 130), is that somewhere behind the Greek-language Gospel of Matthew lay a much earlier work written in the Aramaic language, to which the later – Greek – Gospel was in some way indebted. Papias actually claimed that the original was written in Hebrew.[10] Modern experts are divided on this and most of them would disagree with this traditional claim, since Matthew carries no linguistic traces of it being a Greek version of an Aramaic/Hebrew original.[11] Perhaps Papias was referring to a collection of sayings that Matthew drew on, rather like the collection called *Q*? The matter is far from certain.

Finally, we come to the Gospel of John. This Gospel is very different to the other three and comes from a quite different literary tradition. Some think it is the work of a single man described in this Gospel as the "disciple that Jesus loved" who, it is claimed, wrote this Gospel, three letters attributed to John, and the book of Revelation. Others argue that there was a group of authors who wrote in a similar style, with numerous layers of careful editing. Although this Gospel is more developed, reflective, and symbolic, it achieves this by focusing in on a narrower set of events and themes. It is, therefore, arguably more theological. But this should not be overstated, as the other Gospels are also clearly focused on making key points regarding belief.

The general consensus among experts is that the Gospel of John was compiled later than the other Gospels but may still have drawn on much earlier oral traditions and even on some written sources now lost to us. More conservative scholars would definitely assert this. It was once fashionable to give it a second-century date but, given that the earliest manuscript dates from about 120 and was probably copied several times before that, and undoubtedly had a back-story of circulating among churches in Asia Minor prior to that, it was almost certainly compiled much earlier than some have suggested. With its emphasis on being thrown out of synagogues due to Christian faith (formal Jewish rejections of Christian belief date from about the year 90, but this was the culmination of a period of conflict) the Gospel could have been compiled any time between years 70 and 100. This would make its date of composition more comparable with the other Gospels.[12]

It will be noted that we have used the names Matthew, Mark, Luke, and John as the names of the writers of these Gospels, but some would conclude this is overly simplistic and that these are actually personal names anchoring these accounts in particular communities scattered around the eastern Mediterranean, rather than the individuals who actually penned them. Some, such as John's Gospel, have been described as the work of a group of writers. In contrast, church tradition, it should be said, has tended to link these compilations to particular high profile members of the early church whose Christian credentials went back to the time of the ministry of Jesus. In this book we shall use these personal names for simplicity, although accepting that things were possibly (probably) rather more complex than this suggests. But, however these accounts finally came together, they were made up of collections of traditions that claimed to represent authentic words and deeds of Jesus. The early church certainly soon differentiated them from other – later – material, which included additional letters and Gospels that never made it into the accepted canon of the New Testament. This brings us to these other potential sources of "gospel" evidence.

There is a possibility that some early material may also survive into some, at least, of the non-canonical gospels which survive from the second century onward. Making sense of these in trying to construct something of the life, words, and deeds of Jesus is very contentious indeed. On one hand some *may* contain some evidence not found in the four canonical Gospels. We know – from Papias of Hierapolis again – that oral traditions (often termed *agrapha*, unwritten things) were still being passed down among Christians who believed they had originated with the first apostles. This was as late as c. 110, and Papias (controversially from our perspective) appears to have valued these collections even more highly than the written Gospels with which we are familiar.[13] As a result, we will at times explore and assess some of this additional material. We get hints about this kind of evidence, paradoxically, within the New Testament itself. In Acts 20:35 the apostle Paul, while staying briefly at Miletus (in modern south-western Turkey), gave instructions to a group of church elders summoned there from the Christian community at Ephesus. Paul famously stated,

> In all this I have given you an example that by such work we must support the weak, remembering the words of the Lord Jesus, for he himself said, "It is more blessed to give than to receive."[14]

The significant thing about this is that this saying is unknown, apart from in this context. It does not appear in any of the four Gospels and it reveals that Paul was aware of sayings of Jesus (probably orally transmitted) that were current among early Christians but did not make it into the Gospels.[15] There were, undoubtedly, many more like this. The *First Epistle of Clement* (written between 70 and 140, and probably around year 96) calls on its readers to remember the words of Jesus but without referencing any particular written account.[16] This may be another piece of evidence concerning circulating sayings (oral and written), in addition to the Gospels.

However, although there is no reason to question the authenticity of the example from Acts, other possible oral survivals are more contentious and constitute a very mixed group. Much of it, we would contend, is not admissible as evidence when attempting to construct a biography of Jesus. This is because – although some survivals of the oral tradition prized by Papias deserve our attention – most are hugely compromised by their origins in groups who were committed to presenting a very different view of both Jesus and "gospel" to those accepted as essentially authentic and authoritative by mainstream early believers. The *Gospel of Thomas*, the *Gospel of Philip*, the *Gospel of Truth*, and the *Gospel of the Egyptians*, are often referred to as "Gnostic gospels" because of their origins among fringe heretical groups and the fact that they were compiled much later than the canonical Gospels. These particular ones (written in Egyptian Coptic with Greek titles) were unearthed at Nag Hammadi, in Egypt, in 1945. There, thirteen manuscripts (containing fifty-two texts) date from the third and fourth centuries.[17] Not all of those discovered there claimed to be gospels or, for that matter, Christian. The Nag Hammadi documents are the only surviving examples of these particular texts. Most were clearly produced by Gnostic sects (named from the Greek word *gnosis*, "knowledge") and contain information deeply at odds with the New Testament. With an emphasis on secret knowledge known only to a spiritual in-crowd, they are clearly a totally different genre of later literature to the earlier canonical Gospels; and the mainstream church never accepted them.

Some, such as the *Gospel of Thomas*, are not of this type and have only come under the "Gnostic gospel" umbrella due to being found with the more extreme texts. The *Gospel of Thomas* may, therefore, be worth exploring for some surviving early material, not found elsewhere.[18] A saying such as "He who is near me is near the fire. He who is far from me is far from the kingdom"[19] may be an *agraphon* worth consideration as a possible saying of Jesus. However, it also contains passages of baffling obscurity which are certainly not accepted as authentic by most modern biblical scholars.[20] A number of these reveal Gnostic influence.

Other Gnostic gospels include the *Gospel of Peter* (the first such text to be discovered in Egypt, in 1886), the *Secret Gospel of Mark*, and the fragmentary *Gospel of Judas*. The *Gospel of Mary* is not actually a gospel, as it has little to say about the life of Jesus and deals more with a purported conversation between Mary (clearly Mary Magdalene) and the male apostles after the resurrection. It has given rise to highly controversial claims about a relationship between her and Jesus.[21] A similar theme of a purported relationship between Jesus and Mary

Magdalene appears in the *Gospel of Philip*. We will examine the evidence for Mary (and the other women among Jesus' followers) in a later chapter, but suffice it to say here that there is nothing about this particular document (or the *Gospel of Philip*) in support of it representing authentic early traditions.

Overall, we will assess whether there is any useful evidence in these accounts, or whether they are simply sensational fictions designed to promulgate the extreme beliefs of marginal groups within the early Christian community. Certainly, the Mary Magdalene we meet there would have shocked and astonished the writers of the New Testament Gospels. But is there any "history" in any of these radical claims? We shall explore and decide.

To this evidence from gospels (canonical and non-canonical) could be added evidence from the very beginning of the Acts of the Apostles. And then there are some clues within the early Christian teachings we find in the letters of Paul. In fact, the letters of Paul form the earliest definite layer of Christian literature since they pre-date the composition of the Gospels as we now have them. Probably dating from the 50s, they were being penned within about two decades of the life of Jesus. However, they contain very little in the way of personal details about Jesus, being mostly statements of what Christians believed about him, along with answers to theological and personal issues raised by the early Christian communities.

So, to return to an earlier question. With all this apparently biographical detail available in the various gospels, who needs another biography?

This is an understandable question. But the answer is very straightforward: none of these are biographies! They are faith statements. They were written to persuade their readers that the Jewish preacher and teacher, known as Jesus, was God's chosen messiah (*Christ* in the Greek of these early documents), sent to complete the revelation of God seen through Judaism, and to save the world from its sins. As a result, the Gospels were not hastily scribbled-down despatches from the front line, as Roman sentries paced the Jerusalem streets. They were not records written by the light of a flickering oil lamp in the evening after the diarist had witnessed the feeding of the five thousand, or the healing of the daughter of a desperate Syro-Phoenician woman who had sought out Jesus. No, they are carefully crafted and constructed to make a point. Furthermore, they were written down some time after the events they describe (although still very close to these events when compared to other ancient sources). As the writer we know as Luke explained to his Roman patron,

> Since many have undertaken to set down an orderly account of the events that have been fulfilled among us, just as they were handed on to us by those who from the beginning were eyewitnesses and servants of the word, I too decided, after investigating everything carefully from the very first, to write an orderly account for you, most excellent Theophilus, so that you may know the truth concerning the things about which you have been instructed.
> **(Luke 1:1–4)**

As we read the Gospels we see reflection, selection, explanation. This is not to catch-out the Gospel writers. Nor is it to reject the historicity of what they wrote. It is simply to recognize the obvious: they were written for a purpose. But if as historians we are to understand the nature of the person and the events they describe, we will need to look at, through, and behind their words in order to decide exactly what led to these words being written in the first place. In a sense these are records of an "earthquake" – the impact of Jesus on these people – and what we need to do is to try to piece together exactly what that "earthquake" was all about. In as far as we can do this, our aim is to try to ascertain why that "earthquake" occurred; its relationship to previous "earth tremors" and "aftershocks"; exactly what happened and who was involved; the impact on those around and on nearby "structures"; and why some people rapidly began claiming that it was an "earthquake" in the first place!

As well as this, there are lots of things that the Gospel writers simply do not tell us. We are left with so many questions. Why would a Roman emperor's edict be able to send a heavily pregnant women off to the ancestral family town at Bethlehem? And did such an edict actually occur? Who was Herod and how come we seem to have two of them, at the start and end of this story? And what was the power play going on between him/them and the Romans? If Jesus was a carpenter's son in Nazareth, did that make him a lowly worker or a skilled artisan? And would that have affected the kind of life he lived, the experiences he had, and his outlook? What was life like in the homes, streets, fields, and towns of Galilee? And why the focus on distant Jerusalem, which dominates key parts of Jesus' life and death? Did everyone see the Pharisees and Sadducees as bad guys (the Gospel writers certainly seem to) and who were they anyway, and what was their problem with Jesus? What was the core of Jesus' teaching and was its biggest impact religious, social, or political (after all, he was arraigned on religious charges before a Jewish court but executed on political charges by a Roman one)? How do we reconcile the accounts of his movements between Galilee, Jerusalem, and elsewhere, and does it matter? Was the man bigger than the message, and what does his view seem to have been on this? Did he actually claim to be the "messiah", or the "Son of God", when his favourite self-description was "Son of Man"? And what about the role of women in his personal life and within his group of followers? What about resistance fighters and political radicals among his innermost group of followers (they were certainly there)? And on, and on... That is why a biography is justified.

Other "voices" in the "conversation"

In order to achieve this, we will need to listen to, and assess, a wide range of "voices". Together they make up the "conversation" (at times an argument) about this man and his impact. As we do so, we will explore the strengths and weaknesses of each different clue, its agenda(s), how it has been used and abused, its problems and its potential. The written sources of evidence are varied. As we have seen, they include the four so-called canonical (official) Gospels of the New Testament and clues within some of the letters of Paul (which preceded the compilation of the Gospels). And there may be some admissible evidence within some of the non-canonical gospels if we use them cautiously. In addition, some of those oral traditions – so venerated by Papias of Hierapolis

– occasionally surface in the writings of Christian authors of the later first and second centuries. These too will repay attention.

Then there are Roman written sources. None of these refer to Jesus' activities from his lifetime – and we would not expect them to do so – but they give us an understanding of the power politics at the time. Through them we can piece together the dynamics of power, the military situation, the interaction between Greek and Roman culture on one hand, and Jewish religion, society, and politics on the other. Then other Roman sources will tell us what early Christians were up to, as the faith spread, and what this reveals about their beliefs regarding Jesus. We can track this back toward him. An interesting example is the possible comment on the execution of Jesus under Pontius Pilate, in Tacitus' *Annals* (Tacitus died c. 120). We will look at this in a later chapter but suffice it to say here, its authenticity is much debated, with a number of experts concluding that this reference, in the sole surviving eleventh-century monastic manuscript, represents a later Christian intervention rather than the original words of Tacitus himself. Less contentious is the letter written to the Emperor Trajan by Pliny the Younger, the Roman governor of Bithynia and Pontus (now in modern Turkey), in c. 112, asking advice on how to deal with early Christians. But this, although very useful in identifying Christian beliefs about Jesus (as expressed by a pagan imperial administrator), offers us no information regarding the life and teachings of Jesus himself.

Jewish written sources help us see things from another perspective and we will explore whether they can be used to discover clues about the life of Jesus; or whether they have been distorted by both later conflicts between Judaism and the rival group that arose from within it, and by later Christian interpolation or alteration of existing Jewish accounts. Josephus (died: c. 100) is a key example of this. The surviving manuscript of his work, the *Antiquities of the Jews*, contains two mentions of Jesus and one of John the Baptist. There is much disagreement over whether these are authentic, partially authentic, or later additions. In the last two options this redaction (partial or entire) would have been the work of later Christians keen to see their beliefs supported by references in this well-known, non-Christian, source. The same thing may have led to an adaption of Tacitus' text, mentioned earlier.

Archaeology will not tell us about Jesus the individual man, but it will tell us about his world; and whether artefacts and sites tend to corroborate the impression we get from written sources. From the remains of the synagogue at Capernaum, to the layout of the Temple in Jerusalem and the nearby Roman military fortress, we can assess whether places actually connect with people, events, and claims. And when they do, we will examine how they add to the impression we get from the written sources.

We will also briefly tackle the challenging question of how we can relate the "Christ of faith" of the emerging Christian community to the search for the "Jesus of history"; and what these categories mean and how they impact on writing a "biography" of Jesus.

This, then, is the aim of this book. It is the story of a man known to his contemporaries as *Yeshua*, to the world as Jesus, to Muslims as *Isa*, and to Christians as the *Christ*. It is the "unauthorized biography" because we will hold up all the claims and evidence to critical scrutiny. Some have claimed it is "The Greatest Story Ever Told".[22]

CHAPTER 2

Back-story...

As we shall see in due course, Jesus was not actually born in AD 0, whatever our modern dating system insists. Nevertheless, his story begins within a decade of that date. Understandably, our usual start for any exploration of the life of Jesus is at his birth. However, in order to really understand what was going on when that occurred we need to explore the life, times, society, and politics in the eastern Mediterranean at the end of the first century BC/start of the first century AD. Consequently, this chapter sets the scene in the society, religion, and power politics of that time period and that geographical area. This will allow us to better examine issues of how the later life and teachings of Jesus related to contemporary Jewish culture: from the experiences of the ordinary men and women on the street to the religious elites of Jerusalem, and religious communities such as the compilers of the famous *Dead Sea Scrolls*. It will also help us get acquainted with something of the political geography of the area, its intrigues, and its conflicts. This will help explain why there were so many "messiah conversations" occurring in his lifetime. The eastern Mediterranean of the time was an unsettled, vibrant, dramatic, multicultural world of both complex cooperation and conflict. *Plus ça change!* And it was into that world that Jesus was born.

Then and now

Were we to superimpose a modern political map onto the world of Jesus we would find that it included the modern State of Israel; the Palestinian-administered areas of the West Bank and Gaza; Jordan to the east of the River Jordan and the Dead Sea; Syria, with the Golan Heights contested with Israel; Egypt and Sinai to the south-west; and Lebanon to the north.[1] It does not take much awareness of twentieth- and twenty-first-century history and politics to realize that these names and political boundaries are today heavily freighted with contested values and meanings. One person's "Palestinian territories" or "occupied West Bank", is another person's "*Eretz Yisrael*" (Land of Israel)[2] being reinforced by Jewish settlers. One person's legitimate boundary is another person's imposition of divisive power. Even to use the term "Palestine" as a geographical term is highly contentious to some because it now has a strong political connotation and can be viewed as implicitly reducing concepts of modern Israeli sovereignty. The offence can easily be repeated in reverse. The modern map and its terminology offers a veritable minefield before the unwary.

In an attempt to avoid this (unintentional) offence to any readers – and to avoid any anachronistic use of political terminology – we will endeavour to use the labels and terms used at the time. However, in order to give modern readers a geographical fix it is inevitable that, from time to time, we will have to use descriptive phrases such as "this site is located in what is now Jordan" or "the closest legionary troops were stationed in what is now Syria" or "this route would have led from Galilee, via the West Bank, to approach Jerusalem from the east", and so on. But we will try to defuse the more contentious and explosive terms by using contemporary labels wherever possible.

The impact of geography

The area that interests us is situated in what has traditionally been described as the "fertile crescent". This "crescent" of land sweeps from the head of the Persian Gulf (north of the Arabian Desert); through the river plains of the Tigris and Euphrates; skirts the Syrian Desert, which lies to its south; then dips down along the coastal strip of the eastern Mediterranean; and onto north-eastern Sinai. Some definitions allow it to leapfrog northern Sinai and include the Nile delta of Egypt, and even extend down the Nile valley. Above the outer curve of this crescent, more mountainous land stretches north and north-westward into Anatolia (modern Turkey) and north-eastward toward the Caucasus and the Caspian Sea (into modern Georgia, Armenia, Azerbaijan, and Iran).

Today, this great sickle of land, often referred to as the "fertile crescent", mostly includes Iraq, Syria, Jordan, and Israel-Palestine (with that possible extension into Egypt). The term has been used for over a century and was popularized by, among others, the archaeologist James Henry Breasted in his books *Outlines of European History* (1914) and *Ancient Times, A History of the Early World* (1916). This remarkable area has historically been one of the cradles of global human civilization, containing early urban centres, high levels of population, and sophisticated material culture. As a result, it has been crossed by major trade arteries and its accessible land (in contrast to the desert and the mountains) has also made it the route-way of choice of many invading armies intent on bringing this area within the orbits of competing early imperial systems. Over time and geography these have included Babylon to the east, Assyria in the centre and to the north, and Egypt to the south-west. And sandwiched between the ambitions of these great (though fluctuating empires) were the competing kingdoms and communities of "Palestine" (used here as a geographical term), with the Mediterranean to their west. From out of the desert these communities were also, at times, menaced by the nomadic tribes of the northern desert areas, where seasonal grass provided fodder for these nomads' flocks and herds. Often referred to as part of the Middle East we might also call the area at its largest extent Western Asia.

It is also sometimes called the Levant, derived from the Italian *levante* (rising) and referring to the rising of the sun in the east. This effectively means "the east" as seen from the perspective of the southern Mediterranean states of Europe. The term Levant has a more tightly focused meaning than the other two terms (Middle East and

Western Asia) and covers modern Syria, Lebanon, Jordan, Israel, and the Palestinian territories.[3]

Heavily contested, it is no surprise to learn that this area is no stranger to the power politics and military strategies of those living beyond it. And that fact has played a major part in composing its mood music over the millennia. It continues to do so.[4] In the century preceding the birth of Jesus this was once again in play and its ramifications would be felt throughout his lifetime. It is to that political context that we now turn.

Enter the Greeks...

By the time of Jesus, the international language of the eastern Mediterranean was Greek. This was despite the area having come within the Roman sphere of influence by that time, with its Latin language. Although by then dominance had shifted from the initial political power of Greece (more on that in a short while), the basic Hellenistic (Greek) influence remained very strong indeed. This extensive Greek influence, already spreading across the eastern Mediterranean, was given a massive boost by the campaigns of Alexander the Great (lived: 356–323 BC). In 334 BC he campaigned down the Mediterranean coast of the Levant, through an area known to Greek geographers as *Palaistinē* (Palestine).[5] For him it was a corridor leading to the wealthy far-flung Persian province of Egypt. Alexander was engaged in a long-running Greek-Persian animosity which eventually led to the defeat of Persia at the hands of this Macedonian king.

The area through which he marched was a mosaic of little states and communities, part of the patchwork of peoples of the Persian Empire, which was itself the successor to the Babylonian Empire which had dominated the area before it. That earlier empire had fallen to the Persian (Achaemenid) ruler Cyrus the Great in 550 BC. All the communities in the area that the invading Greeks called "Palestine" were living in the administrative region known by the Persians as the *satrapy* of *Abar Nahara* (across the river). It stretched from the Euphrates to the Sinai Peninsula.[6]

Here were found Jewish and Samaritan communities, among many others. None of them were living in independent states at this time. The Jewish community around Jerusalem was descended from the southern Jewish kingdom of Judah which had earlier been conquered by the Babylonians. The Samaritans were descended from the northern Jewish kingdom of Israel, ruled from Samaria. Having broken away from the southern kingdom on the death of Solomon (c. 931 BC) it had been conquered by the Assyrians (c. 722 BC). Large numbers had been deported by the conquerors. These constituted the so-called "lost tribes". Due to the mixing of the remaining Jewish population with other groups brought into the area by the Assyrians, the Jewishness of its inhabitants was rejected by its southern neighbours. Differences in practices added to the estrangement. This explains why there was little love lost between Jews and Samaritans by the time of Jesus. North of Samaria the relatively high and rocky area of Galilee was also ethnically rather mixed. As far back as the prophet Isaiah (Isaiah 9:1), it had been described in Hebrew as "*g'lil ha-goyim*" or "Galilee of the nations". Traditionally composed in the eighth century BC, parts of Isaiah have been assigned a sixth century or later date by a number of modern biblical scholars. However, the reference to Galilee comes from a part of the work that may well be late eighth- or early seventh-century in date.

The campaign by Alexander brought the area under Macedonian (Greek) rule and opened it up to a fresh influx of Greek culture. When Alexander died in 323 BC, the region changed hands a number of times as his successors fought over his empire and carved off pieces for themselves. These wars are sometimes referred to as the wars of the *Diadochi* (the successors) and these were followed by the Syrian Wars. The latter being six wars fought between the Seleucid Empire and the Ptolemaic Kingdom of Egypt; both of whom were successor states of Alexander the Great's extensive empire.

The area that would later be known to Jesus ultimately fell to the Seleucid Empire between 219 and 200 BC. This empire was based on Babylon and it was not the first time that the Jewish communities and their neighbours had come under the authority of a state based there. Indeed, it had been the Babylonians who had conquered Jerusalem and destroyed the first Jewish Temple there in 587 BC. In 116 BC, a civil war in the imploding Seleucid Empire gave opportunities to those semi-independent client-states who were unhappy with Greek rule from Babylon. One of the areas which benefitted from the Seleucid weakness was the Hasmonean principality in the Judean mountains, which asserted its independence. The opportunity for increased assertiveness allowed this hill-country statelet to extend its influence north into Samaria; east into Transjordan; and south into Idumea (which straddled land south of the Dead Sea and earlier had been called Edom) where the inhabitants were given the choice of conversion to Judaism or expulsion. They converted.[7] Hasmonean power was extended further north into Galilee under the Hasmonean king Aristobulus I (reigned: 104–103 BC). This reasserted and entrenched Jewish culture in the area; although it would still be regarded as something of a backwater in the time of Jesus (from the perspective of the Jerusalem elites anyway) and still possessed recognizable signs of ethnic complexity.

The Hasmoneans were a Jewish dynasty which was descended from the family of the Jewish nationalist leader, Judas Maccabeus, who had led resistance against the imposition of Greek religion and culture by the Seleucid ruler, Mithradates (also known as Antiochus IV Epiphanes) who died in 164 BC. The Old Testament book of Daniel (with its staunch defence of Jewish faith in the face of pagan persecution) is thought, by many modern biblical experts, to have been written in its current form during this time of pagan persecution of Judaism and the resulting Jewish fight-back. Antiochus IV persecuted both Jews and Samaritans. This radical Hellenization involved attempts to eradicate Jewish religious beliefs and culture, alongside the promotion of Greek religious cults, language, and culture. Although the religious campaign of Antiochus IV failed, the influence of Greek language and its culture (from theatres to gymnasia) continued to spread.

Tension between this Greek way of life and Jewish traditional culture provides a backdrop to much of life in the area in the period leading up to the ministry of Jesus. This could lead, as we shall see, to some interesting complexities. For example, the city of Sepphoris (with its theatre and mosaics featuring Dionysus and Heracles) was a mere 3.7 miles (6 kilometres) north-north-west of Nazareth and yet Jesus never appears to have visited it and it is not mentioned in the Gospels. It was just an hour's stroll away, yet it is as if it was not there. It is going too far to describe it as a "Greek city", but perhaps there was something about its Hellenization that brought its Jewish character into question? This may explain the absence of references to some other Galilean towns too, as we shall explore in due course. Less ambiguous was the huge impact of Greek as an international language and the presence of Greeks and Greek communities (such as that of the *Decapolis* – the "Ten Cities") that do appear in the Gospel accounts.

From 110 BC, the Hasmoneans extended their authority over much of what the Greeks called Palestine, creating an alliance (even if at the point of a sword) between Judeans, Samaritans, Idumeans, Itureans (living north of Galilee), and Galileans. The dominance of the Judeans over an expanded region led to the state being referred to as "Judea". Before this, the label had only been applied to the much smaller region of the Judean hill country. It was a return to independence for a Jewish state such as had not been experienced since the fall of the kingdom of Judah, with its capital in Jerusalem, in 587 BC. It was not to last.

Enter the Romans...

Between the years 73 and 63 BC, the leaders of the Roman Republic extended their influence into the region as a result of what is known as the Third Mithridatic War. They conquered Judea in 63 BC, and broke up the once-independent Hasmonean kingdom. Under Roman influence it became five districts. This was done by the Roman general, Pompey the Great. He intervened in a civil war being fought by rival members of the Hasmonean family and appointed one of the rivals, Hyrcanus II, as high priest of the Jerusalem Temple. However, Pompey downgraded him by refusing him the title of "King", which had been used by his predecessors. Instead, he was allowed "High Priest and *Ethnarch*" (governor of a people but not a king). Clearly, the Judean kingdom was being brought into line by the new power in the region. As evidence of this reduction in status, Pompey also imposed Roman taxes on the Jewish population and restricted Jewish influence outside its heartland of the old southern kingdom. This was demonstrated when Pompey granted what amounted to virtual autonomy to a group of Hellenized cities, afterward known as the *Decapolis*, placing them under the jurisdiction of the newly appointed Roman governor of the province of Syria (annexed to the Roman Republic in 64 BC). All but one of them (Scythopolis) lay beyond the River Jordan (immediately east of Galilee, Samaria, and Judea). Today these sites are in the modern states of Jordan and Syria.

The arrival of the Romans was a game-changer and other political players scrambled to adjust their strategies in order to make the most of the new realities and possibilities. After the death of Pompey, the person that he had installed as high priest, Hyrcanus II, was eclipsed by the strategies of a man named Antipater. He was an Edomite, the son of the governor of Idumea, and would be remembered as the father of the future king, Herod the Great. Although the Edomities/Idumeans had converted to Judaism, their ethnic and religious purity had aspersions cast on it by Jews living in the old Judean heartland of Judah. This goes a long way toward explaining Herod the Great's later attempt to show himself as a benefactor to Judaism in the rebuilding of the Jerusalem Temple. The snake pit of contemporary politics goes a long way toward explaining his murderous paranoia. But more on that in due course.

Antipater played his cards with some skill. In return for backing Julius Caesar in the turmoil of Roman politics, he received both Roman citizenship and the title of "procurator of Judea" (Latinized as *Iudaea*). The family was on the up. His sons, Phasael and Herod, were appointed by the Romans as *strategoi* (governors) of Jerusalem and Galilee, respectively. It was part of a well-developed Roman strategy of ensuring that border areas were administered by loyal client-rulers. Hyrcanus II was marginalized by the power politics occurring around him.

Then, in 40 BC, the applecart was upset in dramatic fashion. The Iranian Parthians briefly conquered the region. Roman ambitions to conquer the empire once ruled by Alexander the Great – up to and even beyond the Euphrates – had set them on a collision course with this state. In 54 BC the Roman general Crassus launched an invasion of Parthia that ended with his death which, according to legend, was caused by molten gold being poured into his mouth in mockery of his thirst for wealth.

The Parthians struck back and invaded Roman territory. They set up a puppet ruler of their own in place of Rome's client. This new ruler was drawn from the Hasmonean family and so appeared more legitimate than the Idumean *parvenus*. He briefly ruled as Antigonus II. Phasael was reported to have committed suicide; Herod went into exile in Rome. Hyrcanus II, who had been high priest (and briefly confirmed by Julius Caesar, in 47 BC, in the rank of *ethnarch*), was mutilated and taken off to Babylon. The cutting off of his ears made him ineligible for the priesthood, so any return as high priest was out of the question. And his chances of achieving kingship were now long gone.

The rise to power of Herod

By 37 BC the Parthians had withdrawn and it was back to Roman business as usual. Herod, in exile in Rome, had done well for himself. He had been recognized by the Senate, as "King of *Iudaea*" in 40 BC. This was due to the patronage of the up and coming Octavian (who would become the first emperor in 27 BC, and is now better known as Augustus) and Mark Antony (who committed suicide with Cleopatra in 30 BC having been defeated by Octavian). Herod returned to his lands in 39 BC. Shortly after his arrival Roman troops expelled the Parthians. Herod's road to power had a little way to go yet since he still faced a threat from Antigonus II, who had been installed by the Parthians. Eventually – and assisted by the Roman military – Herod seized Galilee and went on to capture Jerusalem and seize Antigonus II in 37 BC. In effect this was the end of a fiercely independent Jewish state, although officially Herod was a semi-independent client king. His official title (as accorded by the Roman Senate) was in Latin: "*Rex socius et amicus populi Romani*" (allied king and friend of the Roman people). This rather obscured the fact that he was totally dependent on Rome and owed Rome everything. The Roman view of things was practically expressed in what happened to Antigonus II. He was executed on the orders of the Roman general Mark Antony, which rather indicated where the decision-making power lay. And his form of death – crucifixion in some accounts,[8] beheading in others[9] – was a brutal reminder of what happened to any ruler who stepped out of line and attempted independence from Rome. Both the Roman historians Cassius Dio (who says he was crucified) and Plutarch (who says he was beheaded) commented that it was unprecedented to inflict such punishments on a king.

After the defeat of Antigonus II, Herod married Mariamne, a niece of the deposed king. It was clearly a gesture designed to win over those who had previously been loyal to the Hasmonean house. Herod's position as head of a Jewish state was complicated by the fact that he was, in effect, an outsider. As an Idumean (Edomite) his Jewish credentials were open to question. Many traditional Jews had hoped for something rather better. Herod was well aware of this, hence the marriage to Mariamne. He also consolidated his power by inviting Hyrcanus II back to Jerusalem from exile in Babylon and then executing him on a trumped-up charge. By this time, Hyrcanus may have been as old as eighty.

Until 4 BC King Herod ruled as an ally of Rome. Although he had backed the wrong side in the civil war between Octavian and Mark Antony, he was reconciled with Octavian after the defeat of Mark Antony (and his Egyptian ally Cleopatra) and had his kingship of Judea confirmed.

By 20 BC Herod had regained the Jewish lands that Pompey had taken from Hyrcanus II, along with land that Herod himself had lost to Cleopatra of Egypt (despite the fact that Herod was an ally of both her and Mark Antony). As a result, his kingdom included not only traditional territories across the diverse area of *Palaistinē*, but also areas to the east of the River Jordan in Perea and Esbus;[10] and tracts of land in what are today southern Lebanon and Syria, including two of the Decapolis cities;[11] and the region of Iturea which lay north-east of Lake Huleh. There is evidence that the Emperor Augustus intended to grant him the wealthy Nabataean kingdom too (which stretched down the eastern shore of the Red Sea). However, when that throne fell vacant Herod no longer had the mental or physical well-being to make him a safe pair of hands. He was no longer in Augustus' favour. His time was past.

Herod's rule was long, peaceful, and stable for the majority of the time. Among many building projects he ordered the construction of a new city at Caesarea (*Caesarea Maritima*) on the Mediterranean coast. The late-first-century AD Jewish historian, Josephus, praised it for its fine port and its impressive drinking water and sewerage system. He established the city of Sebaste on the deserted site of ancient Samaria. Both were Greek-inspired communities, more pagan than Jewish. Both were named after Herod's patron Augustus (taking their names from his adopted family name "Caesar", and "Sebaste" the Greek form of "Augustus"). This was typical of Herod's strategy of signalling his loyalty to the Roman superpower and also acting to secure the loyalty of his pagan as well as Jewish subjects. At Sebaste he ordered the building of a temple dedicated to the worship of Emperor Augustus; and Caesarea included another pagan temple, as well as the usual Hellenistic amenities of a theatre and hippodrome. Herod was clearly trying to ensure he had all his bases covered.

In the Judean desert he built a fortress palace named Herodium and extended the fortress of Masada beside the Dead Sea. In Jerusalem he built the fortress of Antonia and a lavish palace. As well as these projects, he built many aqueducts, fortresses, theatres, and other public buildings across his kingdom. He donated money to building projects outside his own kingdom and was even a patron of the Greek Olympic Games.

Most significant of all was his rebuilding of the Jerusalem Temple. The resulting construction was magnificent, with its huge central building set within a great sanctuary surrounded by colonnades, and with its inner and outer courts of increasing sanctity and religious exclusivity. This was the building that Jesus would have known, although today it has vanished except for the surviving retaining West Wall (once called the "Wailing Wall"). This was designed to overcome the stigma of his foreign origins which affected how many of his contemporaries viewed him. For example, he was frequently in conflict with the Pharisees, the leading faction within Judaism, because they regarded him as a foreigner. In order to buttress his Jewish credentials he built new enclosures around the traditional burial sites of the Old Testament Jewish patriarchs at Hebron and Mamre. But his more orthodox Jewish critics knew that he had also built pagan temples, and centres of Greek-style athletics which offended traditional Jewish cultural norms.

Herod ruled as a Hellenized king in grand style. He is often titled Herod the Great. Though not how we normally recognize him from the Christmas story. Toward the end of his reign, however, things began to unravel. Having married nine wives and fathered many children, the succession was anything but clear. It was in the intra-family bloodletting that arose from this that Herod executed his wife, Mariamne, and his sons by her, Alexander and Aristobulus. In this bloody purge he was egged on by his sister Salome and – shockingly – by Mariamne's own mother, Alexandra. The charge was adultery. Herod went on to kill Mariamne's brother, her grandfather, and her mother (despite the latter's part in denouncing her own daughter). He changed his will three times and finally disinherited and then killed his firstborn son, Antipater.

It was this Herod – an increasingly paranoid and vengeful ruler – who was king of Judea when Jesus was born and whom we will come across again in the next chapter.

Second Temple Judaism

The term "Second Temple Judaism" is used to describe the Jewish community between the construction of the second Temple in Jerusalem in about 515 BC, and its eventual destruction by the Romans in AD 70. It was this Jewish community into which Jesus was born.

As a community with a strong religious as well as ethnic sense of identity, political power and religious authority were connected in a complex web. This highly politicized the office of high priest of the Jerusalem Temple with predictably divisive results. Under the Hasmoneans, royal and high priestly powers were combined. Indeed the significance of the latter role was such that their coins often simply carried the formula "X the high priest and the congregation of the Jews". It seems that they were intent on presenting themselves "first and foremost as religious leaders" on these high priestly coins.[12] In this they stood out from other Hellenized rulers in the surrounding area. It was clearly a key part of their cultural identity. This was further emphasized by the fact that the high priestly title was always presented in Hebrew script, whereas any royal titles would also use

Greek or Aramaic script.[13] When the Romans first intervened heavily in the area they initially suppressed the kingly title, while allowing the continuation of the high priestly one. Attempting to combine both roles in one person had been a factor leading to the end of the brief period of Judean independence.[14]

This emphasizes the extreme importance of the Jerusalem Temple, its priests, sacrifices, and cult[15] in the life and culture of the Jewish people. Alongside the temple priests, there were educated Jewish religious elites – that we will meet again – who played a major role within the life of the Jewish community. The two most prominent ones were the Pharisees and the Sadducees. As a broad generalization: Sadducees tended to be wealthy aristocrats, and their centre of power was the Jerusalem Temple with its chief priests and high priest, Pharisees had greater connection with the masses and controlled the synagogues; Sadducees did not believe in the existence of an unseen, spiritual world, Pharisees believed in angels and demons; Sadducees accepted aspects of Hellenization whereas Pharisees opposed it; Sadducees stressed the rites and role of the Temple, whereas Pharisees emphasized the detailed daily observance of Mosaic Law; Sadducees recognized only the written Torah (in the first five books of the *Tanakh*, the Hebrew Bible), whereas Pharisees emphasized the Oral Torah, the books of the Prophets (the *Nevi'im* in the Hebrew Bible), the Writings (the third part of the Hebrew Bible, called the *Ketuvim*), and the resurrection of the dead. The Sanhedrin, the seventy-member supreme court of the Jewish religious community, contained both Sadducees and Pharisees in its membership but the Sadducees had a majority.

In addition to the great religious sacrificial centre of the Temple, there is mounting evidence for the spread of synagogues among Jewish communities. These first appear in documentary sources in the third century BC, though most of the evidence regarding them dates from the first century AD onward. But their widespread nature by then, both in the Jewish homeland and in communities across the Mediterranean indicates that they were well established by the time of Jesus. As places for communal gathering to study the Jewish Law and to be reminded of its precepts, they were both teaching centres and statements of community identity. Synagogues would also be the location of local courts, secure places for depositing community funds, and places for local meetings. We will return to them in greater detail when we explore their role within the ministry of Jesus, but suffice it to say at this point that in the last century before the Christian era, we can assume that they were a major part of Jewish community life, whether that was in Jerusalem, the villages of Galilee, or the Jewish diaspora from Alexandria to further afield. In this veneration of sacred literature, the Jewish people stood out from the non-Jewish peoples around them.

A further group within Judaism under Herod were the Essenes. The New Testament does not mention them but written references to them exist in the writings of Josephus (writing in the AD 90s), Philo of Alexandria (died: c. AD 50), and Pliny the Elder (died: AD 79). The first two were Jewish historians, the latter Roman. These accounts differ in significant details, which may indicate that the Essenes were not a homogenous movement with uniform beliefs.

It is thought that the origins of the Essenes lay in the second century BC and that they were a reaction to the seizure of the office of high priest (combined with secular power) by the Jewish nationalist leaders Jonathan Maccabeus and, later, Simon Maccabeus. Essenes – protesting at this and facing persecution as a result – fled into the wilderness. The one they described as the "Teacher of Righteousness" may have been the leader at this point or may always have been a future apocalyptic end times figure. One biblical scholar has suggested that Hyrcanus II was the figure known as the "Teacher of Righteousness", and that Antigonus II was the figure known as the "Wicked Priest", in the scrolls (*Pesher Habakkuk* or *MS.1QpHab* and *Pesher Nahum* or *MS.4QpNah*) found in the vicinity of Qumran.[16] Or this identification may have varied over time, with differing apocalyptic interpretations of changing contemporary events.

The Essenes' conflict with the temple authorities, along with the upheavals of the time, caused them to develop an apocalyptic outlook, focusing on God's decisive action to overthrow the "wicked priests" based in Jerusalem and vindicate their Essene critics as the true priesthood and the true representation of Israel. It has been suggested that their communal meals were thought to pre-figure the messianic banquet in which God's elect would partake.

Forming monastic communities that, generally at least, excluded women, property was held in common and a programme of disciplined communal life and manual labour was followed. Having fallen out with the Jerusalem priestly elite they shunned worship at the Temple. There were never huge numbers of Essenes; Pliny assessed their number as c. 4,000. Like Pharisees, they were rigorous followers of the Law of Moses, with its detailed rules regarding Sabbath observance and ritual purity. Like the Pharisees, they believed in life after death and a future judgment, but saw this in a purely spiritual form with no bodily resurrection.

It is thought, by many modern experts, that Qumran, on the north-western shore of the Dead Sea, was one of their communities. It was near here, in 1947, that the *Dead Sea Scrolls* were discovered in a cave. Since 1949, excavations at a site called Khirbet Qumran (which is situated less than a mile from the Dead Sea and north of a waterway called Wadi Qumran) have unearthed the ruins of a large number of buildings. It is not proven beyond doubt, but many believe that this site was occupied by a community of Essenes, who were the owners of the *Dead Sea Scrolls*. It has been postulated that the Essenes established the community at Qumran in the middle of the second century BC. This may have occurred during the reign of the Hasmonean Simon Thassi (ruled: 142–135 BC) and no later than the reign of John Hyrcanus (ruled: 134–104 BC).[17] Later rabbinic literature remembered the latter as *Yoḥanan Cohen Gadol* (John the High Priest).[18]

During the reign of Herod the Great, an earthquake (in 31 BC), and accompanying fire, caused the temporary abandonment of Qumran. Despite this, the community resumed its life there and this lasted until it was destroyed in AD 68 by Roman troops suppressing the First Jewish Revolt. These appear to have remained at the site (as a garrison) until c. AD 73. When the Second Jewish Revolt occurred (AD 132–135), Jewish rebels briefly established a base there.

There is much debate regarding whether any Essene ideas can be detected in the later teaching of Jesus. The New Testament makes no mention of them or their beliefs. We will return to that question in due course. Suffice it to say at this point that the Essenes contributed to an atmosphere of apocalyptic expectation which grew during the years of Hasmonean rule (with its politicized high priesthood), Herod's reign (with its increasing, and controversial, gentile influences), and then accelerated under Roman occupation. As a result, as Jesus was growing up, a great many "messiah conversations" were happening in Judea and Galilee. This was a significant legacy of the century leading up to AD 0.

CHAPTER 3

"O little town of Bethlehem"

All that we know about the birth of Jesus comes from the New Testament Gospels of Luke and Matthew. Luke contains all the main traditions now associated with Christmas. These include (in chapter 1): the miraculous birth of John the Baptist to elderly parents, as fulfilment of an angelic promise; the visit of the angel Gabriel to Mary[1] in Nazareth, with the announcement of her forthcoming virgin pregnancy and birth of a son who is to be named Jesus; Mary's visit to Elizabeth (the pregnant mother of the future John the Baptist); the birth of this forerunner of the Messiah. Then, in chapter 2, we have the well-known account of a Roman census; the journey of Joseph and his betrothed (not actually his wife at this point, according to Luke, although this may simply mean the absence of consummation) to Bethlehem; no room for them to stay, so Jesus is placed in a manger; angels appearing to the shepherds who hurry to Bethlehem; the circumcision and naming of the child; his presentation in the Temple. This is all in one very full chapter of Luke, which goes on to include a visit by the twelve-year-old Jesus to Jerusalem (although it must be remembered that the division of the New Testament into chapters and verses was not a feature of the original and did not appear until the ninth century and only became established from the thirteenth century). This, as recounted in Luke, is the structure of the familiar Christmas story.

Matthew, on the other hand, contains no birth traditions at all. In chapter 1, verses 18–25 we hear of: Mary's pregnancy by divine power; Joseph's plan to set her aside, due to her pregnancy; an angelic messenger who reassures him in a dream that "the child conceived in her is from the Holy Spirit" (Matthew 1:20); instruction that the child should be called Jesus "for he will save his people from their sins" (verse 21); a statement that this fulfils a prophecy in the Old Testament book of the prophet Isaiah; Joseph's rescinding of his original divorce plans and his subsequent marriage to Mary but having no sexual relations with her until after Jesus is born. Then, in chapter 2, Matthew recounts the visit of the – unnumbered – *magi* (the "*We three kings*" of the carol and school Nativity plays) to Jesus in Bethlehem, guided by a star. This clearly is not a birth tradition, as such, since there are indications within this account which suggest that Jesus may have been as old as two years when this event occurred.

The account of the magi starts with a visit by them to Herod in Jerusalem; is followed by their arrival at a "house" (no stable here) in Bethlehem, to see Jesus; the giving of the famous gifts; dream warnings to the magi and to Joseph concerning Herod's murderous intentions; the magi leaving without returning to Herod; the threatened family fleeing to Egypt; Herod's massacre of the children in Bethlehem. After Herod's death, another angelic messenger tells Joseph it is safe to return but Joseph fears the intentions of Herod's son, Herod Archelaus, and so the family move from Egypt to Nazareth, in Galilee. Throughout his account, Matthew anchors events on what he describes as prophecies fulfilled (virgin birth, messiah born in Bethlehem, the flight to Egypt, the massacre of the children, Jesus "a Nazorean").

It should be noted that there are no birth narratives whatsoever in Mark's Gospel (probably the first written) or in the Gospel of John. In Mark, Jesus bursts onto the scene as a man – sometime, we assume from other evidence, around the year 30. In John (probably the last canonical Gospel to be written) there is the famous prologue which reflects on the divine nature of Jesus. This includes a dramatic and memorable exploration of a being described in Greek as the *Logos* (the Word) and the incarnation (becoming a human being) of the Logos/Word. This famous reflection in the fourth Gospel provides a profound insight into how Jesus came to be regarded by his early followers, after his death and the resurrection that they declared so determinedly. But it does not provide us with any biographical details – whether these details found elsewhere are regarded as persuasive historical information or carefully crafted faith statements. They are simply not found in Mark, nor in John.

It seems that both Luke and Matthew (in different ways) felt the need to add a birth narrative to the earlier Gospel of Mark, as part of their development of what they found there. This is possibly because in Mark the declaration of Jesus' divine sonship only occurs at his baptism by John, as we shall see in due course (Mark 1:9–11). This *could* give the impression that it was at this point that God "adopted" Jesus or that this was, in some way, the result of John's baptism.[2] If so, Luke and Matthew headed off this misinterpretation with their birth accounts which emphasize the divine status of Jesus. So, it is to Luke and then Matthew that we will turn.

Before we do so, a note of caution. The compilers of these two Gospel accounts were trying to do more than simply record traditions that they believed correct. They were also writing faith statements. As a result, it is not easy to bolt their accounts together, although so-called "harmonizations of the Gospels" are fairly common. This is what many Christians often tend to (unconsciously) do when they read the Gospels. However, the reality was more complex. Since this will occur again and again, it is important to be clear about this from the start and the birth of Jesus is a good place to do this.

The Gospel writers selected traditions known to them and presented them in order to make a point. They also adapted features from these traditions in order to communicate things to their readers. Much time can be spent (and, arguably perhaps, wasted) trying to make the accounts do what they were never intended to do in the first place. They need, instead, to be read on their own terms. When it comes to the birth of Jesus, Luke is different to Matthew. But this leaves puzzles…

Why did Matthew leave out the Roman census? For Luke this was why Jesus' birth occurred in Bethlehem. Did Matthew not know of it? Did he think it all started in Bethlehem? Or was he sidestepping the Nazareth tradition so as to make Jesus' conception start where his life would climactically finish – in the vicinity of Jerusalem, the cultural capital of Judaism? This is possible.

Why did Luke leave out the dramatic tradition regarding the magi, Herod's attempt to murder Jesus through the "Massacre of the Innocents" (as it later came to be known), and the escape of the family to Egypt? Perhaps he did not know of it from his sources. Or perhaps, contra-Matthew, he wanted the epicentre of his dramatic story of Jesus' life to be firmly *rooted* in Galilee. From there it flowed over to the vicinity of Jerusalem at the birth, then Jesus' visit to the city as a twelve-year-old (Luke 2:41). Then back to Galilee, before a reference to Jesus being briefly taken to the pinnacle of the Jerusalem Temple by the devil during the temptations (Luke 4:9). Then it's back to Galilee again as the main focus, until the end of Jesus' life. Incidentally, Matthew only takes Jesus to Jerusalem the once after the birth accounts; in the final weeks of his life (Matthew 16:21).[3] We will explore the issue of the Jerusalem-connection later and none of this precludes Jesus from going annually (or more often) to the great city and its amazing Temple. All it means is that these Gospel compilers don't tell us about it and that may have been simply because they were constructing particular lenses through which we see and understand the significance of Jesus.[4]

Each had points they wanted to make. These points differed, although they shared common ground in principle, if not in historical detail. Each worked their material to do this. Each adapted and explained what they had before them. Each had a "take", a "point of view". Each had a bigger goal in mind than the minute detail of each aspect being subjected to historical scrutiny and forensic comparison. We usually ask, "Is it true?" The original readers asked, "What does it mean?"[5] This is not to say that veracity regarding details does not matter. Rather, that there were, for the writers, even more pressing issues. And there may be features whose detailed historical accuracy we might question.

So, as we shall see, there will be complications. Some things may not entirely dovetail with other evidence. There will be uncertainties. The accounts may differ (although we should not assume that "difference" necessarily involves "contradiction"). We will avoid a lot of stress by admitting that now.

That said, the writers definitely thought that things actually happened and that these were important and revealing. That is why, again and again, similar things occur in the Gospels. Things are insisted on. They thought they were grounded in fact, even if the details varied and sequences of events might change. That is the approach of this book too: that these accounts are grounded in traditions that are cogent and rooted in real events. And, even when we cannot verify something (no modern historian can prove the virgin birth or that angels appeared to shepherds, for example), we can still explore *why that mattered* to the compilers of the Gospels. And *what it was intended to communicate* to readers. Modern readers can decide whether it occurred. That is not the job of this book.

For some, that is simply *not going far enough* in accepting the accounts as given. For others, it will be *going far too far* in giving them credence. It is a matter of balance. In exploring the birth accounts, the approach of this book is that here there is historical evidence; but evidence that needs scrutiny and questioning. And that, even when there appears to be issues of historical accuracy, the message and meaning is crucial and was what we were meant to grasp. Furthermore, the kinds of world and society described certainly can be scrutinized, analyzed, and verified in order to better understand the points being made.

When was Jesus born?

This is not as obvious a matter as it first appears. The earliest Christian accounts – as recorded in the New Testament and as early oral traditions that might survive in some non-canonical literature – have no dates attached.

Today we are very familiar with a Christian dating system of AD (*Anno Domini*, "in the year of our Lord") for events after the birth of Jesus. And BC ("Before Christ") for events before that. This has become so widespread across the globe that it has been adopted regardless of Christian faith by vast numbers of communities. Increasingly, it has been adapted to reflect this in the form: CE ("Common Era") and BCE ("Before Common Era"). But the pivot point of Jesus' birth remains central to both systems. Even in many Muslim communities (which have their own, *Hijri*, calendar, dating events from AD 622 when Muhammad and his followers migrated from Mecca to Medina and established the first Muslim community), the AD/CE dates are often used alongside the Islamic year as numbered in the AH calculation.[6] So AD/CE 2020 in the AH calendar would be AH 1442. Among traditional

Jewish communities, the system used since the Middle Ages is the AM or *Anno Mundi* one ("in the Year of the World"), in other words, from the creation of the world). For example, the year AM 5780 began at sunset on 29 September 2019. But as with Muslims, the usual dates used in communication are the AD/CE dates. These dates have become global norms.

So, it may come as a surprise to discover that the AD/CE dates are incorrect. The Bulgarian monk Dionysius Exiguus, who devised the AD dating system, thought he lived 525 years after the birth of Jesus, although he never clearly said how he calculated this. There is no evidence that he had before him any more evidence than we do in the twenty-first century; and this was the evidence found in Luke and Matthew. Both these writers say that Jesus was born during the reign of King Herod (Luke 1:5; Matthew 2:1). In addition, as we shall see, Luke later tells us that "Jesus was about thirty years old when he began his work" (Luke 3:23). Earlier in that same chapter he has said that the preaching ministry of John the Baptist (which rapidly includes the baptism of Jesus, at the start of *his* ministry) occurred,

> In the fifteenth year of the reign of Emperor Tiberius, when Pontius Pilate was governor of Judea, and Herod [Antipas] was ruler of Galilee, and his brother Philip ruler of the region of Ituraea and Trachonitis, and Lysanias ruler of Abilene, during the high-priesthood of Annas and Caiaphas.
> **(Luke 3:1–2)**

A number of these people will be key players in the later story as we piece together the adult biography of Jesus. But at this stage their importance lies in their assistance with chronology.

We know, from well-attested multiple sources, that Tiberius became Roman emperor in AD 14. Allowing for no more than a year from the start of John the Baptist's ministry ("In the fifteenth year of the reign of Emperor Tiberius") to the start of the ministry of Jesus (who was "about thirty years old when he began his work"), and subtracting thirty years, takes us back to AD 0. This is, apparently, right on target for the birth of Jesus. And that is clearly what Dionysius Exiguus did.

However, he made mistakes. First, he had no understanding of the concept of zero. Both as a placeholder and as a symbol for nothing, it was a late arrival in Europe.[7] Consequently, in his calculation he omitted the year 0, so that in his system we jump from one year *before* Jesus' birth to one year *after* his birth. It is as if we had 1999 and 2001 but no year 2000! In addition, he decided, for no particularly persuasive reason, that Jesus was born 753 years after the legendary founding of Rome. Plus, he assumed that Jesus was exactly thirty years old when he started his ministry (which is not what Luke actually wrote). As a result, he identified the year of Jesus' birth and established a dating system which today is universally used. But things are more complex than this. Which takes us to the census referred to by Luke, by way of the death-date of King Herod.

The death of Herod and that Roman census...

From other evidence we know that Herod the Great (so-called due to his building projects and to differentiate him from other Herods) died in (according to the BC/AD system) 4 BC. This would place the birth of Jesus in or before 4 BC, according to both Matthew and Luke (due to the references to Herod in their accounts). It was probably two or three years before this as children up to the age of two were killed by Herod, according to Matthew. This suggests Jesus was born about two years before this event.

However, things are yet more complex. In a passage now famous from Christmas celebrations and carols, Luke explains that,

> In those days a decree went out from Emperor Augustus that all the world should be registered. This was the first registration and was taken while Quirinius was governor of Syria. All went to their own towns to be registered. Joseph also went from the town of Nazareth in Galilee to Judea, to the city of David called Bethlehem, because he was descended from the house and family of David.
> **(Luke 2:1–4)**

This is extremely important in Luke's account because it explains why Bethlehem was the birthplace of Jesus. According to the Jewish historian, Josephus, this census took place in AD 6, when Publius Sulpicius Quirinius took up his post of governor (imperial legate) of the Roman province of Syria, at a time when Judea was annexed to it following the deposing of Herod Archelaus.[8] This was ten years after the death of Herod the Great.

So, according to Matthew, Jesus was born before 4 BC (the death of Herod). According to Luke, he was born between that date (the reference to Herod) and AD 6 (the reference to Quirinius). It seems that, as it stands, Luke's account cannot be entirely accurate (in other words, one cannot date the event *both* from Herod *and* from Quirinius as governor). It is possible that Luke meant a different governor or a different census.[9] Perhaps Luke's sources indicated that "this census was *like* the one that took place during Quirinius's [later] governorship"?[10]

However, other evidence indicates that Quirinius was conducting military operations in the region while Quintillus Varus was imperial legate in Syria between 6 and 4 BC. The Greek term in Luke, that is usually translated as "governor" (*hegemoneuontos*) actually covers a number of governmental capacities. This could cover the earlier role held by Quirinius. This fits very well with the Herod evidence, so there may have been some kind of imperial administrative event at this time which involved him. Or he might have served two terms as imperial legate of Syria: the one mentioned by Josephus and other sources regarding AD 6, and an *earlier* appointment as well. A fragmentary inscription (unfortunately not including the name) found at Tivoli, near Rome, in 1764 records a man who had served twice as imperial legate (governor) of Syria. This may have been Quirinius.[11] In which case, Herod and Quirinius can be placed together in the right place at the right time. We should not automatically assume that a complication implies an error.

Finally, Luke says that "Jesus was *about* thirty years old" at the start of his ministry, so he clearly never claimed exact knowledge of this, despite the fact that this has then been used as the basis of specific calculations which go beyond Luke's actual statement. In short, a few years could easily be added or subtracted from the calculations regarding both Jesus' birth date and his exact age at the start of his preaching ministry. Pontius Pilate's governorship (AD 26–36) fits this broad pattern but the Gospels do not tell us exactly when within this governorship Jesus was crucified, nor his exact age at that point.[12] The best we can say is that Jesus was probably born sometime between about 7 BC and AD 6. This date-outline combines Pilate's governorship with the age of "about thirty" we referred to earlier; and Herod's death and the possibilities regarding Quirinius.[13] Most likely, Jesus was born in about 7 BC.

Both Matthew and Luke had access to traditions that this occurred while Herod was king of Judea, and Luke explains that a Roman census occurred at around this time, which brought Mary and Joseph to Bethlehem. The evidence suggests that the apparent conundrums are solvable.

The issue of apparent illegitimacy and the virgin birth

Both Matthew and Luke believed that there were questions about Jesus' legitimacy. The dramatic account of the angelic visit ("the Annunciation") in Luke underscores this, as does Joseph's consideration of breaking off the engagement in Matthew. This is a striking feature of both accounts. Even in John's Gospel – where there is no account of Jesus' birth – the assertion of the Jewish opponents of Jesus that "*We* are not illegitimate children; we have one father, God himself" (John 8:41, emphasis added) makes one wonder if they were trying to make more than a theological point about their spiritual status. It may also be why the people of Nazareth later refer to him as "the son of Mary", with alternative readings in some manuscripts of "son of the carpenter and of Mary" (Mark 6:3), which again emphasizes the position of Mary in an unusual fashion.

Be that as it may, Matthew and Luke were clear that there was an issue here that required explanation. Mary was pregnant before marriage and before sexual relations with Joseph had occurred. Although neither Mark nor John refer to the virgin birth, there is nothing in their accounts which clash with this as a strong Christian tradition rooted in the earliest beliefs of the church. Mark's opening claim that Jesus is the "Son of God" (Mark 1:1)[14] and John's account of the incarnation (John 1:1–18) make sense alongside this belief. Not all would accept this, but it seems a reasonable conclusion and there is simply no justification for pitting the Gospels against each other on this issue. Similarly, although the absence of any theology of the virginal conception of Jesus in the writings of Paul is striking, his highly exalted view of Jesus as the Christ (his *Christology*) is certainly not at odds with it. He states belief in,

> The gospel concerning his Son, who was descended from David according to the flesh and was declared to be Son of God with power according to the spirit of holiness by resurrection from the dead, Jesus Christ our Lord.
> **(Romans 1:3–4)**

This is certainly not a theology of the virgin birth but it does not contradict it either. It could be asserted that there is a hint of "adoptionism" about this, with Jesus' divinity being marked more by his resurrection than by belief in his miraculous birth or pre-existence. But the overall theology of Paul indicates this is not the case and is a warning about making too much from individual verses. Nevertheless, whereas the virgin birth was not a major theme for Paul, it clearly was a significant one that was explicitly stated by other early Christians. There is no Jewish parallel to this and attempts to present this as a Christian version of pagan myths involving gods having sex with human women falls far short of the mark. Whatever it is, the Christian claim about the virgin birth (there is not the slightest hint of sex) is far distant from Greek mythology and the behaviour of Zeus and other Greek deities.

Neither is it convincing, as has been done, to assume that there was nothing unusual about Jesus' conception, but that the whole complexity, as we now have it, was the invention of the later church in order to provide a mythical origin for the man they had come to consider was the Christ, the Messiah.[15] It is too freighted with possible scandal for that.

The woman at the centre of this event is already betrothed. The word implies much more than the modern word "engagement", which appears in some modern translations. To break it was virtually to divorce. Luke does not say why Mary has "found favour with God" (Luke 1:30) but most interpretations are that her depth of faith and her moral uprightness caused her to stand out. The child she is to have will be called Jesus. That is the Latin form of the Greek name, *Iēsous*, which appears in the Gospels. This, in turn, was a Greek form of the Aramaic name *Yeshua*, which was a first-century version of the older Hebrew name, Joshua. It means "Deliverer", "Rescuer". *Yeshua*, and its longer form, *Yehoshua*, was a common name in the first century. In the Gospels we hear of two other men with this name. The first is Jesus Barabbas, the criminal released by Pilate instead of Jesus (Matthew 27:16–17). Some manuscripts omit the first name, and this may have been because their transmitters had become protective of the name Jesus. But at the time many men would have carried the name. When Saul and Barnabas later visited Cyprus on a missionary journey they met, at Paphos, "a certain magician, a Jewish false prophet, named Bar-Jesus" (Acts 13:6). The name was not unique.

Yet the angel insists that the child is. In Luke's account, we read that he will be "great". This is a word earlier applied to John. But then the status climbs. The phrase "Son of the Most High" could have been understood as applying to a divinely blessed king, since the idiom of sonship was used in early Jewish discourses on human monarchy.[16] The reference to "the throne of his ancestor David" could also be read in this light, as Jewish hope focused on a divinely appointed and anointed messiah (Hebrew *mashiach,* Greek *christos* hence "Christ") ruling in the style of the Old Testament King David and from his royal line (either literally or in spiritual descent). However, the next descriptor – that this ruler "will reign over the house of Jacob for ever, and of his kingdom there will be no end" – clearly broke the boundaries of most contemporary understandings of the status of the looked-for messiah. Although there is much about first-century Jewish messiah-expectations that we do not know, its limited duration, leading to the establishment of God's eternal kingdom, seems apparent in much of it. This, the angel declares in Luke, is not how it will be. Instead, the Messiah himself will have an authority that is exponentially greater than expected. This angelic assertion reveals the way that Christians were recounting and expressing the significance of Jesus by the time that Luke compiled his Gospel sometime in the 80s. The social and religious implications of this are staggering. Socially, an unmarried woman is going to have to manage a situation of extraordinary scandal, as her neighbours would view the situation. Theologically, the claims about this baby would break the boundaries of first-century Judaism.

Most modern people reading the Gospel accounts jump straight to the main narrative and ignore the genealogies that we find in both Matthew (chapter 1) and Luke (chapter 3), or simply refer to them as evidence that early Christians considered Jesus' descent from King David to be a defining feature. But in Matthew there is rather more to it than this. There are women where we would not expect them, in this list of patrilineal descent (emphases added): "Judah the father of Perez and Zerah *by Tamar*" (verse 3); "Salmon the father of Boaz *by Rahab*, and Boaz the father of Obed *by Ruth*" (verse 5); "And David was the father of Solomon *by the wife of Uriah*" (verse 6). These are highly significant women. Tamar, Rahab, and Ruth were definitely Gentiles. Rahab, in addition, was a prostitute. The wife of Uriah, Bathsheba, may have been foreign too but, even if not, the adulterous action by David cast a shadow over her status. And yet here they are, listed by Matthew as ancestresses of Jesus. Clearly, he was making a point. If questions were raised about Mary, then there were others through whom God had worked who also would have been discredited by contemporaries. The radical nature of the statement being made is extreme.[17]

That Luke also recognized this is apparent in the challenging nature of the "Magnificat" (Luke 1:46–55) which he states is declared by Mary. Phrases such as "he [God] has looked with favour on the lowliness of his servant", "he has scattered the proud", and "He has brought down the powerful from their thrones, and lifted up the lowly" remind us of the radical roots of Christianity, its counter-cultural message, and its openness to attack by those who questioned its legitimacy. This is firmly embedded in the birth narratives but is often obscured by our modern – rather sanitized and tinselled – version of the Christmas story. Whether a later Christian poet composed this and Luke put it in the mouth of Mary, or Mary composed it in the style of Hannah in the Old Testament (1 Samuel 2:1–10) no one can say for certain.

Later Jewish opponents recognized the importance of this to emerging Christianity, claiming that Mary was made pregnant by a Roman soldier. A lowly member of the occupying power was clearly included to add depth of insult. Worse, Mary is presented as a prostitute.[18] In some later Jewish traditions she is described as "Miriam" the "long haired woman" which was clearly meant to imply a prostitute (loose hair in public being culturally taboo) and represented a fusion of Mary the mother of Jesus with Mary Magdalene (who herself had been combined with the woman "who was a sinner' referred to elsewhere in the Gospel of Luke).[19] It should be emphasized that there is no evidence whatsoever to support this allegation and it was clearly designed as an insulting attack on Christian assertions regarding Jesus' birth. The Babylonian Talmud also has a curious and convoluted tale about the offspring of a mule that can possibly be interpreted as a biting ridicule of the Christian belief in the virgin birth.[20]

No twenty-first-century study of Jesus can prove the angelic visitation or the virgin birth, but what we can say is that it clearly mattered to the early followers of Jesus and they were clear that there was something shockingly unusual (by contemporary standards) about his conception. And for that they had a dramatic and challenging answer. It is this that lies behind the account of the visit of the angel Gabriel to Mary. The fact that angels appear in the accounts of the conception of both John (the Baptist) and Jesus was clearly Luke's way of making clear that what he thought of as the "Age of the Messiah" was breaking into human experience in a miraculous form.[21] We will return later to John the Baptist and his role. But now we need to turn to Bethlehem.

No room at... "the inn"?

The order to return to the ancestral home for the census is an unusual one and has caused its historicity to be questioned, but we know that something like this happened in Egypt in AD 104. Bethlehem was the original home of the Old Testament king, David, and was closely associated with the Davidic line.[22] What is clear in Luke is that, though Mary is heavily pregnant, they cannot find lodging. The word traditionally translated as "inn" is actually less specific and means "living space". As such, it could refer to any home opened up to paying guests. The Greek word is used again by Luke, later in the Gospel, when he describes the room used at the final Passover meal, where it is translated as "guest room" (Luke 22:11).[23]

The mention of a "manger" has usually been taken as indicative of location in a stable, but could easily have been in an open courtyard. A second-century Christian tradition was that it was in a cave, used for stabling.[24] We cannot tell. The "bands of cloth" are fully in line with care of infants which emphasized both keeping them warm and also arose from an early idea that they assisted in limbs growing straight.[25] More importantly, the poverty and desperation is clear.

The same applies to the shepherds who come to the scene, explaining that angels sent them. Shepherds were a rough lot. Looked down on for their perceived lack of adherence to strict religious practices, they could not be witnesses in a court of law. For Luke they represent yet more evidence of the new Messianic Age being for the poor and dispossessed and that this was evident from the very start of Jesus' life. When we read one commentator's view that these shepherds must have been "devout men, else why should God have given them such a privilege?"[26] one feels he has rather missed the point.

Luke's account explains that the angel describes Jesus as "Saviour" (the only time this word appears in any of the synoptic Gospels) and "Christ the Lord" (a phrase unique in the whole New Testament). The contrast between contemporary expectations of the Messianic Age and what is actually happening in a cattle feeding-trough is profound.

Modern interpretations vary over whether shepherds "living in the fields" (Luke 2:8) can be used to give a seasonal fix on the birth of Jesus as described in Luke. In Judea (a drier area than in Galilee) they may well have been there throughout most of the year. One thing seems clear, though, the date of 25 December was a fourth-century Christian strategy to take over the pagan Roman feast of *Sol Invictus* (the Unconquerable Sun) celebrated on that date. The date had been mooted in Christian circles (for example by Hippolytus, lived: 170–236) for a century before this. This assumption seems to have been reinforced by the belief that the Annunciation (the appearing of the angel Gabriel to Mary) occurred on 25 March, although there is no evidence for this in the Gospel account. Dionysius Exiguus (who made the mistake in calculating Jesus' birth-date) also accepted this date for the divine conception because of the contemporary Christian belief that God had begun the creation of the world on 25 March. This argument all became extremely circular – and lacked Gospel evidence.

Overall, it is not contrived to read the subtext of Luke's account as representing the birth of Jesus in terms of liberating Israel from Gentile oppression (the Roman census authorities); embodying emancipation, like an Old Testament "Jubilee year" (by echoing language found in Leviticus 25); but being rejected by Israel (no room provided in King David's town, despite Mary's condition).[27] However, the truth is revealed to – and accepted by – the marginalized (the shepherds).

It is reasonable to assume that Luke's assertion that "Mary treasured all these words and pondered them in her heart" (2:19) is a claim to authenticity based on access to church traditions uncovered by the compiler that stretched back to Mary herself. That Quirinius (Roman governor of Syria according to Luke) minted coins at Antioch (where Luke may have compiled his Gospel) showing a star above a sheep, has been suggested as inspiration for Luke's account.[28] Christian tradition, though, would protest that this is too reductionist and minimalist an explanation.

What Matthew brings to the discussion

As we have seen, for Matthew the story of Jesus begins in Judea under the rule of King Herod. We last met Herod engaged in massive building projects and in shoring up his Jewish credentials as ruler of Judea. Here he is presented as a new pharaoh set on the murder of children (as Pharaoh did in the book of Exodus); but failing to kill the targeted one (Jesus), just as Pharaoh failed to kill the one appointed to God's special task (Moses). However, one greater than Moses is targeted here. The account of Jesus' birth is also implicitly linked to King David by the explicit reference to "Bethlehem of Judea" (David's home town), to avoid any confusion with another Bethlehem, in Zebulun (at the southern end of the Galilee region).

The arrival of people described as *magoi*, with their gifts of gold, frankincense, and myrrh was clearly meant to underscore the message that God's relationship with the Jewish people has broken out of ethnic boundaries since these travellers are clearly non-Jews, and are representatives of pagan culture (*magoi* is related to "magician", though we often sanitize it as "wise men") who have been brought to recognize God's messiah. The term *magoi* is derived from a Persian word (*magush*) referring to a class of astrologer.[29] It is clearly such star-studying experts that Matthew is asserting travelled in search of the newborn king. This stands in stark contrast to Herod and the people of Jerusalem, who are clearly intended to represent the Jewish people.[30] One must remember that by the time Matthew wrote his Gospel (probably in the 80s), Judaism and the Christian community were parting ways.

There are no parallels to the star/magi in the other Gospels and the Greek contains expressions characteristic of Matthew's Gospel which suggests that this was a tradition unique to Matthew and his source(s). As historians we cannot categorically test his account against any other evidence other than to state that on 17 April 6 BC Jupiter had a heliacal rising (appearing as the morning star).[31] Other modern writers have suggested that Jupiter crossed the paths of both Venus and Saturn in 7 BC;[32] or the sign represented a regal portent based on an eclipse of Jupiter by the moon (seen by pagan astrologers as representing the god Aries) in 6 BC;[33] or the magi saw two meteors seen at different times but moving in the same direction;[34] or it may refer to a comet which (according to Chinese sources) appeared for seventy days in 5 BC.[35] Such phenomena as these may have been regarded as highly significant by astrologers from (probably) Zoroastrian Persia (modern Iran).[36]

On the other hand, Matthew states that the star went "ahead of them" and "stopped over the place where the child was" (Matthew 2:9) which does not seem to describe the kind of phenomena that we have just suggested. In which case, Matthew had something in mind either more miraculous (that we cannot test) or theologically symbolic. In the Old Testament, in Numbers 24:17, we hear that "a star shall come out of Jacob, and a sceptre shall rise out of Israel". The second-century AD Jewish nationalist (messianic?) leader, Simon *Bar Kokhba*, appears to have adopted this name, meaning "Son of the Star", as a result of its messianic connection. So, Matthew may have had something more symbolic in mind than astronomical phenomena. On the other hand, he may have known that a celestial phenomenon had certainly occurred about the time of the birth of Jesus, and seen it as a sign of an event of cosmic significance.[37]

Intriguingly, the Greek writer Ptolemy explained that heliacally rising planets can appear "stationary". [38] And Geminus of Rhodes used the same verb that lies behind Matthew's "ahead of them" to describe what is called planetary retrograde motion.[39] Consequently, Matthew's account may be more accurate than is sometimes given credence and based on astrological terms to describe a historical phenomenon; albeit one then presented in a messianic way. We would contend that it is incorrect to detach Matthew's account from historical events and to interpret his Gospel as a reading-back of celestial events (such as the comet of AD 64) into the birth of Jesus in order to highlight messianic significance to that birth.[40]

The reaction of Herod to the magi's assertion – though undocumented in other sources – is entirely consistent with the final years of this increasingly unstable and paranoid king.

A flight into Egypt is also entirely plausible, although Matthew also sees it as being highly significant – with God later calling his Son out of Egypt, as once before he had called the Jewish people out of that same nation under Moses. History and theology are closely connected in these accounts.

The intended geography of the birth and early-childhood accounts

In Matthew the occasion of the angelic message to end the Egyptian exile is the first appearance of Nazareth in this Gospel account, which to this point has been entirely focused on Judea (Bethlehem and Jerusalem being the only places mentioned). For the compiler of Matthew's Gospel, without an angelic dream Joseph would not have taken the family to Nazareth in Galilee. This is curious since, if that was where he had lived before journeying to Bethlehem and then fleeing to Egypt, one might expect it to have been the obvious place to which to return.

From Matthew we would assume that the story starts in Bethlehem. However, he doesn't actually state this, so there is nothing to preclude the earliest part of the story starting elsewhere. Nevertheless, Matthew's statement that Jesus "will be called a Nazorean" (2:23), after the first mention of Nazareth, suggests that, for Matthew, this is the first appearance of Nazareth in the tradition with which he was familiar (hence the association of words). Interestingly, the word "Nazorean" appears not to be derived from the place-name Nazareth (see Chapter 4).

It seems that Luke and Matthew had contrasting mental maps in mind. For Luke it was: Galilee, then to Bethlehem in Judea, and then back to Galilee. For Matthew it was: Judean focused (Jerusalem/Bethlehem), then to Egypt, and finally to Galilee due to specific threats being located in Judea. Both clearly knew that Galilee was the epicentre of the movement that grew up around Jesus, while understanding that Jerusalem was both the spiritual heartland of Judaism and the crucial location of the dramatic conclusion of Jesus' life and ministry. For Luke, the story started in Galilee. For Matthew it started in Jerusalem. They simply focused on different places, both of which played major parts in the life of Jesus.

Although harmonization of such different accounts is not possible (nor necessary) it must be stated that they do not actually contradict each other. There is nothing in Matthew to preclude a start in Galilee, even if he was not sure why the family ended up there (hence the "Nazorean" suggestion). Similarly, there is nothing in Luke to rule out the magi, who are so central to Matthew, since Luke knew (or recorded) nothing about Jesus' life between his birth and his eventual return to Jerusalem aged twelve. So, we do not have to bolt together the mental maps of these two accounts; neither do we have to divide them.

After Herod... more Herods

When Herod the Great died in 4 BC his kingdom was divided among his sons. Under Roman direction, Herod Archelaus was given the title *ethnarch* of Judea, Samaria, and Edom (central and southern Palestine); Herod Antipas was given the title *tetrarch* of Galilee and Perea (east of the River Jordan); Philip was given the title *tetrarch* of Trachonitis, Batanea, and Auranitis (between the Greek cities of the Decapolis and Damascus in Syria). None were accorded the title "king".

Philip ruled the northern area until he died in the year 34 and another Herod – Herod Agrippa I – inherited his land, and then a wider area after the year 37.

Herod Antipas reigned in Galilee and Perea until year 39 and will play a part in Jesus' ministry and execution (he was then banished by the Emperor Caligula). His tetrarchy lands were then added to those of Herod Agrippa I.

Herod Archelaus was removed by the Romans, at the request of his subjects, in the year 6 and his region (consisting of Judea, Samaria, and Edom) became incorporated into the province of Syria, under direct Roman rule. It was administered by the *praefectus Iudaeae*, who was subordinate to the governor of Syria.[41] One of its prefects, Pontius Pilate (in position: 26–36) will play a key role in the trial and execution of Jesus. Later he would be removed for the massacre of Samaritans. In the year 41 the territories of Judea, Samaria, and Edom were added to the lands of Herod Agrippa I.

From then until his death, in 44, Herod Agrippa I ruled the same kingdom that his grandfather, Herod the Great, had ruled from Jerusalem.

Then, in 44, the entire kingdom passed under Roman rule and was reconstituted as the Procuratorial Province of Judea.

That is the political framework for the rest of this exploration of the life of Jesus. And to it we will return, in more detail, in due course.

CHAPTER 4

Growing up in "Galilee of the Gentiles"

Galilee and Nazareth play a major part in the life and mission of Jesus. But was it a social backwater, a multicultural community, or a political hotbed? What was Galilee really like and why was it so important in the life of Jesus and his followers? And what was the status of the small-town community of Nazareth?

The brief evidence for the childhood of Jesus from the canonical (official) Gospels, and the apocryphal gospels will also be critically examined to see if they contain any relevant evidence. Other first-century evidence gives us insights into this relatively quiet period in the life of Jesus. And just what was the social status of a carpenter and what impact did this have on Jesus and his life?

Galilee: social backwater, multicultural community, or political hotbed?

The centre of most of Jesus' work lay in Galilee. The region of Galilee lay in the north of what is today the modern State of Israel. The regional term Galilee is traditionally used to refer to the upland area within this region, and is often divided into Upper and Lower Galilee. Today, Upper Galilee lies to the north-west of the Sea (lake) of Galilee and borders the state of Lebanon. In its north-eastern corner the mountain cluster of Mount Hermon is the southernmost of the Lebanon mountain chain and straddles the Israel–Syria border. South of this lies the much-disputed area of the strategically important Golan Heights, which lies to the east of the River Jordan.

Lower Galilee lies to the west of the lake and Nazareth (more on this place shortly) is situated in the far south of this area, near Mount Tabor. In the first century the regional administrative centre of Tiberias was located on the eastern edge of this region and lay on the shores of the large lake which dominates this part of the Jordan Valley.

This division of the area is found as far back as the deuterocanonical – or apocryphal – *Book of Judith* (Judith 1:8) which may have been written at the beginning of the first century BC.[1] The division also features in the writings of the Jewish historian, Josephus, in the late first century AD and in the second-century Jewish Mishnah writings. The latter used vegetation to differentiate the regions, with sycamores found in the valleys of Lower Galilee but absent from Upper Galilee.[2]

The name Galilee, as it appears in English, is ultimately derived from a Hebrew term, *Haggalil* (the district), via Latin *Galilaea* and Greek *Galilaia. Haggalil* itself is a compressed form of *Gelil haggoyim* (district of nations) as referred to in Isaiah 9:1 and translated as "Galilee of the nations".[3] This intriguing assessment of the region is important and we shall return to it shortly when trying to decide exactly what Galilee was like as a community.

The so-called Sea of Galilee is a freshwater lake with the remarkable characteristic of being the lowest freshwater lake on earth. It is also the second-lowest lake on earth since the Dead Sea – the lowest – is a saltwater lake. Lake Vostok, the largest of Antarctica's subglacial lakes may challenge both these records but that is a geographical detail we do not need to get further into. Suffice it to say at this point, that this lake in Galilee is a remarkable place. Its modern name – Sea of Kinneret – is derived from the Hebrew name for it in the Old Testament. In the Babylonian Talmud, as in the writings of the Jewish historian Josephus, the name used for it is the Sea of Ginosar, which is derived from the Hebrew name, "Kinneret". In the Greek New Testament Gospels of Matthew and Mark it is called the Sea of Galilee; although the Gospel of John also refers to it three times as the Sea of Tiberias (for example John 6:1), a name used to describe it in the late first century AD. This Roman-influenced name is found in a number of Roman sources and also in the later Jewish text, the Jerusalem Talmud. Interestingly, Luke calls it "Gennesaret" (Luke 5:1) which is a Greek version of the Hebrew name Kinneret. Its impressive size caused the writers of both the Old and New Testaments to describe it as a "sea". The exception to this is the Gospel of Luke where it is described as "the lake of Gennesaret" (Luke 5:1).

The combination of water and surrounding hills makes the lake subject to sudden and violent storms as the wind, passing over the eastern mountains, drops suddenly onto the lake. Storms are especially likely when an east wind blows cool air over the warmer air that covers the water. The cold air (being heavier) drops as the warm air rises. This sudden change can produce surprisingly furious storms in a short time. It is unpredictable and we will find that this meteorological phenomenon appears in the Gospels in the dramatic calming of the storm by Jesus.

Galilee in the first century contained many small towns and villages. Josephus claims that there were 204 small towns in Galilee.[4] Although some modern writers have questioned this number, others have pointed to archaeological and other evidence which substantiates his account of a well-populated region.[5] Many of these towns were sited on the shores of the Sea of Galilee, which contained large fish stocks and combined this with fertile land away from the lake itself. The fishing industry and its associated processing businesses produced salted, dried, and pickled fish which generated a significant level of income for the local population.

The lake and its hinterland frequently feature in the Gospel accounts of the ministry of Jesus. He recruited no fewer than four of his close companions from the shoreline villages: the fishermen Simon (later named Peter), his brother Andrew, and the brothers James and John (called *Boanerges*, "Sons of Thunder", by Jesus). Mary Magdalene was named from a town called Magdala on the western shore of the Sea of Galilee. Its full name was Magdala Tarichaea, meaning the "Tower of Salted Fish". But it was the lifestyle not the maritime produce that captured contemporary attention. In the later Jewish Talmud, a document called the *Midrash on Lamentations* or *Lamentations Raba*, states that the town of Magdala was condemned and destroyed by God (it was attacked by the Romans in AD 66 during the First Jewish–Roman War) because of the sexual sin (extra- and pre-marital) that was taking place there. Whatever the truth in that accusation, these brief glimpses give us insights into the economy of the area.

In 4 BC, a rebel named Judah plundered Sepphoris, Galilee's largest city (which was then its administrative centre) and made it a base for his revolt against the Herodian rulers, who were allies of Rome. In response, the Roman governor of Syria, Publius Quinctilius Varus, sacked Sepphoris and sold the population into slavery.

Administratively, the areas of Galilee and Gaulanitis (to the east of Galilee and part of the tetrarchy of Philip) under the rule of Herod Antipas (reigned in Galilee and in Perea, 4 BC – AD 39) and Philip (ruled the region between the Greek cities of the Decapolis and Damascus in Syria, 4 BC – AD 34) was organized from the towns of Tiberias, Caesarea Philippi, Bethsaida, and Sepphoris.

Tiberias was founded about the year 20 by Herod Antipas who made it the capital of Galilee and named it after the Roman Emperor Tiberius. It was then that he moved his capital there from Sepphoris. It was a spa town with some seventeen hot springs nearby. In the time of the adulthood of Jesus, Jewish influence was slowly growing in what had been, at first, a Hellenized and pagan foundation. By the late first century, the Sea of Galilee came to be called the Sea of Tiberias. It appears by this name in the Gospel of John and as a place from which boats had sailed (John 6:23) to Capernaum in order to find Jesus. There is no evidence that Jesus himself ever visited this royal capital with its pagan connotations. However, the increased taxation involved in building this new capital almost certainly put great pressure on the lakeside Galilean communities. This time of stress and anxiety, as it must have been experienced by many across the region, was the background to the ministry of Jesus, which occurred within a decade of the start of construction.[6]

Caesarea Philippi was the administrative capital of Philip's large tetrarchy of Batanaea and was renamed (as Paneas) in the year 14 after the Emperor Augustus (Caesar). The New Testament calls it Caesarea Philippi to differentiate it from Caesarea Maritima on the Mediterranean coast. Josephus called it Caesarea Paneas, in his late-first-century work, *Antiquities of the Jews*. Like Tiberias, it had strongly Hellenized characteristics. Herod the Great – in a characteristic act of religious plurality – had erected a temple there in honour of Augustus.

Just as Jesus was starting his ministry (c. 29–30) Philip minted a coin-issue celebrating the city, which carried his image on it, which offended non-Hellenized Jews. The city is mentioned twice in the New Testament and neither reference indicates that Jesus actually visited it. One records his presence in "the district of Caesarea Philippi" (Matthew 16:13) and the other, describing the same incident, refers to him travelling "to the villages of Caesarea Philippi" (Mark 8:27). As with Tiberias, we get the impression that he avoided these Hellenized administrative centres.

Bethsaida – located, it seems, near where the River Jordan enters the Sea of Galilee – was also in Philip's territory and had an economy heavily dependent on fishing. Its name means "house of fishing". There is some debate as to whether all the New Testament references are to the same Bethsaida, but we will assume that they all refer to one place, within the jurisdiction of Philip, as this seems a fair conclusion based on varied evidence (both within the Gospels and in later evidence). It was the home town of the apostles Peter, Andrew, and Philip; and, unlike Tiberias and Caesarea Philippi, was well known to Jesus who visited it on a number of occasions. According to Josephus, in c. 30–33 Philip raised the village of Bethsaida to the rank of a *polis* (an administrative centre) and renamed it Julias in honour of Livia, who had been the wife of the Emperor Augustus.[7] However, during the time of Jesus it may have been less cosmopolitan and more Jewish than the other administrative settlements. This may explain Jesus' frequent visits. It was also outside the jurisdiction of Herod Antipas who, as we shall see, executed John the Baptist and this may also have added to its appeal. The circumspect words of Luke 9:9–10 give the impression that there was some connection between this execution, Herod's interest in Jesus, and Jesus' decision to withdraw "privately to a city called Bethsaida". Matthew explicitly indicates that this re-location was connected to the execution of John (Matthew 14:11–13). More on this later, but suffice it to say that the geo-politics of the time can easily be missed as we read the Gospels.

Then there was Sepphoris. Described by Josephus as "the ornament of all Galilee" it was chosen as an administrative centre by Herod Antipas as far back as 4 BC, when he succeeded his father. This was before the later foundation of Tiberias, which cost Sepphoris its capital status. This well-defended city had strong Hellenistic characteristics with its colonnaded main street, theatre, and representational mosaics (including one famous today for its portrayal of a women termed "Mona Lisa of the Galilee").[8] Its streets were paved with crushed limestone and it possessed two market areas. Josephus referred to a citadel which suggests the existence of a fortress located within the upper city. As an administrative centre it would have employed a number of its citizens on government business for Herod Antipas. Its basilica building was decorated with brightly painted plaster walls and white mosaic floors. Later Jewish Mishnah writings refer to the archive of Sepphora, which is probably an echo of its role within the bureaucracy of Herod Antipas. Two aqueducts supplied the city with water and fed into a large underground reservoir. No first-century bathhouses have yet been discovered but we may surmise some were located here from later evidence for these structures. Its hilltop setting made it visible for miles. Perhaps Jesus was thinking of it when he said that "A city built on a hill cannot be hidden" (Matthew 5:14).[9] Although it lay about one hour's walk from Nazareth it seems that Jesus never visited it. This may indicate something of its cultural character. In the First Jewish–Roman War, the citizens of the town – wishing to distance themselves from the nationalist ideology and actions of their revolutionary neighbours – declared for Rome and the invading Roman commander, Vespasian, used the town as a Roman base. Coins then minted at the town declared it to be a "city of peace" in Greek script and also carried the letters SC (meaning *Senatus Consulto*), in imitation of Roman imperial coinage,[10] on the obverse.[11]

The mention of Sepphoris brings us to the multicultural nature of parts of Galilee during Jesus' lifetime. Historians disagree about the extent to which the Jewish nature of Galilee had been diluted in the first century AD. It was certainly ringed by Greek-speaking towns and cities such as Ptolemais, Scythopolis, and Gadara (to give them their first-century names).

In addition, Galilee was distinct from the southern province of Judea and this stood out in its history, politics, and culture. It was separated from the holy city of Jerusalem in Judea by the non-Jewish territory of Samaria. And it was separated from Jewish populations in Perea (to the south-east) by the Greek-speaking cities of Decapolis.

Its history since Isaiah had marked it out as distinctive and culturally complex. Since the Assyrian conquest of the northern tribes in the eighth century BC, it had experienced a more mixed population. This had increased under Greek and Roman influence and it is notable that the Herodian family sponsored Greek (and pagan) style buildings and institutions as both a bid for imperial support and in recognition of the mixed nature of their subject population. It was Greek pagans, rather than indigenous Jews, who were initially settled in the Hellenized centres of Tiberias and Sepphoris. As a result, we can picture more "Jewish" towns such as Nazareth and Capernaum being close neighbours to more Greek (and pagan) cities, such as Tiberias and Sepphoris; and Jewish and pagan merchants, travellers, and landowners having to develop some kind of *modus vivendi*, as fellow-citizens of the ruling (Herodian) house which considered itself rooted in both cultures and which attempted to conciliate both. This was a multiculturalism that hid inner tensions, which exploded in the 60s and 70s during the First Jewish–Roman War.

Moreover, Galileans spoke a distinctive form of Aramaic, whose pronunciation stood out to Judeans and which meant that Peter, at the time of the arrest of Jesus, could be identified as a Galilean. There clearly was a north–south divide. Southern opinions of uncouth northerners exacerbated Judean prejudices that Galileans were lax in their observance of proper Jewish ritual, increased by the distance of Galilee from the Jerusalem Temple and the religious leadership, based in Jerusalem.[12] Lack of Jewish purity, it was inferred, accompanied openness to Hellenistic influences, and was indeed intertwined with it.

We learn from John's Gospel, a source probably dating from the 90s, that Jesus' status as a prophet was compromised in the eyes of some Judeans by his northern origins.

> But some asked, "Surely the Messiah does not come from Galilee, does he? Has not the scripture said that the Messiah is descended from David and comes from Bethlehem, the village where David lived?" So there was a division in the crowd because of him.
> **(John 7:41–43)**

This shows the north–south divide in the assessment of the messianic credentials of the northern preacher.

However, we should not over-emphasize questions regarding the Jewishness of Galilee. Although no first-century synagogue has yet been excavated at Sepphoris (in contrast to ones of the fifth and sixth centuries), beneath the floors of most of the houses explored to date Jewish ritual baths or *miqvaoth* have been discovered. Cut into bedrock, with steps leading down to watertight-plastered pools, the owners of these clearly took their Jewishness seriously.[13] At the same time, the discovery of stone vessels at other sites also points toward inhabitants intent on ritual purity. The limited use of figurative art also points toward Jewish cultural concerns deciding matters of decoration.[14] The situation in Galilee was culturally mixed but it seems that the complications of being far from Jerusalem (rather than the fundamental Jewishness of its inhabitants) loomed larger in southern attitudes toward their northern compatriots.

The division was further complicated by the fact that Galilee (especially Lower Galilee) enjoyed better agricultural and fishing resources than the more mountainous southern territory of Judea. First-century olive presses have been found in every first-century Galilean site archaeologically excavated.[15] So, its edgy non-conformity was compounded by it having, arguably, greater economic prosperity.

These cultural and economic divisions were underscored by the political divisions which emphasized the difference between Galilee and Judea. Since the tenth century BC they had been under different administrations. After a brief reunification under the Maccabees (see Chapter 2), they were divided again as Jesus grew from child to man with Galilee theoretically independent under a Herodian prince, whereas Judea and Samaria rapidly came under direct Roman rule. It was ironic that the cultural core of Judaism was occupied by a foreign and pagan power, whereas the slightly less orthodox and culturally less pure north was ruled by an Idumean prince who claimed Jewish legitimacy. And, to add to the complexity, many first-century Galileans may have been descendants of Judeans who settled there under Hasmonean rule, rather than the descendants of northern Israelites.[16]

What does seem clear from modern studies is that there was something of a "Galilean self-awareness" in the first century AD, which meant it was something of a political hotspot with its own peculiar brand of aggressive regional Jewish nationalism which was almost a century old by the time Jesus started his ministry. For a Jewish teacher from Galilee, a visit to Jerusalem was probably met with both political and religious suspicion.[17]

Even within Galilee, though, there were internal complications and prejudices.

"Can anything good come out of Nazareth?"

In John's Gospel, Philip, one of Jesus' disciples excitedly invites a friend named Nathanael to come and meet "Jesus son of Joseph from Nazareth" (John 1:45). To which Nathanael witheringly replies, "Can anything good come out of Nazareth?" (John 1:46). It is a very revealing comment and raises questions about just what kind of place the home town of Jesus was.

We are today familiar with the designation "Jesus of Nazareth". In 1977, the British-Italian TV miniseries carrying this title had a big impact on the way many people of a certain generation imagine Jesus. Directed by Franco Zeffirelli and co-written by Zeffirelli, Anthony Burgess, and Suso Cecchi d'Amico, its casting of Robert Powell as Jesus created a strong visual image. Though, it must be said, the blue eyes do not immediately speak of the Middle Eastern origins of the real man. But the key point is that title. It is instantly recognizable as a geographical but also a biographical descriptor because it is used so frequently in the Gospels. The Greek New Testament uses the form "Nazarene" six times (in the Gospels of Mark and Luke), and the form "Nazorean" thirteen times (in the Gospels of Matthew, Luke, and John, and Acts, and in some manuscripts of Mark) to identify Jesus. Consequently, the phrase "Jesus of Nazareth" can also be translated as "Jesus the Nazarene" or "Jesus the Nazorean". This would seem an unambiguous reference to his origins in the town of Nazareth, but the matter is a little more complicated.

The tradition in Matthew's Gospel highlights the complication. As we have seen (in Chapter 3) when Matthew recorded the movement of Jesus and his family from Egypt to Nazareth he asserted that this was "so that what had been spoken through the prophets might be fulfilled, 'He will be called a Nazorean'" (Matthew 2:23). However, the form of this irregular Greek word, with its additional vowel, does not obviously arise from the place-name "Nazareth".[18] Matthew rather adds to the complication by assuming it fulfils an Old Testament prophecy when there does not seem to be one. In fact, there is no reference to Nazareth anywhere in the Old Testament. And outside the Gospels the place-name is not recorded until c. 200 when it is mentioned by name in the writing of Sextus Julius Africanus.[19] This raises the matter of exactly what Matthew meant.

Modern scholars are divided on the issue and have suggested a number of interpretations. The first is that he meant it as a reference to Isaiah 11:1, which reads "A shoot shall come out from the stock of Jesse, and a branch shall grow out of his roots", which is usually understood as a messianic prophecy. This makes no reference to Nazareth, but the Hebrew word *netser* (branch) may have suggested a messianic title – Nazorean – which was then connected to the place-name Nazareth (or *Nazara* in the Hebrew of biblical times). The other suggestion is that he was thinking of Judges 13:5 which describes Sampson in these terms: "No razor is to come on his head, for the boy shall be a nazirite to God from birth. It is he who shall begin to deliver Israel from the hand of the Philistines." When translated from Hebrew into Greek (and early Christians used the Greek *Septuagint* version of the Old Testament) the word "nazirite" is very close to Nazarene. The term "nazirite" means "one separated" or "one consecrated", which may have seemed appropriate as a messianic term for one chosen for God's purpose of deliverance. This then nicely dovetailed into the name of Jesus' home town.

This has led some biblical experts to suggest that the word originated as a religious term and was only later connected to origins in the Galilean town of Nazareth. There are some grounds for this suggestion. In the original Greek of the Gospels, Jesus is more commonly called "Jesus the Nazarene/Nazorean", than "Jesus of Nazareth", although it is the latter which predominates in English translations. The best attested manuscripts of Mark only ever use the form *Nazarēnos* (clearly linked to Nazareth). This form is also found in Matthew (four times) and Luke (twice), but the remaining instances in these Gospels is *Nazōraios*' (Nazorean). This is the form found in Acts and in John.[20] In Acts 24:5 early followers of Jesus are described as "the sect of the Nazarenes [Greek: *Nazoreans*]". By this time there was no connection whatsoever between followers of Jesus and the eponymous town apparently used to identify them. Indeed, as we shall shortly see, Jesus himself left Nazareth when he began his preaching ministry. Tertullian, writing in 208, also refers to "Nazarenes" – as a term used by Jews to describe Christians.[21] By this time the term may also have been applied, by Christian writers, to describe fellow Christians who were Jews and still lived a Jewish lifestyle. Later the term came to be used within the church for believers classed as heretics; probably due to them continuing to follow the Jewish Mosaic Law.[22] It has been suggested that the term had a prehistory which preceded the rise of Christianity and that, originally, Nazorean may have been applied to an ascetic Jewish sect and was then used by orthodox Jews to describe the new group, which they considered a schismatic sect.[23]

So one can see how the word has been interpreted as implying a religious title and not a geographical location. The modern Hebrew term *Notzrim* to describe Christians is derived from this usage. The same root has given rise to the word for Christian in Syriac (*Nasrani*) and also in Arabic (*Naṣrānī*). In the Qur'an, Christians are called "*Al-naṣara*".[24] When so-called Islamic State were conducting their murderous persecution of non-Islamic groups (and also those that they considered the "wrong sort of Muslims") they painted the Arabic letter "N" on the doors of Syrian Christians slated for destruction.

For New Testament writers, the matter of a connection between Nazareth and Old Testament terminology may have been encouraged by a possible origin for the actual place-name in the word *netser* (branch).[25] That would mean that – quite independent of each other – the place-name and the verse in Isaiah shared a similar linguistic root (*netser*, branch). This then coincided with the appearance of the word *nazirite* (one separated/one consecrated) used in the book of Judges to describe Sampson.

To conclude that the connection of Jesus with Nazareth is actually a later invention, in order to provide a geographical location for a *religious term* originally used to describe Jesus, as is occasionally suggested, is unconvincing and assumes no historical basis for the strong evidence in the Gospels. This evidence, despite the complications already noted, clearly indicates that early followers of Jesus were sure he came from Nazareth. This appears in an early statement of Christian belief found in Acts:

> That message spread throughout Judea, beginning in Galilee after the baptism that John announced: how God anointed Jesus of Nazareth with the Holy Spirit and with power; how he went about doing good and healing all who were oppressed by the devil, for God was with him.
>
> **(Acts 10:37–38)**

The best texts of Mark – the earliest of the Gospels – uses the form "Nazarene" (which is closely linked to the form of Nazareth) rather than "Nazorean" (which is not). But even Matthew (whose preferred form is "Nazorean") contains the revealing formula: "The crowds were saying, 'This is the prophet Jesus from Nazareth in Galilee'" (Matthew 21:11). This is in addition to the clear linkage between place-name and (apparent) religious term used in his reference to the return from Egypt. And then there is that famous put-down by Nathanael found in John. All of this is consistent with other New Testament terminology where we find references to Saul *of Tarsus* and Mary *of Magdala*, to name two other famous examples (and there are more).

Rather than being a later Christian attempt to invent a geographical location for Jesus, the simpler and obvious explanation is that Jesus came from Nazareth and this place-name became linked with messianic and deliverance terms used in the Old Testament by the time the New Testament was being compiled. And this association may well have occurred during Jesus' actual ministry in Galilee. The root-word *netser* (branch) may have united both geography and theology.

So, what kind of place was Nazareth? Clearly, Nathanael was not impressed. We know very little about it. It is not mentioned in the Old Testament, nor by Josephus, nor in traditional Jewish writings such as the Talmud or Mishnah. The first record of its existence outside the Gospels dates from the third or fourth century AD and was found at Caesarea Maritima. Discovered in the remains of a synagogue there, an inscription refers to "Happizzez of Nazareth". The lack of literary evidence (outside the Gospels) – combined with the "Nazorean" complication – caused some sceptics to suggest that Nazareth did not exist in the time of Jesus and that references to it simply localized beliefs in a supposedly real place that was not actually established until after the year 70.[26] This was a scepticism which rejected all the evidence in the Gospels and has now itself been undermined by recent discoveries. Since 2009 Israeli archaeologists, working in the modern settlement of Nazareth have discovered structures dating from the time of Jesus. The unlikely scenario that later Gospel writers invented his connection to the town has been fundamentally challenged. We can assume its population was no more than four hundred people. Perhaps no more than fifty households lived there.[27] Although the term is anachronistic, there is something to the description of it as "a tiny hick town in the middle of nowhere"![28] It was certainly in the shadow of nearby Sepphoris.

In terms of geographical hierarchy: Ptolemais, Caesarea Philippi, Hippos, Sepphoris, and Tiberias were cities; Migdal and Gamla were large towns; Capernaum was a village; Nazareth was a very small village.[29] What is interesting is how few, if any, of the towns and cities feature in the activities of Jesus. Indeed, he seems never to have entered the cities. Not even once. This prompts some thought – but we shall return to that in another chapter.

Whatever the nature and influence of Nazareth, it was not to remain his base once his preaching ministry had started. We learn that, "He left Nazareth and made his home in Capernaum by the lake [the Sea of Galilee]" (Matthew 4:13). But before we explore that momentous beginning of his ministry, we need to pause for a moment to consider his childhood.

Jesus' childhood and youth – the few surviving clues from the "silent years"

Many Christians will be familiar with the carol, "Once in Royal David's City", by C. F. Alexander (1818–1895). It contains a verse which reads:

And through all his wondrous childhood
He would honour and obey,
Love and watch the lowly maiden,
In whose gentle arms he lay:
Christian children all must be
Mild, obedient, good as he.

From this one would imagine that we possess a range of traditions concerning the period of Jesus' life between the birth-stories and the beginning of his preaching ministry. We don't. In fact, we know very little about the childhood and the early adulthood of Jesus.

To start with, we know next-to-nothing about Mary and Joseph. Within medieval and modern Catholic traditions this can appear otherwise. Mary (*Maryam* or *Mariam* as she would have been known in Aramaic) is given an entire extended family in later tradition, with Joachim and Anna named as her parents (in the mid-second-century *Gospel of James*, also known as the *Protoevangelium of James*, and the *Infancy Gospel of James*). In it, Mary as a child is dedicated to life in the Temple through a vow of chastity. This work also claims that Mary was perpetually a virgin. This assumes that the siblings of Jesus (for example referred to in Matthew 13:55–56) were half-brothers and half-sisters, born to a previous wife of Joseph's. It also describes Joseph as being much older than Mary (age not specified, but in the fifth-century *History of Joseph the Carpenter*, it is stated as being ninety). This extreme age was clearly part of a developing belief in the total absence of sex from their marriage. It contrasted with the description of Mary being in her early teens (probably fourteen years old).

Later Catholic doctrine built on this exalted status, with the belief in the "Immaculate Conception": Mary was conceived without the stain of original sin. (This is not to be confused with the belief in the virgin conception and birth of Jesus.) This belief was tentatively explored from the early fifth century onward but was not formally stated as Catholic Dogma until 1854. It also became associated with an idea of her being sinless in all aspects of her life that appeared in a number of early medieval writers. From the fourth century we also find the emergence of the belief in the "Assumption": Mary being lifted body and soul up to heaven at her death. Some versions of this belief claim that this occurred without Mary actually dying.

The Gospels contain none of this (with the exception of the virgin birth). All we know of her family is that she had a sister (John 19:25). The form of the Greek leaves it open as to whether this sister is unnamed or (another) Mary – the wife of Clopas. In the second century, this other Mary was viewed as a sister-in-law. Luke says that Elizabeth (mother of John the Baptist) was a relative, but is not specific about the exact relationship. This has led some Christian commentators to suggest that the genealogy in Luke is that of Mary, whereas that in Matthew is that of Joseph.[30] This would give Jesus descent from King David through the family of his adopted-father (Joseph) and his mother (Mary).

Taking the Gospel accounts at face value – without reading them through a lens of pre-conceived Mariology – Joseph's refraining from sexual relations with his wife only lasted until after the birth of Jesus (Matthew 1:25). In this case, James and Joseph, Simon and Judas, along with unnamed sisters (Matthew 13:55–56) were the children of Mary and Joseph and younger siblings of Jesus. This is the most obvious reading of the text. In short, Jesus was the oldest sibling in a large family, with at least six other siblings. More on this later.

This was a family that acted within the expected boundaries of Jewish behaviour. Forty days after the birth of Jesus, Mary and Joseph went to the Temple in Jerusalem to make a sacrifice to achieve ritual purification and to dedicate Jesus to God as he was a firstborn male (Luke 2:22–38). These actions were in line with Old Testament instructions (Leviticus 12:1–8). It is then that Luke records messianic prophecies about the child by Simeon (later famously to become the canticle, *Nunc Dimittis*, the Latin for its opening words) and the prophetess Anna. Luke then says they returned to Nazareth in Galilee (Luke 2:39), but in Matthew they remain in Bethlehem for up to two years. The only other evidence for Jesus before his adult ministry is also found in Luke, who recounts a visit to Jerusalem to attend Passover, when Jesus was twelve years old, which resulted in him becoming separated from his parents. But he is found in the Temple three days later, amazing religious teachers by his insights.

Luke was clearly aware of the tension between Jesus' confident pursuit of his mission and contemporary expectations of young people's obedience to parents. After the reunion of the family in the Temple he says, "Then he went down with them and came to Nazareth, and was obedient to them" (Luke 2:51). The only other information he gives (and this is more than in any other Gospel) to bridge between this event and the later ministry period is: "And Jesus increased in wisdom and in years [or stature], and in divine and human favour" (Luke 2:52). This reminds us that, even given the developed Christology of early Christians at the time of the compilation of Luke's Gospel, there was an acceptance of the human development of Jesus. Sometimes the Gospel's appreciation of his humanity is more apparent than in the thinking of later Christians. Clearly, he grew, reflected, and matured.

That is it. There are no other accounts from his childhood and certainly no hints of anything to give support for Blake's "And did those feet in ancient time/Walk upon England's mountains green" (1804). They didn't. The poem was inspired by a much later legend that young Jesus, travelled to what is now England and visited Cornwall and Glastonbury (Somerset), in the company of his uncle, Joseph of Arimathea, a tin merchant.[31] To be fair to Blake, he did pose it as a question. And the answer is that there is not a shred of evidence in support of this attractive (and very popular) English fiction.

Carpenter: poor worker or respected artisan?

We get few hints concerning the status of this family. At Mary's purification accompanying Jesus' presentation at the Temple, we are told that "they offered a sacrifice according to what is stated in the law of the Lord, 'a pair of turtle-doves or two young pigeons'" (Luke 2:24). This indicates they were relatively poor since the law in Leviticus stated that this should be the offering "If she cannot afford a sheep" (Leviticus 12:8).

We learn later – during Jesus' ministry – that the family business lay in the building trade. When he later returned to Nazareth the locals ask: "Is not this the carpenter, the son of Mary" (Mark 6:3). Some other early manuscripts of Mark read at this point: "son of the carpenter and of Mary", as does Matthew (Matthew 13:55).[32] The Greek word *tektōn* meant a worker in stone, wood, or metal and only the context would have clarified which was meant. Jesus' family may have been the village builders.

Bible commentators differ over which was the original form and why there are these differences. Some have argued that the omission of Joseph may have been due to later Christian emphasis on God alone being the father of Jesus. But there are some interesting issues here. It may well have been an insult to omit his father and reference only his mother. In which case, we have an early insight into negative responses to Jesus.[33]

On the other hand, some early Christians (such as Origen, died: 253) were very defensive about Jesus being described as something as lowly as a carpenter by the Greek writer Celsus (who opposed Christianity).[34] On balance, it seems best to conclude that Jesus came from a *tektōn*-family and may well have been a builder/carpenter himself, in the family tradition. The later disparaging attitude toward him as a mere manual labourer (so offensive to Origen) reveals something of the radical nature of the Christian movement with its crucified lower-class founder; and how later Christians were sometimes active in trying to counter this image. However, it should be remembered that in a Galilean village the builder/carpenter would have been a pillar of the community – even if far down the social scale to contemporary and later educated elites.

The first-century Jewish historian, Josephus, stated that most Galileans supported their family with agriculture. Given that many of Jesus' parables use the language of the fields and orchards, rather than the carpentry shop, it is possible that the family business was one in which building work supplemented small-scale farming.[35]

Jesus' childhood in the Infancy Gospel (Story) of Thomas

The lack of information about Jesus' childhood and growth to manhood clearly prompted some second-century writers to fill in the gaps. The so-called *Infancy Gospel* (or *Story*) *of Thomas* (late second- or early third-century) is a case in point. Some modern scholars now refer to it as the *Paidika* or *Childhood Deeds* (of Jesus), which avoids confusion with the Coptic *Gospel of Thomas*.

Although no mainstream biblical expert would accept it as rooted in any authentic traditions, it shows how some later believers imagined the childhood of such a dramatic and unusual person. The result is, to put it mildly, controversial. Aged five, Jesus performs a playful miracle and turns toy birds into real ones which then fly away. On the very same day, Jesus curses a village boy who drains a pool of water that Jesus had made. The image is of a child with superpowers who wields them erratically (as a child might). The matter grows even more shocking when Jesus kills a boy who knocks against him; and causes some adult villagers to go blind but later restores the sight of all those he has cursed. With regard to his education, Jesus baffles one teacher with arcane knowledge (a nod toward the manuscript's Gnostic origins no doubt); a second teacher is cursed and collapses; a third praises the wisdom of Jesus and is spared any harm or humiliation.

At home, when Joseph tries to correct Jesus' behaviour, Jesus rejects his parental authority and reacts with a veiled threat. However, when a snake bites his brother, James, Jesus saves his life. All this occurs before the visit to Jerusalem at twelve years old. It is clear that neither his family nor the villagers of Nazareth understand this strange boy.[36] The writer of the *Infancy Gospel* (*Story*) *of Thomas* offers us nothing authentic to add to our limited picture of Jesus as he grew up.

What is clear from the canonical Gospels is that the man who finally emerged, amazed, puzzled, excited, and shocked those around him. This occurred against a background that gives us little insight into the formation of his self-awareness and outlook. So it was that Jesus stepped out of the relative obscurity of his first thirty years and began a short ministry that would end in his conflict with the religious authorities, execution by the Roman occupying power, and changing the world.

CHAPTER 5

"A voice crying in the wilderness"

Exactly who was John the Baptist? What kind of bridge does he provide between contemporary Jewish beliefs and the experience about to explode in the person of Jesus? In order to decide, we will explore his teaching, actions, and relationship with both the religious authorities and with Jesus himself. And why he ended up in deep trouble.

Today John is held in high regard in Christianity, Islam (where he is known, in Arabic, as *Yaḥyā ibn Zakarīyā*), the Bahá'í Faith, and in Mandaeism (historically based in Iraq). All of these faiths regard John as a prophet, and he is honoured as a saint among many Christians. Among the Mandaeans, John is revered as the Messiah and these views can be found expressed in their holy books, including the *Ginza Rba* and the *Draša D-Iahia* (*Book of John*).[1] This may well be derived from Gnostic beliefs about John the Baptist that emerged from the second century onward.

For the first generation of Christians, as they compiled the Gospels in the second half of the first century (as for modern Christians), John the Baptist is the dramatic forerunner to the ministry of Jesus. There is something reminiscent of the Old Testament in this austere, uncompromising prophet who declares the coming of God's kingdom and the imminent arrival of the Messiah (Greek: Christ). And yet he rapidly fades from view.

However, it is possible that we now underestimate the original dynamism and then the later potential rivalry between emerging

Christianity and what we might call the "John the Baptist movement". The Gospels reveal that, even after John was imprisoned, his followers constituted a recognizable sect in contemporary Judaism, within the context of Galilee. And they seem to have been ascetic and puritanical. When criticizing the (apparent) relaxed behaviour of Jesus' disciples, when it came to socializing with those considered outcast "sinners", a complaint was addressed to Jesus by the Pharisees and the teachers of the law that "John's disciples, like the disciples of the Pharisees, frequently fast and pray, but your disciples eat and drink" (Luke 5:33). This gives an intriguing insight into the social as well as theological dynamic of Jesus and his followers to which we will return in another chapter. But, at this point, it is important to note it as an insight into the kind of community associated with John. It was a community that did not dissolve at his arrest. And, as we shall soon see, it did not dissolve after his execution either.

There is evidence that this complicated relationship between the two groups ran on into the middle of the first century and even beyond that. Written perhaps as early as the year 70, the New Testament document known as the book of Acts refers to disciples of John active long after his death (in Acts 18:25; 19:1–7). In addition, as late as the third century, documents known today as the *Pseudo-Clementine Recognitions* and *Pseudo-Clementine Homilies* record garbled traditions suggesting the continuation of, what it describes as, a sect of "daily baptizers" active long after the death of John the Baptist. We know little more about such people or their beliefs but it looks as if a radical group continued to reference John as its founder. And it preached some kind of baptism-based ideology long after John had been executed. It may even have been seen as a potential rival to the Christian community.

This tension may also explain the emphasis in the Gospel of John (3:30) that, in the words of John the Baptist, "He [Jesus] must increase, but I [John the Baptist] must decrease". Recorded in a Gospel written perhaps as late as the 90s and conscious of continued competition between the two groups of followers, it was determined to set out theological priorities clearly. The message was transparent: John *was* the honoured but passing prophet; Jesus *is* the Messiah, the saviour, the revelation of the eternal nature of God.[2]

All of this makes us more curious about exactly who John the Baptist actually was. And in order to decide that we will first look at the presentation of his work through the words of those Christians writing in the second half of the first century. Then we will attempt to explore behind these explanations in order to see if there is more that we can learn about this important and yet enigmatic figure.

John in the Gospels

As part of his preparation for the account of the birth of Jesus, the compiler of Luke introduces us to John the Baptist. In Luke chapter 1, we are told that he was the son of a priest named Zechariah, and Elizabeth his wife. Both, we are told, were descendants of Aaron, the brother of Moses. In this way John is given impeccable Old Testament prophetic roots which set him in the context of the great story of God revealing himself to the Jewish people. The reference to Aaron takes us back to the Exodus of the Jewish people from slavery in Egypt. We are, no doubt, meant to read this as a reminder of the great action of God about to be revealed.

According to Luke, Elizabeth was of advanced years and could not have children. For this reason, her pregnancy with John is seen as a miraculous intervention by God. This is revealed to Zechariah by an angel, while he is going about his duties within the Jerusalem Temple. Later Christian tradition claimed that the birthplace of John (and hence the home of Elizabeth and Zechariah) was at Ein Karem, south-west of Jerusalem. Situated about five miles from Jerusalem it would be a suitable location for the home of a temple priest.[3]

The extraordinary nature of the child to be conceived is made clear in the angel's description of his role and status.

> He will be great in the sight of the Lord. He must never drink wine or strong drink; even before his birth he will be filled with the Holy Spirit. He will turn many of the people of Israel to the Lord their God. With the spirit and power of Elijah he will go before him, to turn the hearts of parents to their children,

> and the disobedient to the wisdom of the righteous,
> to make ready a people prepared for the Lord.
> **(Luke 1:15–17)**

John's status within the ancient prophetic tradition (the spirit and power of the revered prophet Elijah) and his bridge to greater to come (to prepare people for the Lord) is clear. Jesus himself later explicitly identifies John as "Elijah who is to come" (Matthew 11:14 and also Matthew 17:11–13) although in the Gospel of John, John the Baptist expressly denies being linked to Elijah (John 1:21), which is intriguing and may indicate that Jesus and John differed in their interpretation of John's role. The synoptic gospels, though, insist on his status as being (in some way undefined) fulfilling the role of that Old Testament prophet. In both Matthew and Mark, John's unusual clothing is described in a way that recalls how Elijah is described in 2 Kings 1:8. We will return to the clothing of John shortly. And we have seen the unambiguous statement in Luke, as expressed by the angel. For the synoptics, John clearly fulfils the prophesied role of Elijah in preparing the way for the Messiah. There is, it should be clearly noted here, no hint of reincarnation, which is quite alien to Judaism, as later to Christianity.

In addition to the specific referencing of Elijah, the role of a prophet fulfilling Old Testament promises is explicitly connected with John. Mark (probably the earliest Gospel written) describes John as a fulfilment of a prophecy from the book of Isaiah concerning a messenger sent ahead preparing the way of the Lord and being "the voice of one crying out in the wilderness" (Mark 1:3). In fact, the prophecy, as expressed in Mark, is a combination of verses from Isaiah, Malachi, and Exodus.[4] Some manuscripts of this Gospel recognize this by substituting the words "as it is written in the prophets". Matthew begins with the same (modified) quotation from Isaiah 40:3 – "In the wilderness prepare the way of the LORD, make straight in the desert a highway for our God" – laying more emphasis on the "voice of one crying out in the wilderness" (Matthew 3:3), whereas Isaiah puts a little more stress on the place in which the preparation will occur. However, the meaning is largely the same. Matthew then moves the verses from Malachi and Exodus to later in his account, where they are quoted by Jesus.

The location of John's later activities in the wilderness of the Jordan Valley places him within the austere tradition of the ancient prophet, in contrast to the settled lives of the majority of the Jewish community in their villages and towns.

But, to return to the account of the birth of John. Due to Zechariah's questioning of the message he is struck dumb and only allowed to speak when, later on, he fulfils the angelic instruction to ensure that the boy is named John. John's name derives from a Hebrew term meaning "YHWH is gracious". All of these dramatic events, as with the birth of Jesus, occur during the final years of the reign of King Herod the Great.

We are told later that Elizabeth is "a relative" of Mary the mother of Jesus, but the exact relationship is not spelled out. However, Luke emphasizes the connection of the two miraculous pregnancies by describing a visit to Elizabeth by Mary. This involves a journey from Galilee to Judea; and the child in Elizabeth's womb leaping for joy as Mary's greeting is heard. This, according to Luke, is reported to Mary by Elizabeth (Luke 1:39–45).

Only Luke refers to this family connection and it is not mentioned in any of the other Gospels. This has led some modern commentators to reject its veracity. Raymond E. Brown judged it "of dubious historicity"[5] and Géza Vermes concluded it was "artificial and undoubtedly Luke's creation".[6] Others have noted similarities between Luke's narrative of the birth of John and the account in the Old Testament of the birth of the prophet Samuel. This has led to the suggestion that Luke's account of this, as of the miraculous birth of Jesus, was modelled on that of Samuel. [7] Countering this, more traditional commentators would point to Luke's intimate knowledge of Nativity accounts and the belief that his sources included Mary herself. There are certainly parallels between Luke's accounts of the births of Jesus and John: each account starts with an angelic annunciation; there is a miraculous conception and a birth that is out of the ordinary; then there is circumcision; hymns of praise to God declare the extraordinary nature of each child and his God-given destiny.

We hear no more about the child John, until Luke returns to him with John as a man, and explains that "the word of God came to John son of Zechariah in the wilderness" (Luke 3:2). This occurs "In the fifteenth year of the reign of Emperor Tiberius, when Pontius Pilate was governor of Judea" (Luke 3:1). The same passage contextualizes the event in the reigns of the Herodian successors to Herod (Herod Antipas and Philip) and the high-priesthood of Annas and Caiaphas, both of whom will feature in the dramatic final week of the life of Jesus. From this we should probably date the start of John's preaching and baptizing to about the year 29.

The message of John the Baptist

According to Luke, John's message was one of personal spiritual renewal, moral transformation, and social justice. It was a transformation signalled by adult water baptism. Luke reports this as a fulfilment of a messianic prophecy in the book of Isaiah: "The voice of one crying out in the wilderness: 'Prepare the way of the Lord'" (Luke 3:4, quoting Isaiah 40:3). In this way John is presented as the forerunner of the actual Messiah. The baptismal events at the Jordan also echo the ancient exodus from Egyptian slavery which involved crossing that very river into the Promised Land.[8]

John's message is uncompromising and extraordinarily blunt. Those flocking to him are greeted as a "brood of vipers", whose only way to escape the judgment of God is to transform the quality of their lives and not to rest on their status as children of Abraham (Luke 3:7–9). The message is one of repentance, followed by actions in line with a fresh start in life. Those with resources should share with those without; tax collectors should take no more than is officially due; soldiers should not extort money using threats and lies; the same soldiers should be satisfied with their wages.

The puritanical nature of the firebrand preaching is matched by a detail provided in Mark and Matthew of a figure "clothed with camel's hair, with a leather belt around his waist, and he ate locusts and wild honey" (Mark 1:6). This argues for an austere lifestyle.

The food source translated as "locusts" is usually taken as the infamous flying insects, since the Greek word used (*akris*) seems a clear reference to the grasshopper. However, other ancient traditions – though lacking the antiquity of the Gospel accounts –

suggest he was a vegetarian, which has led to the suggestion that the word referred to beans of the carob tree, but this seems hard to square with the Greek word used in the Gospels. There may be a clue in the fourth-century *Gospel of the Ebionites*, as reported by their opponent, the orthodox Christian Epiphanius (died: 403), in his work entitled *Panarion*. Though a very late source this states that John's diet was based on honey cakes (Greek *enkris*). Bearing a close similarity to the Greek *akris* (locust) this is the word used to describe the "manna" eaten by the Israelites on their way to the Promised Land in the Greek version of the Old Testament. So it is possible that this might be a pointer to what John ate. On the other hand, the Ebionites may simply have taken the word used for "manna" and applied it to John (adjusting the Gospel spelling) in order to emphasize his prophetic authority as one comparable to Moses. The Ebionites were a sect about whom not a lot is known. They appear to have combined some aspects of Christian belief with Jewish asceticism, vegetarianism, and ritual bathing. These last two possible characteristics may also have led them to a particular and peculiar view of John the Baptist.

Whether John survived on insects or honey cakes it was an extremely pared down lifestyle. Elsewhere he is contrasted with Jesus in that John neither ate bread nor drank wine (Luke 7:33). It was a lifestyle that prompted either admiration or shocked dismissal and condemnation. When Jesus is defending himself from the charges of being a glutton and a drunkard he remarks that the very people who accuse him of these excesses, regarded John's minimalist lifestyle in the wilderness as evidence of demonic possession. Clearly, both Jesus and John sharply divided contemporary opinion regarding their lifestyle.

The baptisms occurred, according to Matthew, "in the wilderness of Judea". The later Gospel of John records the tradition that they took place in Bethany across the Jordan (John 1:28). Unlike Jesus, John the Baptist was not from Galilee and so it is not surprising that the focus of his activities were in the Judean lower Jordan Valley. The site at Al-Maghtas, Jordan, on the eastern bank of the river (seven miles north of the Dead Sea), has been venerated as the location of his work since the Byzantine period. Today, the ruins of a Christian monastery have been excavated there and it was added to UNESCO's

World Heritage List in 2015. As with so much in the Middle East, the location is contested and a rival site has been postulated as being on the western bank, in Israel.[9]

The potential political radicalism of John's message is not fully explored in the Gospels – which focus more on his spiritual role and message – and has been completely removed from Josephus's account, with its agenda of reducing ideas of political conflict between Judaism and Hellenistic and Roman culture. However, at the time, John's message was both socially challenging and politically charged. His denunciation of Herod's marriage undoubtedly presented Herod with the very real danger that (what he would consider to be) radicalized Jewish subjects might combine with his Arab subjects in opposition to his rule. He acted to ensure that no such potential alliance could occur. The uncompromising moral stance of John the Baptist led to his arrest and eventual execution.

John the Baptist in the context of contemporary Judaism

The eventual execution of John occurred during the ministry of Jesus but, suffice it to say at this point, his movement both fascinated and horrified contemporaries. This was, no doubt, both a product of his condemnation of wrongdoing at all social levels, and the fear of a mass movement in the volatile atmosphere of Judea in the late 20s and early 30s. In such a context John was always in danger, as one who attracted mass support outside of the officially sanctioned and managed boundaries of official religious practice. That he criticized elite behaviour made his destruction certain.

The later Jewish historian Josephus, when recounting (in *Antiquities of the Jews*) the execution of John in the fortress of Macherus in the Judean desert on the orders of Herod Antipas, indicates that the reason was the popularity of John and the danger that this might have given him a platform for rebellion. With a message to all Israel, proclaimed by himself and so circumventing the Temple and its priestly hierarchy and sacrificial activities, John was a huge challenge to the Jewish establishment. He was living on borrowed time.

Luke is more specific about what led to John's downfall. It was, he says, caused by John criticizing Herod Antipas for divorcing his wife and taking as wife, Herodias who had been married to his brother (her uncle), Philip (sometimes referred to as Herod Philip). Herodias took John's condemnation to heart and, as we shall see, organized his eventual death. We can assume that, whatever her specific role was, Herod Antipas himself would not have taken kindly to John's intervention in royal personal relationships and dynastic politics. This, despite the fact that the later parts of the story indicate he was fascinated by this latter-day prophet and was highly reluctant to kill him. Nevertheless, he arrested him and the baptizing and preaching ministry of John the Baptist came to an end.

This raises the question of how should we read John's activities in the context of contemporary Judaism? It has been suggested that John was connected in some way to the contemporary community at Qumran. This has been argued on the basis of perceived similarities in terms of their mutual asceticism and End Time theology. Given the relative proximity of Qumran to John's centre of activity (less than fifty miles) this would have been more than possible. John's food of locusts and wild honey were foods acceptable at Qumran, according to the Jewish food laws enforced there. In addition, if John had accepted the Qumran vow not to receive clothing or food from outside this exclusive group (Rule of the Community 5.16) then this would be consistent with his strict diet and clothing. But the similarities go far deeper than food and appearance, for both John the Baptist and the inhabitants of Qumran held, it seems, similar apocalyptic views that were expressed in similar terms. For both of them the impending end of the current world order, due to God's judgment, were vivid beliefs. Both drew heavily on the prophetic language and imagery found in the Old Testament book of Isaiah. They were, as it were, on the same page. This is strikingly shown in the way that they both similarly interpreted Isaiah's "A voice cries out: 'In the wilderness prepare the way of the LORD, make straight in the desert a highway for our God'" (Isaiah 40:3) with the "wilderness" symbolizing a place of spiritual renewal and preparation for the End Time actions of God.[10] Both also emphasized the place of ritual cleansing; indeed it was the distinguishing mark of John's activity at the Jordan. It was a personal preparation for End Time testing and, eventually, salvation. It was water that had been made "living" by the faith of those entering it. They even shared the same way of describing opponents, and those they considered to be under God's judgment, as vipers. This was part of the binary world view that each held.

However, the comparison has its limitations which might cause us to question the Qumran credentials of John. He called all Israel to repent and he sought to win converts from among the whole Jewish community, but at Qumran there was an inward concentration on the preparedness of community members: those predestined as "Sons of Light". John was inclusive, whereas Qumran was exclusive. Despite his wilderness location, John was open to all the community. Baptism, unlike circumcision, could be experienced by women as well as men.[11] Indeed, we know that prostitutes – seeking access to the promised salvation – were among those who travelled to the Jordan (Matthew 21:32). Those baptized, then returned to their homes. Qumran, on the other hand was a separatist, withdrawn group of the spiritually pure, a gathered holy elite who made up (in their view) the true Israel. And it was a community of men. These were significant differences. The specific language and terminology used at Qumran was coined to reflect their exclusivity and their creation of a whole new language of holiness. Nothing like this is ascribed to John. Nor did John stress the strict study of the Mosaic Law as Qumran did. Even the common emphasis on water can be misleading. There was a real difference between Qumran's ritual bath as used by the exclusive community and John's river-water baptism of the multitudes who flocked out to him. His baptisms of those who were already Jews, but chose spiritual renewal, was also different to the Jewish practice of baptizing converts to Judaism,[12] as it was also different to regular Jewish ritual bathing. Finally, the Qumran group and the wider community of Essenes appear to have been closely connected and were geographically spread across the geographical region of Palestine. In contrast, John's geographical focus never extended beyond the southern Jordan Valley area.

So, what are we to make of this complexity: this similarity and dissimilarity? We might conclude that John and Qumran drew on similar theological roots but developed and applied them differently. Or that John "might have once lived at Qumran but that he left the community for a variety of possible reasons, not least of which was to lead his own disciples and prepare 'the way of the Lord,'" as he understood it.[13]

It has been speculated that John's group was one of a number of groups operating in and around the Jordan Valley preaching an End Time message. The later Jerusalem Talmud claims that twenty-four such sects were operating by the year 70.[14] If so, the supposed similarities with the practices at Qumran, suggesting some kind of connection, may be misleading.[15]

John the Baptist and Jesus

Luke indicates that many people wondered if John was the looked-for Messiah. For Luke as for other early Christians, John's role was preparatory. It was to challenge existing beliefs and lifestyles and prepare people for the preaching of Jesus. Luke later refers to tax collectors (pariah quislings in the view of many of their contemporaries) who had been baptized by John and then turned to Jesus. There is a direct connection made between this earlier baptism and then being open to Jesus' message (Luke 7:29). In contrast, the Pharisees and lawyers are presented as rejecting Jesus' message and, therefore, God's purpose for them and this being explicitly connected to the fact that they had earlier refused to be baptized by John (Luke 7:30).

The last of the canonical Gospels to be written – the Gospel of John – reflecting on late-first-century perspectives on John the Baptist concluded that "He himself was not the light, but he came to testify to the light" (John 1:8). In this famous prologue to the Gospel the writer(s) contrast the *Logos* ("the Word") and "the light" – that is, Jesus – with the person of John. There is exalted status here – John was sent by God as a witness – but it is combined with a clearly prioritized relationship with Jesus.

Islam continues this interpretation of John as a prophet heralding the coming of Jesus (Arabic: *Isa*). The Islamic tradition describes John as one of the prophets whom Muhammad met on the night of the *Mi'raj*; when, Muslims believe, Muhammad was taken on a journey from Mecca to Jerusalem (the *Isra*) and then to heaven itself. It is a belief similar to earlier Christian views regarding John.

Exactly what the relationship between Jesus and John was, in the year 29, has led to much speculation. It has been fuelled by the fact that John's ministry preceded that of Jesus and Jesus accepted baptism (which for everyone else was a sign of repentance) at the hands of John; yet the Gospel writers insist that Jesus (not John) is the Messiah and the Son of God. And later believers would assert Jesus' sinlessness, which makes that key point of baptism more complex. It is perhaps significant that in John's Gospel there is no mention of John the Baptist having an Elijah-anointing and there is no mention of Jesus' baptism by John. John the Baptist becomes more of a "voice" than a personality and any questions concerning Jesus' baptism are avoided. This may well have been a product of the emphasis of this Gospel on the exalted nature of Jesus the Christ, in combination with a wish to defuse problems (potential or actual) caused by continuing adherents of John the Baptist who were still operating at the end of the first century.

Simon J. Joseph has argued that the accounts, as they survive in the Gospels, actively demote John,[16] by presenting him as the prophetic forerunner to Jesus, whereas his actual ministry may have complemented that of Jesus, before John was arrested and removed from the scene.[17] It has even been speculated that Jesus was originally a member of John the Baptist's sect.[18] This was clearly not how the Gospel writers saw things, nor traditional Christian commentators over two millennia. And a careful reading of the surviving evidence suggests that there was always something significantly different between the two men, their message, and its implications. As John Dominic Crossan memorably put it: "John had a monopoly, but Jesus had a franchise." In this interpretation, John dominated the baptism movement and to stop it entailed simply arresting him. In contrast, Jesus preached and modelled a new and ongoing community lived within the "kingdom of God". Even without his physical presence, such a community was set up so that it could continue.[19] This may, though, over-stress the rapidity of the collapse of the "John the Baptist movement" following his arrest and execution. As we have seen, there are hints that it proved rather more robust in the face of this catastrophic set of events.

All four Gospels insist that Jesus was baptized by John and that this signalled the start of his own preaching ministry. Why this occurred, its significance, and what this meant we will explore shortly. For this is where John the Baptist surrenders centre stage in the Gospel accounts in favour of Jesus. Just what happened at this point and the kind of relationship that continued between these two related men, will be explored later. But for the writers of the Gospels, this is the point at which the forerunner steps aside.

CHAPTER 6

"The kingdom of heaven is at hand"

Modern interpreters of the New Testament have offered differing opinions regarding the outline dates and the duration of the ministry of Jesus. These range from a start date c. 27–29 and the end of his work c. 30–36.[1] As we saw in Chapter 3, the most probable start date was c. 29–30, shortly after the fifteenth year of the reign of Emperor Tiberius (whose rule began in the year 14). Traditionally, it then lasted until 33. We will look, a little later, at the reason why some commentators have suggested a year-long ministry rather than the traditional three-year-long one, but at this stage we will work with the traditional framework of a three-year-long ministry.[2] Luke tells that: "Jesus was about thirty years old when he began his work" (Luke 3:23). The Gospel accounts place the beginning of the ministry of Jesus in the countryside of Judea, near the River Jordan. This was in an area administered by Rome west of the river and by Herod Antipas east of it.

Why is Jesus' baptism and his temptation in the wilderness so important?

After the brief childhood accounts regarding Jesus' upbringing, there is silence. We know nothing more until he explodes on the scene as a mature adult and begins his preaching, teaching, and healing. And in each of the synoptic gospels this is signalled by his baptism by John the Baptist and a period spent in the harsh environment of the Judean wilderness. For the man from Galilee this is the prelude to three dramatic years...

The baptism...

It is thought that some of the earliest statements of Christian belief can be found in the Acts of the Apostles. In Acts 10:37–38, Peter visits the home of a Roman centurion named Cornelius and provides a résumé of the ministry of Jesus and the expansion of the Christian community. He explains how,

> That message spread throughout Judea, beginning in Galilee after the baptism that John announced: how God anointed Jesus of Nazareth with the Holy Spirit and with power; how he went about doing good and healing all who were oppressed by the devil, for God was with him.

It is clear from this that the events of Jesus' ministry are dated from the period of the work of John the Baptist. And, although Peter does not specifically refer to it in this explanation, this also involved the baptism of Jesus himself. This was a highly important moment in Jesus' life and (possibly) in his personal understanding of his role and mission. We get little insight into the inner world of Jesus' thinking and that which we do get is gained via writers compiling their work after the mid-first-century. Nevertheless, as we shall see, there are reasons for thinking that this event was a decisive one.

As we saw in the last chapter, the later Gospel of John specifies the location where John was baptizing as "Bethany across the Jordan" (John 1:28). This was not the more famous village of Bethany, located east of Jerusalem, which Jesus used as a base in Judea. Rather, it was a village of the same name in Perea.[3] Perea lay east of the Jordan, and was under the rule of Herod Antipas (who reigned in Galilee and Perea, 4 BC – AD 39). The New Testament does not actually mention Perea by name. However, the Gospel of John refers to the general area again when it states that John was baptizing in Aenon, near Salim, "because water was abundant there" (John 3:23). The first-century Jewish historian Flavius Josephus also wrote, in *Antiquities of the Jews*, that John the Baptist was imprisoned and then killed in the fortress of Macherus which lay on the border with Perea.[4] A sixth-century Byzantine map – the *Madaba Map* – shows Bethabara (Bethany) west of the Jordan, with Ænon (Aenon) on the eastern bank. However, Aenon may have actually been west of the Jordan because, while at Aenon, John the Baptist's disciples refer to the place where John had first met Jesus as being "across the Jordan" (John 3:26) which one would assume was located east of the river. The key thing, though, is not the exact location but the event itself.

The baptism of Jesus is clearly presented as a definitive moment in his life in the Gospel accounts.

> In those days Jesus came from Nazareth of Galilee and was baptized by John in the Jordan. And just as he was coming up out of the water, he saw the heavens torn apart and the Spirit descending like a dove on him. And a voice came from heaven, "You are my Son, the Beloved [or my beloved Son]; with you I am well pleased"
> **(Mark 1:9–11)**

This makes the point that in doing this, Jesus has moved out of his home territory in Galilee. The Gospel of Matthew makes the same point.

Looking at the details of the baptism itself, Matthew and Luke contain similar accounts to that found in Mark, but with slight (though significant) differences. Matthew adds the detail of John feeling he is unworthy to baptize Jesus but being told, "Let it be so now; for it is proper for us in this way to fulfil all righteousness" (Matthew 3:15). Matthew and, to a greater extent, Luke present the opened heavens and the heavenly voice less as a private experience of Jesus and more an event which (one presumes from their accounts) others could have seen and heard. Two manuscripts of the Old Latin Version of Matthew even go so far as adding "and when he was baptized a huge light shone from the water so that all who were near were frightened" which adds an explicit stress which is way beyond anything in the original version of Matthew. The heretical *Gospel of the Ebionites* (adapted from Matthew's Gospel) included something similar.[5] Justin Martyr (died: c. 165) wrote, rather enigmatically, that when Jesus went down to the water, fire was kindled in the river.[6]

John's Gospel explicitly states that John the Baptist saw the Spirit (John 1:32–34). Luke even adds the words "in bodily form" to describe the dove's descent, as an emphatic statement of objective reality.[7] It is, though, perhaps significant that the earliest form of this account (in Mark) "represents these things as seen only by Jesus".[8] Both the opened heavens and the descent of the Spirit are preceded by the words "he saw", which clearly roots the experience in Jesus' personal perception. This may suggest that the event was a key moment in Jesus' self-awareness and confirmation of his mission. It is perhaps indicative of this that Luke's account – though stressing the public nature of the event – indicates that it occurred while Jesus was praying. Although it could be argued that baptism and prayer could well have been simultaneous events, this *could* also indicate that the revelation occurred after the baptism and while Jesus was engaged in (perhaps private) prayer. Luke's surprising reference to the baptism only in a subordinate clause could support such an interpretation.[9] For this Gospel compiler, the moment of revelation seems more significant that the baptism itself.

More perplexing than this, other ancient manuscripts of Luke 3:22 have the heavenly voice declare, "You are my Son, today I have begotten you". This appears in the fifth-century Greek-Latin bilingual manuscript known as *Codex D*, and was the form known to the earlier Christian writer Justin Martyr.[10] The same form appears in the writings of other early church Fathers (as they are often termed): Clement of Alexandria (died: c. 215) and Origen (died: c. 254). Clearly, they either did not see these verses as implying adoptionism – despite the controversy raging around them at the time – or they were sure that this verse, as they quoted it, represented the original wording of Luke, regardless of any complications it caused in the church of their day.[11] It is also found in manuscripts from places as varied as Asia Minor, Palestine, Egypt, North Africa, Rome, Spain, and Gaul (modern France).[12]

This appears to express a very different view of the relationship of Jesus with God (compared with later creeds) and prompted much debate in the early church, as these words can be read in what is termed an "adoptionist" way (Jesus *became* God's Son, rather than always holding that status). There are clear echoes here of Old Testament beliefs in a newly crowned monarch being *adopted* (begotten), in some way, as God's son (Psalm 2:7). The better attested (and the bulk of) manuscripts do not contain this formula but, clearly, the alternative form reveals debates within the early church regarding the nature and status of Jesus. It has been suggested that these other manuscripts (usually described as the "oldest and best" in translation-terminology) represent an attempt to suppress what was the original wording of Luke, because later Christians were becoming uncomfortable with these words, in the context of what some other believers were making of them.[13] This is a tricky area, to put it mildly, and a case can be made for a poorly attested reading actually constituting the original form in a number of cases, with the "better attested" manuscripts representing an alteration of the original text.[14] That the "less well attested" form quotes Psalm 2:7 gives pause for thought, since it was very common in the early church to quote Old Testament passages which were considered to have messianic meaning, and this is often found in the New Testament.

The appearance of just such a verse at this pivotal point in the life of Jesus would not be at all unusual and would be consistent with other New Testament evidence. Indeed, this very verse from the Psalms is also quoted by the apostle Paul (Acts 13:33) and twice by the writer to the Hebrews (Hebrews 1:5; 5:5) referring to the exalted status of Jesus. Interestingly, Paul connects this verse to the resurrection. In Hebrews it is used to differentiate Jesus from the angels and then from earthly high priests, and no exact point in time (or outside time) is linked to this use. There certainly is no evidence that Paul held an adoptionist view of the resurrection, but the key point is that the appearance of this verse from the Psalms at Luke 3:22 is no aberration. It is consistent with early Christian usage. There are echoes of it (but without the reference to "begotten") in accounts of the transfiguration, as we shall see in due course.[15] But the key thing, from our point of view, is that for the compiler of Luke's Gospel, the decisive moment of declaration/realization was at the River Jordan.

It has also been suggested that Greek translations of Isaiah 42:1 (the servant Davidic king anointed, says God, with "my spirit") and Genesis 22:2, 12, 16 (Isaac, the beloved son of Abraham, being prepared for sacrifice), along with Psalm 2:7, formed a feature described as a "composite echo, the combining of catch-phrases from two or more Old Testament passages in a New Testament context."[16] Such composites relied on the trigger-effects of such words as "beloved" and "son" to call to mind various passages which were thought to interpret or illuminate each other, and to throw light on an event or concept being examined. This appears to have been a Christian continuation of Jewish practice in the first-century synagogues;[17] and it survives, in a fragmentary form, in parts of the New Testament.[18] The voice reported at the baptism, therefore, combines and brings to mind passages from the Jewish scriptures, as found in "the Law", "the Prophets", and "the Writings" of first-century Judaism. It appears to be an example of a synagogue practice, applied to early Christian apologetics designed to root claims about Jesus in the Jewish Scriptures and using methods familiar to anyone who had attended a synagogue. This was a Jewish way of reading scripture that was being carried forward into the increasingly Gentile world of the early church.

In short, the baptism of Jesus in the Jordan was obviously highly significant, however it was later understood, and the wording involved more than simply a tussle between early Christians concerning the matter of adoptionism. Instead, the voice recorded to have spoken at the Jordan signalled (to the Gospel compilers) dramatic evidence concerning the status and mission of Jesus. It clearly signalled the launch of Jesus' own ministry and seems connected to his own self-awareness regarding his mission. More than this latter point we cannot say from the available evidence. Did this constitute an audible miraculous experience (which a historian cannot test), an insight within Jesus' private reflections, or the interpretation of the event by later Christians? The essential point is that it was a seminal moment in the life of Jesus. And later Christian writers clearly knew this.

It is, though, particularly complex since John's baptism indicated repentance for sins and an action to escape God's judgment. This, not surprisingly, has caused some interpreters to suggest that Jesus' view of his own nature was less exalted than that held by his later followers;

and that he felt that he, too, needed baptism. This is not the mainstream interpretation, which would see his decision as representing obedience to God and living out a particular form of repentance which was not implying sins to repent of, but rather the obedience "to live in the world wholeheartedly devoted to God."[19] Or it should be seen as revealing in Jesus a willing identification with sinful and flawed people. In much the same way, Jesus' description of himself as "Son of Man" (something to which we will return) conveys a sense of identifying with people, *alongside* its reference to a messianic descriptor used in the book of Daniel.

The apocryphal *Gospel According to the Hebrews* reflected on this apparent conundrum by imagining Mary and Jesus' brothers discussing how John the Baptist baptized for the forgiveness of sins and Jesus responding with the rhetorical question of what sins did he need baptism for? But then adding an enigmatic conclusion that perhaps what he had just said constituted a sin of ignorance. Suffice it to say, that there is not the slightest hint of such a conversation in the canonical Gospels. However, there clearly were people who later speculated what kind of thought processes might have led Jesus to travel down to the Jordan from Galilee.

Finally, the event raises questions regarding Jesus' relationship with John the Baptist and *his* ministry with that earlier one. At first reading, Jesus' baptism and the meeting with John occurs without any previous contacts between Jesus and John and is the only time they are brought together in any of the Gospels. It stands as a dramatic, but isolated, event. However, there is an intriguing reference from the Gospel of John which describes events, apparently sometime after Jesus' baptism (although that event is not actually described in John's Gospel). It states that "Jesus and his disciples went into the Judean countryside, and he spent some time there with them and baptized" (John 3:22). The next verse explains that John was also baptizing at this time; this is the point at which his location is stated as being at Aenon near Salim. It then adds that this occurred, not surprisingly, before John was put in prison (John 3:24). This is interesting because it is the only time that Jesus is associated with conducting baptisms.

Later Christians differentiated their rite of baptism from the one practiced by John. John's involved repentance in anticipation of God's coming judgment. The Christian rite involved this (with its imagery of washing symbolizing inner cleansing) but was more about entering into a new life, a new community. And, for later Christians, it also evoked ideas of dying and being raised to life with Christ – which occurred in the inner life of the believer who put their faith in the one that they believed was both crucified and resurrected. In short, it was a post-Easter rite because it was a post-Easter faith. So, it is no surprise to learn that none of the synoptic gospels mention Jesus continuing the baptism practices of John the Baptist. Yet the witness of John 3:22 seems unambiguous and, as if that was not enough, just a little later in that same Gospel we hear John the Baptist being informed by his followers, "Rabbi, the one who was with you across the Jordan, to whom you testified, here he is baptizing, and all are going to him" (John 3:26). Again, this seems unambiguous: at the start of his ministry Jesus continued the baptism practices that had brought crowds flocking to the Jordan.

The matter is made more complex because Mark insists that Jesus did not start his public ministry until after John was put in prison (Mark 1:14). However, Mark does not preclude a Judean ministry occurring before the more famous Galilean one, but this is not the impression one gets from a first reading of his words. Yet the tradition in John's Gospel clearly indicates that their activities overlapped at the start. And in John this baptizing episode follows an account of a miracle at a wedding at Cana (though it should be added that this precedes Jesus' decision to begin to preach), a cleansing of the Jerusalem Temple (at the start of the ministry, not the end as in the synoptics), and a famous conversation with a leading Pharisee named Nicodemus (presumably in the vicinity of Jerusalem) concerning what is necessary to be "born again". And it is then followed by John the Baptist explaining the superiority of Jesus and his message, compared to himself and his message. The image is powerful: Jesus is the bridegroom (the implication being that Israel is the bride), whereas John is only the bridegroom's friend. Jesus is from heaven, whereas John is of the earth (John 3:27–36).

Now this illustrates the difficulty of relating the chronology of the synoptic Gospels to that in John's Gospel when the latter is more concerned with exploring spiritual truths in a way in which "chronological placing is not the determinative thing."[20] That is why this biography is based on the synoptics, with the addition of insights from John's Gospel. But there may still be something intriguing here about the start of Jesus' ministry and that is the possibility that it developed out of the earlier activities of the "John the Baptist movement" and that, for a short time, Jesus continued John the Baptist's methods before abandoning them in favour of a new and radical approach. As if to block this line of thinking, John's Gospel adds a later parenthesis to a statement comparing the two ministries:

> Now when Jesus learned that the Pharisees had heard, "Jesus is making and baptizing more disciples than John" – although it was not Jesus himself but his disciples who baptized – he left Judea and started back to Galilee.
> **(John 4:1–3)**

It is perhaps not surprising that it has been suggested that the clause between verses 1 and 3 "may be an insertion by an editor who was anxious to distinguish between Jesus and John",[21] since it appears to contradict the statement in John 3:22.

So, whether these particular baptisms were conducted by Jesus *and* his followers, or by his followers *only*, there is the real possibility that a closer connection existed between Jesus and John the Baptist, and between the two ministries, than we sometimes assume.

But what is clear is that the distinctive ministry of Jesus exploded onto the scene *in Galilee*; and that followed a dramatic period in the wilderness of Judea.

The temptations in the wilderness...

The synoptic gospels associate Jesus' baptism with a time of testing in the Judean wilderness which immediately follows. As if to further emphasize the point, Mark adds "and he was with the wild beasts" (Mark 1:13). The emphasis on a place of wild abandonment, outside the Law of Israel, is clear. It is a place of testing and of trial. The sense of a place of desolation and uncleanness was later vividly conveyed in the poem "In The Wilderness", by Robert Graves (1918) with its striking description of the broken, blind, wild, and monstrous things of the wilderness that were drawn to the company of this "Comrade with ragged coat". For Graves, the striking thing was the idea of Jesus living outside the norms of comfortable existence and settled (acceptable) society. But for the Gospel writers, it was a time in which the nature of Jesus' ministry was tested and decided.

This period is often simply termed "The Temptation" and was, according to the synoptics, a period of forty days fasting in the wild country, in which the devil tempts Jesus with various options regarding how his ministry might develop. There is no mention of this in John's Gospel; Mark briefly refers to it; Matthew and Luke (clearly drawing on an additional collection of material) refer in detail to the conversation that occurs between the devil and Jesus. Mark records simply that Jesus was tempted by the devil, to which Matthew and Luke add the nature and detail of the temptations that he faced.

Each of the temptations is something which would divert him from his focus: if he is the Son of God command the stones to become bread to relieve his hunger; worship the devil in return for political power; leap from a pinnacle of the Temple since God will save him from harm (Luke 4:1–13). The second is the most shocking suggestion, but all reveal ways in which the ministry could potentially be diverted from its proper course. The first may be a reference to the wider satisfying of human physical need when his mission is to re-focus people on God. The second clearly condemns the power politics of the world and the way that these represent a world view that is in line with evil rather than with good. Jesus is not going to be a political revolutionary (despite the radicalism of his message) nor a military leader. The third suggests a use of miraculous power to confirm his identity and, perhaps, gain public attention. That the first starts with the words "if you are the Son of God" indicates a questioning of his status and may reveal the way the expectations of others (here voiced by the devil) challenged his self-belief as he set out on his unique path.

By the time that Luke was compiling his Gospel, Christians were proclaiming the divine Sonship of Jesus, but these words remind us of the competing contemporary viewpoints of how such a messiahship *might* have been revealed in political power and meeting physical needs. It may also give an insight into the self-reflection of Jesus, as he wrestled with the siren voices about him calling him from the path that he was determined to follow. It is at this point that modern readers must decide whether this was self-reflection that had been shared by Jesus with his disciples (by way of bringing them into his confidence) or the reflection of the later Christian community on the different routeways that had lain before Jesus at the start of his ministry. What is clear, is that a decisive moment had occurred in the wilderness regarding the kind of route Jesus would take.

"The kingdom of God has come near": the beginning of Jesus' ministry in Galilee

For the synoptic gospel writers, the temptation in the wilderness is immediately followed by the beginning of Jesus' public ministry. It starts in Galilee and it is separated from any earlier activity of John the Baptist.

Mark tells us: "Now after John was arrested, Jesus came to Galilee, proclaiming the good news of God [some manuscripts: the kingdom]" (Mark 1:14). Luke expands on this with, "Then Jesus, filled with the power of the Spirit, returned to Galilee, and a report about him spread through all the surrounding country. He began to teach in their synagogues and was praised by everyone" (Luke 4:14–15). Returning to Galilee – following the defining moment at the Jordan and the testing of his concept of his mission in the wilderness – he preaches around the region of Galilee and begins to recruit his first disciples. With these followers he begins the itinerant ministry of teaching, preaching, healing, and exorcisms that are so characteristic of his work.

It is instructive that the breaking in of what he calls "the kingdom" is the defining feature. For Mark it is "the kingdom of God", for Matthew (more aware of Jewish sensibilities over the use of the divine name) it is "the kingdom of heaven". Its announcement is dramatic and arresting, by one who clearly speaks with authority and confidence. Charismatic in the purest use of the term he is, in Luke's phrase, "filled with the power of the Spirit". In total, some fifty of Jesus' sayings and parables concern the kingdom.[22] It had End Time meaning, rooted in the Old Testament; focused on the revealing and establishing of God's rule on earth. In this sense "kingdom" was used in the sense of "kingship". It was where God's sovereign reign was experienced. It was apocalyptic and personal; a future hope and a present process working toward it; God's future definitive action and a present programme of change. These varied senses exist in Jesus' use of the term. He was "both expectant of the future and demanding in the present".[23] The declaration of its nearness injected urgency into the statements Jesus made about it. Jesus clearly believed he had decisive insights into the workings of the kingdom and its revealing. As we shall see, the man could not be divorced from the message. That in itself was both distinctive and explosive.

Response to the kingdom involved repentance and acceptance of the good news being preached (Mark 1:15; Matthew 4:17). Exactly what this "good news" is, we will explore in due course. But repentance implies a radical change of direction, lifestyle, and orientation. It was a turning from sin and a turning toward God.[24] It was this radical message that Jesus proclaimed.

The base for these operations was not Nazareth. Instead, Jesus relocates to Capernaum. This was a fishing village on the northern shore of the Sea of Galilee, which had been established in the second century BC, and in the time of Jesus had a population of between 600 and 1,500.[25] Archaeological evidence suggests that this undefended site was prosperous and had Gentiles as well as Jews living there.[26] However, although the later Christian community rapidly expanded beyond the boundaries of Judaism, it is clear that the focus of Jesus' ministry was on fellow Jews within settlements and territories that were largely Jewish in terms of population. There were only a few occasions when he moved into predominantly Gentile territories: healing two demon-possessed men in the "country of the Gadarenes [or Gergesenes]", a region of the Greek *Decapolis* or "Ten Cities" (Matthew 8:28–34); speaking with a Samaritan woman at Sychar (John 4:5–42); healing the daughter of a Canaanite woman in the district of Tyre and Sidon (Matthew 15:21–28). This last example included the famous words, "I was sent only to the lost sheep of the house of Israel" (verse 24). Other encounters with Gentiles are due to the mixed nature of the area, rather than a deliberate foray into Gentile communities: among ten lepers healed, one was a Samaritan (Luke 17:12–19); a group of Greeks visiting Jerusalem ask to speak with him (John 12:20–21); the servant of a non-Jewish military officer is healed (Matthew 8:5–13).

There are hints in these encounters of Jesus' message being for more than the Jewish community. After the request from the Greeks, Jesus declares "I, when I am lifted up from the earth, will draw all people to myself" (John 12:32). After the faith of the military officer is apparent, Jesus says "many will come from east and west and will eat with Abraham and Isaac and Jacob in the kingdom of heaven" (Matthew 8:11). Nevertheless, it is clear from the Gospels that his primary mission, during his ministry, was to the Jewish people.

On Jesus' return to Capernaum, Mark reports Jesus as being "at home" there (Mark 2:1) which some have interpreted as indicating that Jesus owned property there. However, in the absence of further evidence and in the light of his apparent lack of possessions elsewhere in the Gospels, it is more likely he stayed with a supporter(s) there. The place will appear again and again in our exploration of the activities of Jesus, since it is mentioned over fifty times in the Gospels, but one should not assume from this that all its inhabitants welcomed the charismatic radical preacher. It, along with nearby Chorazin and Bethsaida, were later condemned by Jesus for their lack of repentance, with the memorable words:

> For if the deeds of power done in you had been done in Sodom, it would have remained until this day. But I tell you that on the day of judgement it will be more tolerable for the land of Sodom than for you".
> **(Matthew 11:23–24)**

Matthew states that this relocation occurred at the start of the ministry (Matthew 4:13), whereas Mark and Luke later simply refer to Capernaum as the base. Luke perhaps suggests that this occurred after rejection of his authority in Nazareth (Luke 4:31, following the conflict referred to in Luke 4:16–30) which was possibly the trigger for the change in location, although there is evidence that he had already been working miracles at Capernaum (Luke 4:23). Either way, the mission would not be based on Nazareth. We will return to this conflict because it gives us an insight into the controversial nature of Jesus' teaching and its impact on some of those who knew him and the family well. There was clearly going to be a price to pay for declaring the closeness of the kingdom – and it was just beginning.

CHAPTER 7

A band of brothers

As Jesus launched his public ministry he drew to himself a group of followers. As we look at his calling of these people, we can begin to gain an insight into the impact of Jesus on those around him. This enables us to ask and begin to answer some important questions about these early followers. What social and political groups can we identify among them? What was the social position of the fishermen who feature so noticeably? How radical was it to call a tax collector in the context of the politics of the time? Do the names of Simon the Zealot and Judas Iscariot reveal the presence of political radicals (even "terrorists") among the core group of disciples? We can also examine the relationship between a wider circle of "disciples" (such as the seventy, or seventy-two, later sent out preaching) and an inner core of "apostles", their different roles, and the dynamics of this varied group of people.[1]

Responding to the call – a mixed bunch

Immediately after Jesus returned to Galilee, following his baptism and time in the wilderness, he began to call disciples to follow him. The word used to describe them –*mathētés* in Greek – literally means "learner", "pupil".[2] It was used to describe both the inner core ("the Twelve") and the wider amorphous group of followers. Through the accounts in the Gospels, these followers play an important role in the ministry of Jesus, although the way in which they are presented varies. In Mark they are often characterized by getting things wrong or misunderstanding key aspects of Jesus' teachings. Particularly in the central part of this Gospel, their concerns, fears, and questions provide a way by which the writer explores and explains Jesus' purpose and the meaning of his teaching. In Matthew, by way of contrast, they are presented rather more positively as communicators of the message that they have received. He uses the word "disciples" far more than the other synoptic compilers (forty-five times) and they are presented more as models of how believers in the early Christian community are called to become part of the mission of Jesus. Matthew, unlike Mark, includes a statement that disciples have authority to forgive sins (Matthew 18:18) and Simon (Simon-Peter) appears more authoritative too (Matthew 16:18–19).[3]

The compiler of Luke's Gospel places the calling of the first followers a little later in his account than do Mark and Matthew, after a confrontation at Nazareth and the healing of Simon's mother-in-law (in Capernaum) who is suffering from fever (Luke 5). In contrast, Mark and Matthew place the calling of his first followers immediately after his return to Galilee. This ordering is rather more persuasive than Luke's, as Jesus comes to Nazareth apparently already quite well known, which suggests he had already been active in Galilee before this (as we shall see in Chapter 9). Indeed, Mark (the earliest account) states that he arrives at Nazareth in the company of his followers (Mark 6:1), which would support this view. Furthermore, when Luke discusses the calling of Simon, he places this *after* the healing of the mother-in-law; a healing in her home which is easier to imagine if Simon was already a follower of some kind. So, we will follow the ordering of events we find in Mark and Matthew and assume that, soon after Jesus returned north, from the wilderness, he began gathering a following.

All the synoptic gospels make it clear that this occurred on the shores of the Sea of Galilee with fishermen being the first called to join him. Those called are Simon who (as Matthew reminds us) would later also be known as Peter and his brother Andrew; along with James and his brother John (who are sons of a man named Zebedee).

These are names that will loom large in the later Gospel accounts and in the history of the church. Simon Peter would become a leading, if impetuous, figure among the core group of followers and would be the one whom Jesus selected for a key leadership role despite his shortcomings. He showed himself both insightful but also flawed. He was determined to do well, but fell short at the time of crisis following the arrest of Jesus. There is something very human about Simon Peter; imperfect and yet with huge potential. Definitely a man with his heart in the right place, even if his words and actions sometimes took a bit of time to catch up. Eventually martyred in Rome, he is still considered by Roman Catholics as the first bishop of Rome and, in effect, the first pope. But that is getting well ahead of our story and the formality of that traditional role (first pope) would be contested by other historians of the church.

John is usually considered to have been the youngest of the core followers of Jesus and is the one who was also known among later Christians as "John the Evangelist" (traditionally considered the writer of the Gospel of John), "John of Patmos", "John the Elder", and "the beloved disciple". The same tradition holds that he outlived the other apostles and was the only one of them to die of natural causes. Modern theologians and church historians disagree over whether these were all one and the same person, but we can set to one side that complex issue as it is not central to our study.

Peter was not the only fiery character among those called. Jesus later referred to the brothers James and John as "*Boanerges*" (Sons of Thunder), which rather suggests they would not go unnoticed in a crowd or a social gathering (Mark 3:17). The tradition is only found recorded in the Gospel of Mark and we would like to know the back-story of this intriguing nickname - but we don't. We do, though, get a little insight into their characters in the form of a Gospel story which relates how the two brothers wanted to call down heavenly fire on an unfriendly Samaritan town (Luke 9:51–56). Some other manuscripts of Luke indicate that they saw themselves as ready to repeat the action of Elijah, at whose prayer, God rained down fire on Mount Carmel during the conflict between Elijah and the "prophets of Baal" (1 Kings 18:36–40). Interestingly, in the Old Testament the fire consumed the burnt-offering, the wood on the altar, the stones of the altar, the dust, and even the water in the trench dug around it - but not the opposition. Clearly, the Sons of Thunder intended to go a step further regarding the unnamed Samaritan village. As Jews well-versed in the

Scriptures, they would have been aware that, although the fire had not killed the followers of Baal in this event, Elijah later had. James and John were not to be messed with. Sons of Thunder indeed! However, Jesus rebuked them. This is a revealing vignette, starkly displaying the difference in his mindset versus theirs. This is not how Jesus does business, is the clear message. Other manuscripts of Luke underscore this by adding that Jesus said, "You do not know what spirit you are of, for the Son of Man has not come to destroy the lives of human beings but to save them."[4]

These snippets of information give an insight into the mixed bunch of men first called as followers by Jesus. All three synoptic gospels state that these core four were recruited quite soon after Jesus returned to Galilee.

The location is not given in any of the Gospels, although in Luke the calling of Simon occurs soon after events in Capernaum, so it is reasonable to assume that was the location. The later apocryphal *Gospel of the Ebionites* explicitly says so, but probably on no firmer authority than the context provided in the canonical Gospels, which it copied and adapted.

The social status of these men is intriguing. There is a tendency to view them as poor fishermen. This, though, goes beyond the evidence of the Gospels which indicates that they were owners of small businesses. Mark specifically says that Zebedee is left in the boat with his "hired men" (Mark 1:20) and Luke talks about James and John, the sons of Zebedee, being Simon's partners (Luke 5:10). So, we should perhaps imagine them as small-scale entrepreneurs, owning a boat or two, and hiring other men. In the same way a small peasant farmer might employ landless labourers to work on the plot alongside the owner and his family. The connection of Simon with the sons of Zebedee suggests a network of shared ownership and cooperation connecting these men.

When they left to follow Jesus they were walking away from the family business. It was a big step, even if they kept their connections with those who stayed behind in the fishing trade.

When we read of Simon and Andrew dropping their nets it seems clear that Matthew is emphasizing renunciation of previous lifestyle as a response to meeting Jesus. The fishing business required large start-up costs, with its acquisition of a boat, or boats, and nets. Giving this up was a real sacrifice and a personal change in lifestyle. Matthew and Mark also make a point of emphasizing that James and John left their father, when they responded to Jesus' call. Mark even underscores this by the illustration that Zebedee is left in the boat, with only the hired men left to assist him. To a first-century audience it will surely have been clear that these men have also abandoned their father. In a traditional patriarchal society such an act would have been shocking. No longer did this father have authority over his sons. Whether this was meant as a point of radical reordering that was to be generally emulated or just indicated that Mark and Matthew intended these two brothers to be understood as particularly devoted is a moot point. Or it may suggest that Jesus expected the imminent coming of the kingdom, the End Time.[5] In which case, the need to abruptly follow him was given additional urgency. When he tells another would-be disciple, "let the dead bury their own dead" (Matthew 8:22), to a man who says he wishes to bury his (apparently recently dead) father, a similar note of abrupt urgency is sounded. Luke extends this command with "but as for you, go and proclaim the kingdom of God" (Luke 9:60). The End Time urgency is plain to see. The familial radicalism would have been equally apparent – and shocking.

Luke describes the calling of Simon as following a massive catch of fish, which had occurred after Jesus told the dispirited fishermen (who had fished unsuccessfully all night) to put out into deep water and put down their nets again (Luke 5:1–11). This – as with the healing of Simon's mother-in-law – hints at a relationship preceding the calling from their nets, since Jesus had already been teaching the crowd from Simon's fishing boat. That Simon, who was washing his nets prior to this, agreed to drop his work and make the boat available may suggest an existing connection with Jesus – or he may simply have been prepared to accede to the wishes of a man who was already regarded as an impressive teacher and healer. We cannot be sure but there are these clues which may suggest that they had got to know Jesus after he relocated to Capernaum from Nazareth, and prior to the invitation to join him.

Mark and Matthew, by way of contrast, give the impression that this event occurs without any previous connection between Jesus and those called. They are at work and Jesus calls them to give up fishing and, in a memorable expression, to fish for people instead. At once they drop their nets and follow him. The impression is dramatic. Jesus briefly speaks to them and they join him. There is no discussion and they abandon their nets without any further communication. This sudden reaction is often regarded, in Christian commentary, as revealing the immediate power of God acting on these men's lives. However, this is not explicitly stated in the Gospels themselves. Although Luke's order of events may not be as compelling as that found in Mark and Matthew, his account, which indicates an existing relationship with Simon may give an insight into a calling that is a little less abrupt than that which appears in the other two Gospels.

The idea that Jesus was already friends with some of these key men is revealed in the later Gospel of John. This contains a tradition that Andrew and Simon (Simon Peter) were disciples of John the Baptist, and began following Jesus soon after he had been baptized (John 1:35–42). Although, it should be noted, the Gospel of John does not actually mention the baptism itself. In this account, John the Baptist identifies Jesus as "the Lamb of God" and this trigger-event causes two of his followers (we later learn that one of them is Andrew) to leave John the Baptist and go after Jesus. They specifically address him as *rabbi* (teacher) and then stay with him, which indicates both the status they ascribe to him and suggests that they are moving allegiance from their previous *rabbi* (John) to Jesus. Andrew then finds his brother, Simon, and tells him that he has found the Messiah (Christ in the Greek of the Gospel). It is at this point that Jesus renames Simon as *Cephas* or Peter ("rock" in Aramaic being *kepha* and in Greek *petra*).

In John's Gospel this event is rapidly followed by Jesus calling Philip, who is identified as "from Bethsaida, the city of Andrew and Peter" (John 1:44). This again suggests a network of connections, rooted in the Galilean community around the Sea of Galilee. It is not stated that Philip had a prior relationship with Jesus but connectivity is possible. Philip then finds his friend Nathanael and excitedly tells him that he has found "him about whom Moses in the law and also the prophets wrote, Jesus son of Joseph from Nazareth" (John 1:45). To which Nathanael replies with his disparaging assessment of the status of Nazareth.

It is not easy to combine the accounts in the synoptic gospels with that in John's Gospel, but suffice it to say that the features in this later account (combined with clues in Luke) indicates that the dropping of the nets may have been the decisive moment of decision, but was not the first time that those making this step had met the *rabbi* from Nazareth.

The calling of a tax collector

The occupation of most of the core followers was that of fisherman. Later in Jesus' ministry he came across a tax collector busy in his booth. The tax collector is called Matthew (Matthew 9:9) or Levi son of Alphaeus (Mark 2:14, and Luke 5:27 who just names him "Levi"). The location is not specified but in Mark and Matthew it follows an event in Capernaum so, if a chronological connection is intended, this suggests the approximate geographical area. It is consistent with Jesus' activities around the shores of the Sea of Galilee from a base in Capernaum. It is usual to consider this tax collector to have been one and the same man, known by two names.

During the ministry of Jesus both Herodian rulers (in Galilee) and Roman administrators (in Judea) hired "tax farmers" (Latin *publicani*).[6] As well as collecting set amounts of tax, their livelihood was achieved by hiking the amount owed where possible. It was a relationship with those so taxed that was "fundamentally oppressive and exploitative".[7] We know, from the later record of Josephus, that these taxes included annual taxes of various kinds (probably on produce and property) and also sales taxes.[8] Rising tax revenues at the time in both Judea and Galilee may reveal an expanding economy – or higher tax rates![9]

Matthew/Levi accepted the call and followed Jesus. He then invited Jesus for a meal with his friends; these included other tax collectors and a group simply defined as "sinners". We may assume that these included anyone living on the margins of acceptable society, since tax collectors were generally considered collaborators and unclean. So, we may imagine prostitutes (they certainly appear in other accounts) and others looked down on by more morally rigorous fellow citizens. Jesus' wider group of adherents included many such morally and politically questionable characters: "there were many who followed him" (Mark 2:15). Once again we see the radical, socially transgressive (to contemporaries), and disruptive impact that had earlier called men away from their familial duties. The calling of disciples was more than just a forming of a group of supporters. It was a modelling of a new community; one that broke expected boundaries both of authority and of those deemed acceptable. Not surprisingly, the religious authorities (scribes and Pharisees) were appalled, causing Jesus to reply in a self-defining statement and a challenge that: it is the sick who need a doctor and that he had not come to call righteous people (we might read this as self-righteous) but sinners (Mark 2:16–17).

The apostles

The word "disciples" covers a wide range of those who followed Jesus but it is clear that there was an inner core immediately around him. These are often referred to as "the Twelve" or are differentiated by use of the word "apostle". The number will have brought to mind the twelve tribes of Israel and evoked images of a new community of God's chosen people being formed by Jesus.

The Greek word *apostolos* meant "one who is sent". Though it is used eighty times in the New Testament, it was rarely used in classical Greek and was clearly a word that the later Greek-speaking Christian community took and made their own. Used in the sense of "delegates of Jesus", it was applied to those with a particularly authoritative mission. It probably represented the Aramaic word *selîha*, which was related to the Hebrew word *saliah* (one sent with authority).[10] Although it could be used by later Christians in a less intense way, to describe a lower ranked – but still authoritative – leader on ground-breaking missionary work, it was more usually used to differentiate an inner core, who had a particular leadership role assigned to them by Jesus. This had a dual aspect since it was both something of a title (Mark for example used it sparingly – just twice), but one depending for authority entirely on the one commissioning them. In short, the authority was not intrinsically theirs but was, rather, entirely dependent on Jesus.[11] This honorific yet dependent title is, therefore, very revealing.

Mark 3:14 explains that from his wider following, Jesus "appointed twelve, *whom he also named apostles*, to be with him, and to be sent out to proclaim the message" (emphasis added). They were thus chosen for particular closeness to him (which suggests that not every disciple followed the master) and were then to go out on his behalf. The Twelve are named as: Simon (Peter), James, John, Andrew, Philip, Bartholomew, Matthew, Thomas, James son of Alphaeus, Thaddaeus, Simon (the Zealot), and Judas Iscariot, who later betrayed him. The same commissioning also appears in Matthew (10:1–4) and in Luke (6:12–16), with some slight variation in names. This takes place after Jesus calls his disciples to a mountain to make his selection. This mountain location has echoes of Moses and the twelve tribes of Israel at Sinai. Matthew expands their mission to include the power of exorcism and the power to heal all diseases. Luke explains that, before the selection, Jesus spent the night on the mountain praying. The importance of the selection is thus underscored.

The fact that Paul later had to defend his position as an apostle indicates the authoritative nature of this selection and the sense that these twelve men had been with Jesus from the beginning, had been personally selected by him, and had witnessed his resurrection.[12] This is a definition rooted in the witness of all three synoptic gospels. Paul, on the other hand, had not been converted until later and so had to defend his status: claiming it as one commissioned by Jesus in a way different to the other apostles (the vision on the road to Damascus). His apostolic status was the exception that proves the usual rule.

There was then the other tier of *apostolic* preachers (which could include women) that was known in the early church[13] but which belongs to the period of the formative years of that body, and not to the period of Jesus' ministry.

Within the group of apostles in the Gospels there were those who constituted a core within a core. These were Peter, James, and John. These three were the only witnesses of Jesus raising the daughter of Jairus from the dead (Mark 5:37), the transfiguration (Mark 9:2), and his agonizing prayers in Gethsemane before his arrest (Mark 14:33). It was Peter and John, alone of the disciples, who prepared the upper room for the last Passover meal (Luke 22:8). That they were aware of their status is clear in that John attempted to stop a non-disciple from exorcising in the name of Jesus, only to be famously told by his master, "Whoever is not against us is for us" (Mark 9:40).

Regarding the Twelve, there may have been a fluid outer edge. Some names appear mutable: Bartholomew has traditionally been considered the same man as Nathanael who appears only in John's Gospel, but is not named as one of the Twelve; Thaddaeus in Mark and Matthew is replaced with Judas son of James in Luke; some manuscripts of Mark and Matthew call Thaddaeus, Lebbaeus. Simon/Peter and Matthew/Levi show a man could be known by more than one name. But it may also be that the membership of the Twelve was not entirely fixed, or that at least one less-well-known member remained obscure in the historic memory.[14] Rather like "the fifth Beatle".

How do the Twelve appear to have related to a wider following?

Specific statements and some clues remind us that although we know the names of the core twelve followers – the apostles – these were drawn from a much larger group. Luke, alone of the synoptic gospels, records a telling point of detail. There is a later moment, as Jesus moves south toward Judea, at which seventy or seventy-two (the Greek manuscripts are almost evenly divided) followers are sent out ahead of him to the places that he intends to visit (Luke 10:1). The key thing at this point is the number involved. This clearly indicates a much wider network of followers. In later Western Christianity, these seventy are usually referred to as "disciples", whereas in Eastern Christianity they are usually referred to as "apostles".

Then there are clues. As we shall see, in due course, when Jesus entered Jerusalem on what we now call Palm Sunday, a donkey and colt are found ready and the disciples sent to untie them are told, if challenged, to simply reply "The Lord needs it and will send it back here immediately" (Mark 11:3). Matthew and Luke contain a similar account with an even shorter response: "The Lord needs it/them" (Luke 19:31; Matthew 21:3).The most obvious way to read this is that it was prearranged, with an agreed code-phrase. A similar thing happens when the room for the final Passover meal is chosen. Jesus says,

> Go into the city, and a man carrying a jar of water will meet you; follow him, and wherever he enters, say to the owner of the house, "The Teacher asks, Where is my guest room where I may eat the Passover with my disciples?"
> **(Mark 14:13–14)**

Once again, this seems to indicate a wider network of followers than we often assume; and prearranged preparations and signals.

The dynamic of a *rabbi* and his disciples

What we see in the relationship of Jesus and his followers is that of a wider core of adherents who do not all leave home and family and an inner core of those who travel with him and had a more intimate relationship with him. Time and again we see those accompanying him listening to his teachings, and witnessing his healings and exorcisms. This is spiritual on-the-job learning and training. And, at times, we see Jesus explaining things to his followers in greater detail than is being experienced by the crowds. Secret things (literally "mysteries") of the kingdom are revealed plainly to those closest to him but in parables to others (Matthew 13:10–11). Mark specifies that this involves private explanations to his disciples (Mark 4:34). Jesus' use of parables is something to which we will return but the key thing at this point is to note the depth and clarity that was experienced by the disciples, whereas the more testing illustrative points were made to the crowds to engage with *and ponder on*.

In the same way, we see Jesus teaching the disciples a pattern for prayer that we now refer to as the Lord's Prayer; but which was clearly meant as a guide to how to approach prayer, rather a fixed formula (Matthew 6:9–13). Luke specifically identifies this as occurring after a request by one of the disciples that Jesus teach them how to pray as John had done for his disciples. As well as illustrating something of the common ground between the two groups of disciples, it also provides a glimpse into the inner dynamic of the rabbi and his closest followers.

This inner group of the Twelve were also sent out on missionary activities with specific roles and for specific time periods. Mark writes of them sent out in twos with Jesus' authority. The particular, and specific, nature of these activities is revealed in them being told to take nothing for the journey but a walking stick; no bread, no bag, no money; to wear sandals and just one tunic (Mark 6:7–13). Matthew includes the instruction not to go to Gentile or Samaritan settlements, for the urgent task is to go to "the lost sheep of the house of Israel". They are to accept no payment (Matthew 10:5–8). This is urgent preaching. Many commentators have read it as occurring with a real sense of impending End Time crisis, implied (it seems) in the statement that the kingdom is at hand.

It was clearly not intended as the commissioning of a permanent community of itinerant poor preachers (like the later Franciscans), but rather as a particular commission, with specific rules, for a specific (and limited) time period. Having been taught by Jesus, they then go out and put into practice what they have been taught.

The same is also done on a wider basis with a larger group of disciples, when Luke records the similar sending out of the seventy (or seventy-two). The modelling of mission in this particular period of action is expanded in this account. They are to greet no one on the road (presumably a sign of urgency); stay in just one friendly house in a town; rely on food and drink provided; cure the sick and proclaim the proximity of the kingdom of God – and the judgment of God on any town that rejects the message (Luke 10:1–12). As with the sending out of the Twelve, this has clear instructions and modus operandi, "limited as to sphere and time" before they return to Jesus and report back.[15] It also appears to have a tone of End Time urgency. The followers are being initiated into the kingdom outlook, actions, and power of their teacher.

Hidden in plain sight – political radicals among the Twelve?

We are used to the idea of fishermen being among the closest companions of Jesus. Thomas, and Nathaniel may also have had experience in this occupation, since John's Gospel refers to them taking part in later fishing activity (John 21:2). And we know of Matthew the tax collector. But radicalized political activists? Men regarded by the Roman and Jewish authorities as revolutionary hotheads, even terrorists? Surprisingly, we know of one among the Twelve. And perhaps two.

One such was certainly Simon. He is referred to variously as "Simon the Zealot" (in Luke and in the related book of Acts) and "Simon the Canaanite" or "Cananaean" (in Mark and Matthew).[16] Luke 6:15 is striking because it explicitly associates Simon with the extreme nationalist party of the Zealots. Even the less threatening surname of "Canaanite" is likely to have been derived from the Aramaic *qan'ana'* – a Zealot.[17] We would like to know more about his political background and how he changed when he joined a group whose rabbi taught transformation without violence. It has been suggested that he was the same "Simon Zealot" later crucified for his political activism by Tiberius Alexander, the reneged-Jewish Roman procurator of Judea (in post: 46–48). The man executed was son of Judas of Galilee who had founded the Zealots.[18] However, there is nothing beyond the coincidence of name to connect the two men.

The second one is less certain but a real possibility. Judas Iscariot, who betrayed Jesus, possibly took his surname from the, unlocated, village of Kariot or Kerioth. However it may be derived from *Sicarii* (knife-men, assassins). In this case he was Judas *Sicarius*.

The complication is that the Zealots and the *Sicarii* came to prominence in the nationalist fervour of the 60s; some thirty years after the ministry of Jesus.[19] Did these terms exist at the time of Jesus? If they did, were they beginning to gain the political meanings that they later carried? Were these terms first associated with these members of the Twelve later, at the time of the compilation of the Gospels? And if so why? Perhaps these men had always been associated with radical politics and the disastrous events of the First Jewish–Roman War (background to the writing of the Gospels) had emphasized how catastrophic this routeway proved to be. In which case, Simon exemplified how a man on a wrong path could be won over to the true way. And Judas *Sicarius* was the prime example of a man on the wrong path, who continued on it. It may contain a hint of discord in the centre of the Jesus-movement over the path the longed-for Messiah should take. Perhaps it was a signpost toward reasons for future betrayal that are not unpacked in the Gospels.

What is clear is that these two men remind us of the variety in experience and outlook that existed among the Twelve. And if they were complex, one can only guess at the level of complexity of outlook among the hundreds who gathered to hear Jesus preach. Perhaps Herod Antipas had cause to be worried about what might happen when such large numbers gathered. Especially so, if their enthusiasm was focused on a prominent leader. The future might become very dangerous, very rapidly, for a young rabbi and his mixed band of brothers.

CHAPTER 8

A band of... sisters

We have explored the calling of Jesus' followers. We have seen how, in addition to the large crowds who came to hear him, there was a fairly large group of disciples (recalled in the case of the seventy-two), an inner core (the apostolic Twelve) and an intimate group of three. All of these were apparently men. Given the social structure, gender roles, and gendered expectations of Galilee and Judea in the first century AD this is not surprising.

However, this leaves us with an important question: what was the role of women? For, hidden in plain sight, we see a radical social experiment going on with regard to the female followers of Jesus. But who were they? What role did they play? And how should we react to controversial claims that have circulated in recent times about Jesus and Mary Magdalene? It is time to explore: A band of... sisters.

The evidence for female disciples

At one point Jesus' family appears and asks to speak with him. He replies:

> "Who is my mother, and who are my brothers?" And pointing to his disciples, he said, "Here are my mother and my brothers! For whoever does the will of my Father in heaven is my brother and sister and mother".
> **(Matthew 12:48–50)**

In reflecting on this we need to recall that Jesus is pointing *to his disciples* and using the phrase "mother and brothers" to describe them. It is hard to think that this was said to a wholly male group. The more obvious understanding is that he pointed to a mixed-gender group of disciples and described them as "my mother and my brothers" and then as "my brother and sister and mother". In short, there were women who were members of the band of disciples.[1]

This is far from being the only evidence. Luke describes how,

> [Jesus] went on through cities and villages, proclaiming and bringing the good news of the kingdom of God. The twelve were with him, as well as some women who had been cured of evil spirits and infirmities: Mary, called Magdalene, from whom seven demons had gone out, and Joanna, the wife of Herod's steward Chuza, and Susanna, and many others, who provided for them out of their resources.
> **(Luke 8:1–3)**

Here we have clear proof. Among those travelling with Jesus were both men and women. These constituted that band of followers who had accepted him as their rabbi and had thrown in their lot with him. Furthermore, the female disciples had ploughed their own monetary resources into supporting the mission. This is intriguing and one wonders what Chuza, steward of Herod's household, thought of his wife going off to join the wandering group of followers accompanying a radical holy man. And, in addition, spending money that she apparently considered was her own to spend as she thought fit. These are clearly empowered women.

Such behaviour – travelling in the company of unrelated males – was frankly astonishing in the first century. And for a woman such as Joanna this meant swapping the high wealth, status, and expectations of the Herodian royal court for the norm-defying experience of membership of a mixed-gender travelling group. And, according to Luke, there were "many others": a phrase that can only have applied to women since is it sandwiched between the named females, and their financial freedom in allocating money to the cause. There is a social earthquake within these simple statements and one that we often miss due to the brevity of the information. But it is there – and it is entirely unambiguous. It does not require us to pit a weaker evidenced group of manuscripts against better attested ones, or Gnostic claims against canonical evidence. This material is clear and solid. These female disciples and their revolutionary lifestyle decisions are hidden in plain sight.

As a result, we should not be surprised to find that women disciples are present at critical points in the Gospel accounts. At the cross, when all but one named male disciple (John) had fled, it was the women who were there. These were – in addition to Mary, Jesus' mother – "Mary Magdalene, and Mary the mother of James the younger and of Joses [Joseph], and Salome" (Mark 15:40). These three unrelated women were later the primary witnesses to the resurrection. That the Gospel writers were willing to record this in a society that did not regard women as valid legal witnesses is truly remarkable and amply demonstrates the central role of these women. These are further examples of how Jesus and his followers challenged social norms.

Another clue to this survives from an unexpected source. In Romans 16:1–7, the apostle Paul greets a number of people prominent in the early church in the Roman capital. Among a number of women named, is this intriguing comment:

> Greet Andronicus and Junia, my relatives who were in prison with me; they are prominent among the apostles, and they were in Christ before I was.
> **(Romans 16:7)**

Junia was a relative of Paul's, became a Christian before he did, and was in prison with him. Despite some attempts to make Junia into a man – via a postulated and otherwise unknown male personal name Junias (the Greek *Iounian* could go either way) – the clear weight of evidence is in favour of it being a female name.[2] Early church tradition thought she was a woman.[3] We must conclude that she was a female apostle.

This may have meant that she was highly regarded "by the apostles" but the Greek does not support this and we must conclude that to translate it as "the apostles held them in high esteem" or "in the eyes of the apostles" is not in line with the linguistic evidence.[4] So, an apostle is clearly what she was – but it might have been "apostle" as used in its rarer sense of church pioneers/missionaries breaking new ground. In this case, Junia was not one who was an – otherwise previously unnamed – member of the Twelve, nor one elevated to this rank after the earthly ministry of Jesus had ended. But, however we should understand this verse, she was clearly an apostle of some kind and had been a believer from an early stage in the history of the Christian community. She may have been one who was regarded as having seen the risen Christ, since she was a believer *before Paul was*. This could apply even if she was later accorded a title in (what we might call) the second tier of apostles, for she had clearly become a believer in the earliest days of the church. This might have even been during the period of Jesus' ministry, if she was a Jew from Galilee or Judea. This is a staggering thought, for it indicates a Jewish woman believer of considerable esteem and authority. Perhaps she was one of the "many others" referred to by Luke.

The case of Junia reinforces the idea of women playing a leading role in the life of the early Christian community. This had deep roots and had started in the days of the Galilean ministry of Jesus. Whether Junia's authority and involvement went back quite that far is uncertain. But it may well have. Other women were certainly playing an important role from the early days and right through to the events of Easter and beyond. We should be on the lookout for a female involvement in the ministry of Jesus. He clearly held women in high regard and this is seen among his group of followers.

Jesus and women beyond his inner circle

The point that Jesus transformed expectations regarding women, applies to his attitude toward women generally. Women appear to a significant degree in the Gospels, interacting with Jesus.[5] He never treats them disparagingly or dismissively. He never reacts to them in line with gender stereotypes. This particularly stands out when the Gospels are compared with other literature of the time.[6] Social norms were actively broken. When a woman with an issue of blood touches his garment, Jesus reacts without any concern for the ritual uncleanness that others would have thought resulted from this (Mark 5:25–34). The total absence of his concern regarding this can mean we miss it – but we need to note it. At Nain, he takes pity on a widow who has lost her son, and, unbidden, Jesus raises the man to life (Luke 7:11–17). Again unasked, he heals a crippled woman who had been unable to stand upright for eighteen years (Luke 13:10–13).

In a similar vein, Jesus refers to women honourably and respectfully in illustrative parables and references (the ten wise virgins, the persistent widow, the poor woman's gift at the treasury, a woman's lost coin illustrating God's love for the lost). He criticized unjust and dismissive divorce, as practiced by men. At the Samaritan village of Sychar he talks openly and frankly with a woman who is on her own; a woman with a problematic relationship track record as well (she has had five husbands and is now living with a man). It is not surprising that, when his disciples return, "They were astonished that he was speaking with a woman" (John 4:27). The point is clear: women have a significant and honourable place in Jesus' regard and in his teaching. Finally, and giving an insight into his personal relationships, when Jesus is not ready to work a miracle at a wedding at Cana, he still does so – because his *mother* asks him to do so (John 2:1–11).

However, to return to the focus on female disciples – rather than women generally – we must now examine the role and significance of Mary Magdalene.

Mary of Magdala

When Luke describes the women who travel with Jesus, the first named of these women is "Mary (called Magdalene)". She appears in all four canonical Gospels as a witness to the crucifixion of Jesus, and to the empty tomb at the resurrection. This demonstrates her importance for all four Gospel writers at this pinnacle of Jesus' mission. A later ending to Mark's Gospel (which originally ended with the women leaving the empty tomb confused and afraid) adds information, also found in Luke, that Jesus had exorcized Mary Magdalene of seven demons (Mark 16:9–11).

Things get rather complex with Mary Magdalene, because the name was a common one. We know of four different Marys in the Gospels. They are: the Virgin Mary; Mary of Bethany (the sister of Martha and Lazarus); Mary Magdalene; and Mary, the mother of James and Joses/Joseph. What is clear is that Mary Magdalene was an important character within the group surrounding Jesus.

What is certainly missing, is the highly charged assertions that have been made about her. Many readers might be wondering what about the prostitution? No sex has entered into the story. Some, if they have read some fairly recent and highly publicized books or watched a Hollywood blockbuster in which she features (with at least a walk-on part) might ask: why do some modern writers suggest that she married Jesus?

It can sometimes be difficult to get a clear view of the women in the band of disciples because of the virtual smokescreen of confusions and allegations that have arisen over the years regarding Mary Magdalene. This has spilled over into extreme assertions regarding women disciples generally. These assertions can cause us to take our eyes off the real story. But because these claims are so high profile it is important to briefly deal with them.

A little digging into the afterlife of Mary Magdalene soon reveals the process by which this occurred. First, there is the demonic possession. This encouraged the idea, and the image, of Mary Magdalene as particularly sinful before she met Jesus. Medieval celibate clergy harboured extreme anxieties about sexuality, and sexual sin. That Mary Magdalene might have been an extreme sexual sinner seems to have been an idea that emerged as males attempted to read between the lines of what the Gospel writers actually wrote.

Then there is the matter of her home town: Magdala Tarichaea (the Tower of Salted Fish). The later Jewish Talmud, in the *Midrash on Lamentations* or *Lamentations Raba*, states that the town of Magdala was condemned and destroyed by God because of the sexual sin (extra- and pre-marital) that was taking place there. Mary's association with Magdala may explain the view in Western Christianity that she may have been a prostitute or promiscuous, before she met Jesus. However, Mary Magdalene is never referred to as a prostitute by any of the Gospel writers and this judgment of sexual promiscuity created associations that none of the Gospel writers intended to be made.[7] Additionally, the fact that she is named after the town of her birthplace or habitation (Magdala), rather than by her husband's or son's name implies that she probably was not married, and she had no children.[8]

But perhaps the biggest reason for Mary Magdalene's peculiarly sexualized "afterlife" in Christian tradition is that she has been conflated with two totally different women. The first conflation is with Mary of Bethany, the sister of Lazarus and Martha. This Mary "anointed the Lord with perfume and wiped his feet with her hair" (John 11:1–2). This dramatic act is described in detail in John 12:1–8.[9] There is absolutely no reason for thinking this is Mary Magdalene, except they both were called Mary.

The second conflation, totally erroneously, introduces sex into the Mary Magdalene story.

This is because another – but unnamed – woman is also credited with pouring expensive ointment on Jesus as an expression of her devotion to him. This event occurred in Galilee.

> A woman in the city, who was a sinner, having learned that [Jesus] was eating in the Pharisee's house, brought an alabaster jar of ointment. She stood behind him at his feet, weeping, and began to bathe his feet with her tears and to dry them with her hair. Then she continued kissing his feet and anointing them with the ointment.
> **(Luke 7:37–38)**

The first event occurred at Bethany, near Jerusalem, whereas this second event took place in Galilee. But the two accounts are so similar in content that the events/women have often been merged together. To complicate things further, although Mary of Bethany has an impeccable moral status, this second (Galilean) woman clearly did not. The description of her as "sinful" almost certainly refers to sexual immorality, and we can safely assume this meant either prostitution or fornication. Sex has entered the story and from this point it will run and run.

This totally unjustified combination of (a) Mary of Bethany with (b) the woman "who was a sinner" was then further compounded by (c) assuming that this composite woman was, in fact, Mary Magdalene. So, in this construction, Mary Magdalene was the woman, in the Gospel of Luke, who washes Jesus' feet with her tears, dries his feet with her hair, and anoints his feet with perfume. From this has arisen the conclusion that Mary Magdalene was an ex-prostitute, whose sexual activities were caused by (or led to) demonic possession. And that her gratitude to Jesus for her deliverance caused this extravagant display of love toward him.

None of this actually refers to Mary Magdalene but this is now so engrained in Christian tradition that it is hard to shake, despite the fact that it has no New Testament basis whatsoever and is clearly completely at odds with the evidence in the Gospels. And it looks like this confusion started early.

In Egypt, at a place called Nag Hammadi, among many other documents unearthed, have been ones called the *Gospel of Thomas*, the *Gospel of Philip* and the *Acts of Peter.* These are Gnostic texts and were written much later than the canonical Gospels. Two of these make highly controversial claims regarding Mary Magdalene. In the *Gospel of Philip*, the disciples ask Jesus, "Why do you love her [Mary Magdalene] more than all of us?" The text goes on to assert: "And the companion of the… Mary Magdalene… loved her more than all the disciples, and used to kiss her often on her…"[10] This fragmentary text has prompted extreme speculations as to what the fully constructed text might once have said. It could mean that to kiss is to share or be born of the same spirit.[11] Others have interpreted the kiss to show that Mary may have been one of Jesus' closest companions.[12] But, not surprisingly, others have read sexual connotations into this fragment. All this, despite the fact that mainstream New Testament experts have dismissed such a Gospel as inherently completely unreliable anyway.

The *Gospel of Thomas* presents the apostle Peter rejecting Mary Magdalene because she is a woman but it then concludes with this strange assertion:

> Jesus said: "Look, I will draw her in so as to make her male, so that she too may become a living male spirit,

> similar to you." (But I say to you): "Every woman who makes herself male will enter the kingdom of heaven."[13]

What this means is anyone's guess, but it is typical of the complex and obscure wording of this Gnostic source.

More controversial again, is the so-called *Gospel of Jesus' Wife*, a Coptic papyrus fragment unveiled in 2012 and appearing to date from between the sixth and ninth centuries, which presents Jesus as speaking of his "wife" as an initiated disciple. The name of this "wife" is not revealed but it is reminiscent of the Gnostic references to Mary Magdalene. Many experts, though, regard it as a modern forgery.[14]

Then there is the *Gospel of Mary*, a papyrus book found in 1896 in a Cairo bazaar. It claims to describe events after the resurrection of Jesus, in which Mary Magdalene is presented as the guide and teacher to the confused male disciples. Peter and Mary are rivals for leadership.[15]

Finally, the third- or fourth-century *Pistis Sophia* (*Faith Wisdom*), discovered in 1773, describes Mary Magdalene as the "blessed one", who possessed mysterious knowledge.[16]

In this way, the clues in the canonical Gospels, that Mary Magdalene was a significant member of the group of disciples, has been added to due to later conflations by Christian writers, and fictional inventions by Gnostic sects. From this has emerged a view of women within Jesus' followers that is highly misleading, to put it mildly. In contrast to a situation where their status can be missed in the sweep of events, an extreme position has been created whereby they are presented as rivals to the male leadership within the apostolic band and one of them has even been reconstructed as the wife of Jesus. As a result, it can sometimes be hard to cut through all these thickets of controversy to the reality as presented (albeit in brief form) within the canonical Gospels. For one does not have to subscribe to extreme conspiracy-theory-theology to feel that, in some sense, Mary Magdalene was an important female disciple. This is not to assume that she was one of the Twelve; and certainly there is no evidence whatsoever to substantiate the Gnostic claims regarding a relationship with Jesus, nor for her having a position analogous to that of Simon Peter (let alone being his superior). Yet her profile is curious: repeatedly (but briefly) mentioned;

present at the crucifixion and resurrection (so central to Christian faith and Christology); but we never quite feel we know here. We see her and yet we don't fully see her. Reviewing this enigmatic and limited evidence – despite her being such an important person – has led to the conclusion that "It's obvious that there's so much unease about Mary Magdalene, even in the New Testament".[17] But this is probably because the sheer radicalism of the Jesus-movement was hard to communicate to many in contemporary society. This led, perhaps, to a reduction in the profile of these remarkable women disciples.

Where does this leave us?

Having looked at this evidence, how should we envisage the role of women within the followers of Jesus? How did the female presence operate within the band of disciples? We might look at it in this rather striking and thought-provoking manner. In Mark's Gospel (for example) women are, quite simply, never mentioned among the disciples. Their speech is muted and the impression is that most of those in Jesus' immediate following were male. This, despite the fact that women appear sixteen times in various contexts. But then, after three named women are identified as being at the crucifixion, we are told: "These used to follow him and provided for him when he was in Galilee; and there were *many other women* who had come up with him to Jerusalem" (Mark 15:41, emphasis added). This sudden appearance is striking and intriguing. They are then prominent until the end of this Gospel.[18]

It has been suggested, in the light of this vital piece of information, that "You have to go back to the beginning of the Gospel of Mark and reimagine just about every scene with women in it."[19] That may be going too far, but it is certainly thought-provoking and it is reasonable that it be done to a significant degree. When we see women at Jesus' tomb, intent on anointing his body, we see non-relatives performing the respectful mourning rituals normally reserved for the female relatives of a deceased man. It is as if a new kind of "family" has been constructed and we are suddenly reminded of Jesus' striking words regarding who constitute his "mother" and "sisters".

However, these are more than simply the subservient women that we might expect in first-century Jewish society. These are the empowered women disciples who have burst through the boundaries of contemporary norms as a result of their meeting Jesus. A new and radical community is being modelled. But would later communities be flexible enough to accommodate such radicalism? Only time would tell.

CHAPTER 9

The "good news": what exactly was it?

At the beginning of Mark's Gospel Jesus proclaims: "repent, and believe in the good news" (Mark 1:15). But what actually constituted this "good news"? In short, what was the fundamental message of Jesus? Exploring this also involves investigating just how radical were both the lifestyle and the message that he proclaimed, and its relationship to what was going on in mainstream Jewish beliefs and practices at the time.

The core of Jesus' message was that the people hearing the "good news" should repent (that is, listen and respond by bringing their lives into line with what he proclaimed). This was because God was directly intervening in human affairs in a dramatic and life-changing way that was set to transform society. The implications of this for his view of world and cosmic history has prompted much debate and will be the subject of a later chapter as we look at Jesus in conflict with the current world order. But, at this stage, suffice it to ask: just what did such an in-breaking of God's kingdom look like?

Even the briefest survey of Jesus' activities in Galilee indicate this involved: teaching principles through stories which challenged his listeners to consider the implications of what they heard; dramatic healings and exorcisms which demonstrated power to liberate people from sickness and demonic possession; a deep compassion for those so bound and restricted and in need of liberation; eating and drinking with a wide range of people, most notably including those regarded as "sinners", "unclean", and marginal in his contemporary society.[1]

All of this took place within an itinerant ministry (although, apparently, with a base in Capernaum) that encompassed preaching in the countryside; in synagogues (none of the upstanding structures of which survive from the period of his activities);[2] in the homes of supporters; and travel, at times, into non-Jewish territory but with a ministry primarily focused on contemporary Jewish communities (mostly in Galilee but also extending into Judea). Interestingly, this was mostly village-focused and he seems to have avoided urban centres such as Tiberius and Sepphoris.

It is clear that he was regarded by many as a prophet (one who spoke a message from God revealed by direct revelation). He clearly presented himself with reference to well-known Old Testament prophetic figures, either by specific reference and use of similar terminology and language (Micah, Ezekiel, Jonah) or by the implication of his message (Ezekiel, Amos). There are also parallels between his teachings and the content and style of Elijah.[3] The amount of times that he is referred to in this way in the various Gospels indicates that this was a tradition that was well-rooted in the period of his ministry. By the time that the first written accounts were produced, his followers were claiming much more about him than this, so the fact that these traditions survive in the Gospels are sure signs that this was a status readily applied to Jesus by many of his contemporaries.[4] Not by all, of course, because he also had his detractors and met opposition.

Synagogues as teaching platforms

It is clear that Jesus was an active participant in the meetings of Jewish males at the synagogues. Later Hebrew terms for them remind us of their roles: *bet ha-tefilla* (house of prayer), *bet ha-kneset* (house of assembly), and *bet ha-midrash* (house of study). Their roots probably lay in the period after the destruction of the first Temple in 587 or 586 BC, when they became locations for the continuation of Jewish religious devotion and community life. Evidence from the time of Jesus refers to numerous synagogues, not only in Palestine but wherever Jewish communities existed, from Babylon to Rome. It seems that morning, afternoon, and evening services were held every day. On the Sabbath and on religious festivals special liturgies guided the meeting.

Mark describes Jesus teaching in the synagogue at Capernaum early in his public ministry (Mark 1:21) and carrying out an exorcism there. Mark goes on to say that this occurred (teaching and exorcisms) "throughout Galilee" (Mark 1:39). The possibility from this is that, as at Capernaum, this occurred within the context of synagogue meetings, although the wording is not exclusive to such locations. Matthew similarly refers to Jesus being active in "all the cities and villages [of Galilee], teaching in their synagogues, and proclaiming the good news of the kingdom, and curing every disease and every sickness" (Matthew 9:35). We hear of another specific healing taking place in the synagogue, presumably at Capernaum (Mark 3:1). And more teaching takes place in the synagogue at Nazareth, which causes conflict (Mark 6:1–6). Luke refers to him preaching in the synagogues of Judea (Luke 4:44), although other manuscripts of this Gospel have "Galilee" and it seems that that geographical area was the main focus of his synagogue attendance and preaching. That Luke felt he had a roving commission involving any synagogue meeting-place is clear in Luke's reference to the healing of a crippled woman "in one of the synagogues on the Sabbath" (Luke 13:10), where the specific *geographical location* has not made it into the tradition he recounts but the *kind of place* where such an event frequently occurred is clearly understood. Although John's handling of evidence differs from the synoptics in a number of ways, he communicates the same understanding when he states that, at his trial, Jesus insists,

> I have spoken openly to the world; I have always taught in synagogues and in the temple, where all the Jews come together. I have said nothing in secret.
> **(John 18:20)**

Although the reference to the Jerusalem Temple stands out in this context (to which we will return in another chapter), the emphasis on public proclamation in places of Jewish assembly is clear. And it is consistent with the mass of evidence from the other Gospels. From this it is clear that both synagogue attendance and preaching and healing at meetings held there was a characteristic of Jesus' ministry. This is not to say that these were the only places that this occurred. There is plenty of evidence relating to his teaching and healing outside of the context of the synagogues, but clearly these were places where this often happened.

Jesus' relationship with God

As well as taking part (we assume) in the formal prayer life of the synagogues he attended, Jesus is frequently described as being engaged in private prayer, often in lonely places. In this he took part in spiritual practices similar to other Jews of his generation,[5] but with a particular concentration on private communion with God.

This sense of an intimate relationship with God is perhaps seen in his use of the Aramaic "*abba*" (father)[6] for God, although this was not unique to Jesus.[7] Modern Hebrew colloquial speech uses the word to convey something like the modern English "daddy" but it did not have this meaning in the first century (although it is often mistakenly stated that it did).[8] The suggestion that it had a strikingly intimate meaning seems to have first been made by the German Lutheran New Testament scholar Joachim Jeremias who, in his 1971 book *New Testament Theology*, explained that *abba* was "the chatter of a small child… a children's word, used in everyday talk" and even "disrespectful, indeed unthinkable to the sensibilities of Jesus' contemporaries to address God with this familiar word".[9] He was later comprehensively taken to task for this linguistic claim;[10] and Jeremias then adjusted his earlier claim in the light of these criticisms. The evidence suggests that, in the first century, there was, in fact, no other word in Aramaic for father. The term *abba* simply meant "the father" or "my father".[11]

To use the term to address God was not unique to Jesus. In Jewish literature of the time, such as *Sirach* 23:1,4, *Wisdom* 14,3, the Joseph Prayer in *ms.4Q372* 1:16, the word is found used in this context. This suggests that Jesus' language in this respect, as with other aspects of his prayer life was consistent with that of other devout Jews of his generation. His use of the term was "distinctive rather than unique."[12]

Nevertheless, although *abba* was a straightforward adult term for one's father, it was certainly not a formal or ceremonial term that one might expect to be used to address the creator of the universe. And the critics of the "daddy" suggestion have still made it clear that the term "belonged to a familiar or colloquial register of language".[13] In first-century Aramaic this form had a character associated with family membership. In the Gemara (the part of the Jewish Talmud made up of rabbinical commentary on the Mishnah) slaves were forbidden to address the head of the family by this title, because they lacked family membership.[14] This is surely of some significance in assessing Jesus' use of the word.

Furthermore, that this Aramaic word is used in the Greek-language New Testament, when it could simply have employed the Greek word *pater*, suggests that it was particularly associated with Jesus, although it only actually appears once in the Gospels:

> He said, "Abba, Father, for you all things are possible; remove this cup from me; yet, not what I want, but what you want".
> **(Mark 14:36)**

That the combined form, "Abba Father", then appears in two of Paul's later letters (in Romans 8:15, and Galatians 4:6) may be because its association with Jesus had caused the phrase to become a very early Christian liturgical formula for addressing God in prayer.

Although it might not have the meaning that is sometimes attributed to it, Jesus' use of the term indicated an intimacy with God which, when taken with other aspects of his teaching style, reveals a confidence in his own authority which was rooted in a personal sense of relationship with and speaking for God. Whether this meant he saw himself as Messiah or Son of God is a crucial question to which we will return. But what it did with regard to his teaching was to infuse it with a sense of authority that needs to be remembered whenever one is assessing the nature and impact of his words and actions. Twice Mark's Gospel comments on the reaction of observers that are relevant to this:

> They were astounded at his teaching, for he taught them as one having authority, and not as the scribes.
> **(Mark 1:22)**
>
> They were all amazed, and they kept on asking one another, "What is this? A new teaching – with authority! He commands even the unclean spirits, and they obey him".
> **(Mark 1:27)**

A number of characteristic features stand out with regard to the style of his preaching, the content of his message, and his actions, but the underlying sense of *authority* must be recalled at each point. For it was particularly this which caused him to stand out and attract attention – both positive and negative.

Celebration, inauguration, condemnation

Jesus' teaching is a striking combination of inclusive celebration of the in-breaking kingdom of God and warnings of judgment and condemnation.

His compassion for the people caused him to describe them as being "like sheep without a shepherd; and he began to teach them many things" (Mark 6:34). Here we see the treatment of ordinary people as being of worth, evidenced in his taking the message directly to them.

On the other hand, he confronts hypocrisy and self-righteousness in a way designed to challenge complacency among his religious compatriots. He describes scribes and Pharisees as being like "whitewashed tombs, which on the outside look beautiful, but inside they are full of the bones of the dead and of all kinds of filth" (Matthew 23:27) and of being a "brood of vipers" (Matthew 23:33) who are threatened with the coming judgment and with hell. He warns Jerusalem (regardless of its possession of the Temple) that it will be left "desolate" (Matthew 23:38). He drives money changers from the temple courts; and more shockingly also predicts its destruction (Mark 13:2). The latter being a significant point held against him at his eventual trial (Mark 14:58), even if this is a garbled version of what he actually said. Even those towns which were his home turf in Galilee did not escape his censure for their lack of response to his message and the imminent judgment of God:

> Woe to you, Chorazin! Woe to you, Bethsaida! For if the deeds of power done in you had been done in Tyre and Sidon, they would have repented long ago in sackcloth and ashes.
> **(Matthew 11:21)**

Which brings us to those "deeds of power" and their role within his announcement of the good news, and the coming of the kingdom of God.

Miracles and exorcisms: the breaking-in of the kingdom of God

Whatever the views of some modern readers and biblical scholars, the simple reality is that the Gospel compilers were convinced that Jesus was the most remarkable worker of supernatural deeds of power. We hear that "he cast out the [evil] spirits with a word, and cured all who were sick" (Matthew 8:16).

John's Gospel describes seven miracles in detail: changing of water into wine at a wedding at Cana; healing of the son of a synagogue official at Capernaum; healing of a man crippled for thirty-eight years at the Sheep Pool in Jerusalem; feeding of the five thousand; walking on water; healing of a man born blind; raising Lazarus from the dead. But the synoptic writers refer to many more: Mark and Matthew both list eighteen healings and exorcisms; Luke gives nineteen. Among other wonders, we hear of lepers healed (the Greek word covered a range of dreaded skin diseases); a storm calmed; walking on water; the blind, deaf, and dumb healed; the dead raised to life.

In addition, we see Jesus' spiritual authority emphatically demonstrated in his driving out of demons, with the Gospel writers explicitly stating "[Jesus] would not permit the demons to speak, because they knew him" (Mark 1:34); "Whenever the unclean spirits saw him, they fell down before him and shouted, 'You are the Son of God!' But he sternly ordered them not to make him known" (Mark 3:11–12). This matter of silencing statements concerning his status is one to which we shall return. But here the key point to make is that, for the Gospel writers, the exalted status of Jesus was seen in his supernatural power. The good news involved liberating people from sickness and spiritual bondage. These "deeds of power" were vivid demonstrations of the breaking-in of the kingdom of God and were as important signposts to what was going on as the table-fellowship with "sinners" and the teaching.

A contested passage in the writings of the later Jewish historian Josephus (even when it is edited of content which was probably added by later Christians) describes Jesus as "a worker of amazing deeds", which can also be translated as "perplexing/controversial deeds".[15]

The significance of the parables

One of the fundamental teaching tools of Jesus was the parable: a new idea conveyed through a familiar theme. These occur with variations in the synoptic gospels and it is likely that these were repeated on various occasions, in different villages, as part of his core teaching which was, nevertheless, adaptable to different situations. This almost certainly underlies the variations that we read.

These stories which conveyed kingdom principles included such well-known examples as: sowing seed on different types of ground; a shepherd seeking a lost sheep; a woman searching for a lost coin; a prodigal son returning home; a good Samaritan helping an injured enemy; invitations to a wedding feast being refused; bridesmaids who do not bring enough oil for their lamps; workers toiling in a vineyard; tenants who kill the owner's son to gain possession of a vineyard that is then taken away from them as a consequence; treasure found in a field; a merchant who sells all to purchase a magnificent pearl.

A number of reasons have been suggested why Jesus found parables such a useful method of communicating his message: they hid powerful and provocative messages in homely stories that his opponents could not use against him; they engaged listeners' attention; they forced people to think about their meaning and differentiated those who were connecting with his message from those who were not; they challenged listeners to make life-changing decisions; their use implemented scriptural promises regarding such methods of communication (Psalm 78:1–4). Given Jesus' intimate use of the Scriptures, his deliberate deployment of the method for this latter reason is very likely.

Such stories cover the range of Jesus' core message: God's love for lost sinners; the need to repent and respond; the real nature of religious devotion; being prepared for the coming judgment; the importance of obedience to God; prioritizing God's kingdom above all else; the raising up of the weak and marginalized.

It is clear that parables were not simply just homely stories designed to make his message accessible to simple country folk. They were, at the same time: proclaimed but concealed; inclusive but divisive; down to earth, but of heaven; familiar and immediate, but pointing to the coming kingdom. It is important to recall that Jesus only explained their meaning to his disciples in private. Many others who heard them must have gone home wondering, "what was that all about?"

Table-fellowship as a radical model... and more

With its rejection of concepts of ritual purity and pollution-by-association, Jesus' meals with tax collectors and other "sinners" went beyond being simply lovingly inclusive. It directly challenged contemporary Jewish notions of exclusivity, moral self-confidence, and the treatment of people as the alien "other". When such aliens were treated as acceptable it undermined a huge range of moral assurances. It challenged the basis of what was considered "proper" behaviour and even national identity (rooted in rigid adherence to certain behaviours) as it was then understood by many ordinary people and certainly by the religious establishment. It also struck at the spiritual power-base of the teachers and elites whose respected status was based on their apparent righteousness and their ability to teach others how they should behave. That this was noted with anxiety, alarm, and outrage is clear from the number of times it is commented on critically and by Jesus' robust defence of his behaviour.

However, as with so much of Jesus' teaching and behaviour, two aspects were inextricably mixed. What he *did* modelled what he was *saying and teaching* – to the amazement or outrage of those listening and observing. And it went beyond this. His table-fellowship practice was clearly presented both as how the new kingdom-society should behave and was also, in itself, a way "in which the kingdom was actually being inaugurated."[16] This is an extraordinary feature of Jesus' behaviour/teaching. It was rather like a "trigger event" setting off a nuclear reaction. Jesus was not just modelling the kingdom-community for others to emulate. Rather, he clearly believed that he was enacting the "trigger behaviour" that would itself bring about the establishment of the kingdom of God. The man was as big as the message. This raises a whole range of questions concerning how Jesus perceived himself and what he claimed about himself (both explicitly and implicitly). This subject is so important that it merits its own chapter. But at this point we need to flag up its crucial and undeniable importance as a central feature of Jesus' actions and speech.

What was distinctive about his style and message?

Jesus' behaviour and teachings set him at odds with significant features of contemporary Jewish society. In a society which was structured around clearly understood parameters of conduct, family commitments, and gendered behaviour, Jesus stood out as strikingly radical. His band of followers included women as well as men and, as we have seen, involved women acting with agency outside of a framework of male family authority (father, brother, husband). This new form of "family" – based on commitment to Jesus and his message – stood in stark contrast to traditional family structures. As a result, Jesus could say, "Who are my mother and my brothers?" (Mark 3:33) and then assert that "Whoever does the will of God is my brother and sister and mother" (Mark 3:35). This was radical, controversial, and provocative, in the contemporary context of patriarchal authority and familial responsibilities and discipline.

As a result, he called followers away from their family businesses in a way which paid no regard to patriarchal authority. It is for this reason that Peter states "Look, we have left everything and followed you" (Mark 10:28). Jesus was central to his message.

Jesus explicitly stated that loyalty to him and his message outweighed family expectations: "Whoever loves father or mother more than me is not worthy of me; and whoever loves son or daughter more than me is not worthy of me" (Matthew 10:37).[17] For "everyone who has left houses or brothers or sisters or father or mother or children or fields, for my name's sake, will receive a hundredfold, and will inherit eternal life" (Matthew 19:29). Immediately before this statement, Jesus indicates that this – as we shall explore in more detail a little later – is closely related to the idea that apocalyptic cosmic change is imminent. "Jesus said to them, 'Truly I tell you, at the renewal of all things, when the Son of Man is seated on the throne of his glory, you who have followed me will also sit on twelve thrones, judging the twelve tribes of Israel'" (Matthew 19:28). Now-time radicalism seems to closely presage a rapidly approaching End-Time culmination and transformation. This is a distinctive feature of the "good news" proclaimed by Jesus.

Another highly distinctive feature of Jesus' message and lifestyle was that, apart from the time in the wilderness, there is no evidence that he fasted. This was a distinct difference from the practices of many contemporaries within Judaism.

Taken all round, Jesus spoke and behaved with a confident authority that drew attention to himself as a prophetic spokesperson for God and as one capable of resolving complex issues of religious understanding. More than that, he was playing a crucial part in the inauguration of the looked-for transformative kingdom of God. In an age in which religious authority within Judaism was becoming increasingly rooted in study and exposition of the Torah,[18] this was bound to lead to conflict with those in authority.

A study of the evidence reveals that Jesus was not the only prophetic figure in this volatile period claiming unique and authoritative revelation from God.[19] Josephus mentions several in the generation after Jesus. There was even another Jesus among these prophetic figures: Jesus son of Ananias.[20] Where Jesus of Nazareth stood out from these other "prophetic" figures was in the focus of his message on personal transformation regarding relationship with God and other people, rather than on political rebellion; the extensive wonder-working associated with him; the extraordinary claims made by his followers after his execution on a Roman gibbet. But that is getting ahead of the story.

CHAPTER 10

"Broods of vipers" or "stalwarts of national life"?

The Pharisees and Sadducees, along with a group described in the Gospels as "scribes" feature prominently in the life of Jesus. Priests also play a key role at the end of the Gospel accounts. Taken all round, they get a very bad press in the New Testament. As a result, it is important to explore their role in first-century Jewish life and assess whether Jesus was always on a collision course with them. This involves identifying the areas over which they clashed and why this conflict occurred. It is also necessary to look at how these groups interacted with both Roman and Jewish political forces and how these complex power politics and religious tensions interacted with the activities of Jesus. Only once we have established this framework will we be able to meaningfully chart the escalating crisis which features so significantly in the Gospel accounts (in Chapter 11).

The Pharisees

The Pharisees – about 6,000 in number[1] – were members of a Jewish religious group whose name may have been derived from *parush* (separated). This implied that they separated from that which was considered unclean or unholy. They were greatly concerned with the Law of Moses, and their aim was to both keep it, but also to adapt and apply it to new situations. This meant that they were concerned with the Law as it stood in the Torah (literally "instruction")[2] as found in the first five books (the Pentateuch) of the Jewish Bible (the Tanakh), where it constitutes the *Torah she'bi'ktav* – the written-Torah – also known as the *chumash*.[3] But the Pharisees were also concerned with traditions that had grown up around its implementation (the so-called unwritten-Torah). In this they developed an organic approach to the demands of religious legality and daily life which is still highly influential in the twenty-first-century Jewish community. Today "Torah" refers to the whole broad body of Jewish traditional learning and not only the *written* legal expectations found in the first five books of the Hebrew Bible.

When the Mishna (the first great written collection of Jewish oral traditions) was compiled c. 200, it built on the work and legacy of the earlier Pharisees. The Mishna along with rabbinical analysis of and commentary on it, is known as the Gemara, and makes up the great compilation of Jewish thought known as the Talmud.[4] Now, this compilation occurred centuries after the ministry of Jesus but it is important to state this, as it reminds us of how much medieval and modern Judaism is deeply indebted to an approach to scripture and its application that can be traced back to the Pharisees. Their active influence extended into the third century AD and their legacy still influences modern Judaism.

We first come across the Pharisees as a recognizable group shortly after the Maccabean Revolt, against the Seleucid Empire and the Hellenistic influence on Jewish life, in about 165–160 BC. As such, they seem to have developed from an earlier group, the Hasideans, who were characterized by their uncompromising observance of Jewish Law and the fight for Jewish religious freedom and the rejection of pagan religious and cultural influences. As such, the Pharisees were a group of laymen and scribes (see below), and distinct from the Sadducees (again see below) who represented elite members of Jewish society around the high priesthood and who had traditionally been the leaders of Jewish society. This characteristic of the Pharisees as a party of the people, in contrast to the social elites, and as representatives of Jewish national character and community in the face of foreign pagan infiltration, is not the way we usually view them on the basis of the New Testament presentation of them.

Why this is so, we will explore in due course because it is extremely important.

Pharisees and the Sadducees differed significantly in their approach to the Torah and its application in the changing circumstances of life. Although the Sadducees refused to accept any rule that was not directly based on the written Torah, the Pharisees stressed both the written Law and the oral Law rising from the Hebrew prophets and the oral traditions that had grown up around these sources. As a result, the Pharisees allowed for evolution and interpretation in the application of Law, whereas the Sadducees stood for a more pared-down approach. The Pharisee-approach allowed for harmonization of different aspects of these regulations and the drawing out of principles implied in them, as applied to new or complex situations. Far from being what we might now term "Pharisaical" (hypocritical or devoid of spiritual character) they would, no doubt, have insisted that they sought out the spirit of the Law and its role within everyday life. They aimed to settle complex questions of ethics and morality by applying general Torah-rules and Torah-principles to them (an approach often termed "casuistry").

Pharisees believed that God could and should be worshipped away from the Jerusalem Temple and its sacrificial cult. This did not set them in opposition to the Temple but it certainly set them apart from those who claimed it had spiritual supremacy. This had within it the seeds of an idea that Torah might one day replace Temple (as indeed it did after the year 70). Given the Pharisees' focus on prayer and active study of the Law it is no surprise to discover that they fostered the institution of the synagogue as a central place within Jewish community life – and one which would outlive the traumatic Roman destruction of the Jerusalem Temple in 70.

As a result, the Pharisees became an active force within Jewish community life across Palestine and the wider Jewish diaspora. Later rabbinical traditions claimed that many Pharisees were drawn from the class of small landowners and traders – the middling kind in society. In their espousal of study, teaching, synagogue-life, and active alms-giving, they represented Jewish cultural resistance against Greek and then Roman rule, in contrast to the militant activities of those who would go on to form the Zealot party. Although they could be considered a high-achieving spiritual elite, their aim was to inspire emulation by others and to advise on the achievement of acceptable spiritual purity. Meeting together and celebrating *havurah* (table fellowship) with like-minded and like-spirited people they modelled a deeply committed community within the wider community. And they held an End Time (eschatological) hope that when all Israel obeyed Torah, the rule of God would be established on earth in fulfilment of messianic prophecy and scripture generally. And here we see a signpost toward why they conflicted with Jesus; to this we will return.

The Pharisees also believed in the resurrection of the dead and had a developed belief in angels and their place and role within the cosmic spiritual order (angelology).

This group appears in eighty-six separate references in the New Testament;[5] all but five of these in the Gospels. As we meet them in the Gospels they frequently clash with Jesus over issues such as daily ritual life and actions (see Chapter 11). The significance of this clash has been contested, with the suggestion made that the Pharisees were a small Jerusalem-based sect and their clashes with Jesus represent a reading-back into his ministry of the severe church verses synagogue conflicts of the next generation.[6] In contrast to this view, the Gospel compilers insist that there was something deeply conflicted in their relationship with Jesus. And the overall evidence certainly does not restrict their influence to Judea.

Commentators disagree as to exactly why the Pharisees were so conflicted with Jesus. One view is that Jesus offered a radical new understanding of Judaism. This new view, it is argued, stressed the merciful rather than the wrathful nature of God.[7] Instead of a "system of rigid boundaries" Jesus preached "a set of personal standards which are at once more demanding and more fulfilling."[8] This involved a "reworking of fundamental assumptions about God, man and the world."[9] In this interpretation, Jesus clashed with fundamental aspects of the beliefs of his day, especially with regard to application of the Torah and the role of the Temple.[10] It was rejection of what he considered religious "petty legalism" which so angered the Pharisees that it led to a political charge being concocted against him in order to secure his death at the hands of the Roman occupying power. Jews of the next generation developed this and presented Jesus as a deceiver of the people, and it is this conclusion that influenced later Talmudic traditions, such as the claim that "Jesus the Nazarene practiced magic and led Israel astray."[11]

Another view is quite the opposite and interprets Jesus as very Jewish, but at odds with certain high profile features of the way Judaism was practiced and with those exponents of these approaches. It also draws attention to the fact that, although Jesus debated aspects of conduct with the Pharisees (especially with regard to the use of "traditions"), he was actually devoted to more intense application of Torah; rejecting not only murder but hatred, not only adultery but lust. He did not reject Torah compliance.[12] Had this not been the case, it is argued, the later church would not have been convulsed with heated debates over circumcision, dietary requirements, and Sabbath observance.[13] As they did so, they were engaged in real-time exploration of the impact on life of the post-Easter faith. But had Jesus, in his ministry, simply rejected Torah, these later debates over the implications of the new faith would have been unnecessary. For Jesus the pressing thing was: what is God doing now? And this was like a spiritual tsunami which did not simply reject the landscape of the shoreline – but was about to totally overwhelm it. It would be others, this approach argues, who then reflected on what the "post-tsunami" world should look like.

Others would argue that, in Jesus' view, it was first-century formal Judaism (and the way it was presented by the Pharisees) which represented disobedience to the God of Israel and was leading toward disaster.[14] This particularly applied to *Jesus' behaviour and personal claims*, rather than *the details of his religious ideas and debates with the Pharisees*.[15] As we shall see, it seems clear that it was, indeed, Jesus' eschatology – rather than simply debates over details of application of law and personal morality – that fundamentally differentiated him from the Pharisees. This becomes particularly compelling if we view the Pharisees' religious practices as being more than simply personal piety. They saw themselves as the guardians of Israel's ultimate nature and identity. Religion and politics were finely intertwined. No less than the militant Zealots, the Pharisees were at war with Rome, Hellenization, and all that threatened the existence of the Jewish community. They regarded themselves as holding the real front line in this war. In contrast, Jesus advocated a totally different strategy as a way to bring in the kingdom of God.

The scribes

A group found in English translations as "scribes" appear in sixty references in the New Testament. Of these references, three appear in the Acts of the Apostles and the rest in the Gospels. Taking account of all these references, they are mentioned in association with "priests" in 26.6 per cent of them, and with "Pharisees" in 15 per cent of them. They are often described as being identical with the Pharisees.[16]

By the first century AD scribes (Hebrew *sofer*) and Pharisees constituted two distinct groups, although it seems that some scribes were Pharisees. The scribes were trained in both secular and religious law, and drafted legal documents such as those necessary for marriage, divorce, land transactions, and inheritance. They also wrote Torah scrolls. One can see here how religious and secular aspects could combine and why scribes and Pharisees overlapped. It is reasonable to assume that most villages of any size would have included a scribe. Scribes were later termed *sofer setam* – the second word made up of the Hebrew initials of *Sefer* Torah (Torah-text), *tefillin* (parchment scrolls worn in phylacteries), and *mezuzot* (scriptural passages fixed to doorways). This may give us an insight into activities practiced by scribes in the first century too. According to the later Talmud,[17] a scholar should not dwell in a town where there is no scribe.[18]

It seems that in Mark's Gospel the main opponents of Jesus in Galilee were scribes; whereas for Matthew they were Pharisees (contrast Mark 2:6, 2:16; 3:22 with Matthew 9:11; 12:2). Given the overlapping nature of these groups this is more a matter of the terminology used in these accounts. Indeed, one account in Mark specifically calls them "the scribes of [and] the Pharisees" (Mark 2:16). Despite this opposition, the Pharisees did not play any significant role in the events that led to the arrest, trial, and death of Jesus. Only Matthew mentions them as playing any part in these events (Matthew 27:62) and they drop out of sight once Jesus reaches Jerusalem in the other Gospels. Although scribes and Pharisees appear to have challenged his interpretation of the Law in Galilee, they never once charged him formally regarding this. It was events and groups in Jerusalem that led to his death.[19] And that brings us to the Sadducees.

The Sadducees

The Sadducees have a lower profile in the New Testament, appearing only fifteen times, and all but five in the Gospels.[20] But, as we shall see, they were highly significant in the dramatic events leading to Jesus' execution. By the time of Jesus, this group had existed for about two hundred years. They took their name from the Hebrew *Tzedoq* (plural *Tzedoqim*), which may have been derived from that of Zadok/ Zadoq, the high priest during the reigns of kings David and Solomon. This family became associated with control of the Temple, such that "Zadokites" formed the temple hierarchy until the second century BC. Clearly, the group who became known as the Sadducees were connected with this elite hierarchy; and celebrated it in their name. Later written sources also link them to the priesthood, with Acts 4:1 stating that "While Peter and John were speaking [in the Temple, at Solomon's Portico] to the people, the priests, the captain of the temple, and the Sadducees came to them".

However, their earliest appearance seems to indicate they were originally a political rather than a priestly group. Josephus refers to an event which occurred in the lifetime of John Hyrcanus, the Hasmonean high priest and ruler of Judah, 135–104 BC, which may present them as something of political grouping.[21] But, if so, it was clearly one with a strong connection with Temple administration and hierarchy. And, anyway, to separate out "political" and "religious" motivations and characteristics is an artificial construct, which fails to recognize the interrelated nature of these areas of life in the ancient (and, indeed, the later, medieval) world.

They constituted a largely Jerusalem-based elite made up of the old priesthood and the landed aristocracy. They may have included some Herodians by the time of Jesus. As a group they either collaborated with Rome or pragmatically accepted *realpolitik* in order to ensure the survival of their national community. No doubt contemporary perspectives will have varied. In the twenty-first century, Pope Francis referred to the Sadducees who had "made it their religious work to make deals with the powers... They were men of power".[22] He was not presenting this as a good thing.

Sadducees did not believe in resurrection, as they decided that there was no Old Testament statement of such a belief. In addition, they also did not believe in angels. This differentiated them from the Pharisees. As the writer of Acts summed it up: "The Sadducees say that there is no resurrection, or angel, or spirit; but the Pharisees acknowledge all three" (Acts 23:8).

Josephus states that the Sadducees depended on scripture alone, in contrast to the traditions accepted by the Pharisees:

> The Pharisees have delivered to the people a great many observances by succession from their fathers, which are not written in the laws of Moses; and for that reason it is that the Sadducees reject them, and say that we are to esteem those observances to be obligatory which are in the written word, but are not to observe what are derived from the tradition of our forefathers.[23]

It is possible that in their origins they represented something of a "back to basics" movement, which sought to challenge traditional outlooks with a return to scriptural purity. Be that as it may be, by the time of Jesus the Sadducees were an elite party of high priests, members of the aristocratic families, and merchants. They had absorbed a lot of Greek influence (rather surprising for a puritanical group) and had established a working relationship with Rome. Perhaps Pope Francis had a point. As such, they dominated the priesthood, the Temple, and Jerusalem. More so than the Pharisees, their elite status separated them from those dismissively described as the *am ha-aretz* (People of the Land): a phrase that described contemporary (less religiously observant) Jews in a term once used to describe the pagan Canaanites. The way they were regarded by ordinary people may be glimpsed in the fact that when Jewish revolutionaries took control of the Temple in late AD 67, as the First Jewish–Roman War descended into bitter infighting, they destroyed the records of debt held there.[24]

Their daily lives and their political authority were both so closely connected with the Jerusalem Temple that, when it was destroyed by the Romans in AD 70, the Sadducees ceased to exist and vanish from the record.

Jesus' conflict with key aspects of the Temple in terms of the practices there, and attitudes toward it, brought him into conflict with this group, alongside key members of the priestly class. For if his message could bring reconciliation with God and spiritual liberation and renewal, then what was left for the Temple and its whole sacrificial system?[25] On reflection, it seems that it was this conflict, even more than conflict with the Pharisees, which eventually led to his arrest and execution. This was intimately connected with conflicting ideas of the nature of the Messiah and the looked-for future kingly rule of God's promised ruler. This was especially so, if Jesus was considered a revolutionary and unsettling influence by *both* the Jewish and the Roman elites in Jerusalem.

We shall return to this in a later chapter in more detail as we look at how this exploded in the final week of his ministry and in his trial(s) and the charges brought against him.

Priests and Levites

The mention of the Sadducees reminds us of the crucial importance of the Jerusalem Temple to Judaism and national identity at the time of Jesus. The existence of the Temple, and the worship and sacrifices that took place there, both ensured God's presence in the Temple and his blessing of the land. It was central to the life of the overall community and to its survival. Given the survival of Judaism for two millennia since the Temple's destruction this needs to be stressed. Before AD 70 most Jews saw the Temple as an indispensable part of their existence and cultural identity.

Priests were trained in religious matters and also in Jewish Law, in literature, and tradition. Long after the end of the effective priesthood in AD 70, some Jewish families still identified as being part of priestly lineages which underscores their importance. But it was a position of authority rapidly replaced by the rabbis and the synagogues in the absence of the Temple.

Alongside priests were Levites. They too were a hereditary order and they manned the temple gates, were responsible for cleaning the Temple, slaughtering some of the sacrificial animals, and performing the music during temple worship.

In the parable of the good Samaritan (Luke 10:29–37), Jesus tells of a priest and then a Levite who refuse to help an injured man. In both cases the reason was almost certainly because they feared becoming ritually unclean by association with a corpse. This would certainly have applied to the priest,[26] although Levites were not so strictly curtailed regarding dead bodies.[27] However, feared association with impurity might have motivated such a reluctance in both of them. The key point of the parable is that both represent Temple purity and practice – but it does not dictate their sense of compassion. Something vital is lacking.

Together, priests and Levites may have numbered about 20,000.[28] They were divided into twenty-four divisions and only performed their temple duties for a few weeks each year. Supported by tithes and temple-gifts, they supplemented their income with other work, including scribing (but not agriculture, which was forbidden). Some aristocratic priests were Sadducees, some others were Pharisees.[29] Josephus considered the priestly theocracy – God's government, mediated by priests – the most appropriate form of Jewish government and more desirable than a monarchy.[30] In many ways it was the high priest who had most governmental authority in Jerusalem, albeit under the oversight of the Roman prefect.

A lethal conflict

Although the well-publicized conflict with the Pharisees is often assumed to have led to the plot to kill Jesus, the simple reality is that this group was not actually involved in his arrest and trial. Instead, it was conflict over the Temple which exploded with such lethal intensity in the days leading up to his execution. And this brings the Sadducees and especially the chief priests and elite rulers into sharp focus.[31] In short, as we shall explore in due course, Jesus and his followers were perceived as a counter-Temple movement and it was this, rather than disputes over details of practice (with the Pharisees), which led to his death.

Claims of messiah-status pointed the same way, for Israel's Temple and its future-king were almost certainly linked in popular as well as elite thinking. Jesus was making a claim to lead and represent Israel, and appeared to undermine the future status of its Temple.[32]

The real issue was over Jesus himself. Although his style of preaching, his *modus operandi* and his devotion to the Law (to Torah) was consistent with many of the practices around him, it was his self-perception and self-presentation that became the most contentious point. As the Gospels indicate, his message is that it is *in him* that the longed-for future kingdom is being initiated. A new Israel is forming around *him*; God's future kingdom is appearing; this is the main event. This rejected the *armed resistance* of the Zealots, as it did the *cultural resistance* of the Pharisees. Suddenly the religious practices of the scribes and Pharisees and the *Temple cult* of the Sadducees and the priestly class was being presented as marginal, indeed passing away, almost irrelevant. This struck at the very heart of much of contemporary Judaism.

This, it has been argued, presented a dramatic manifesto to Jesus' listeners, which had End-Time meaning and now-time effects. In this understanding of his words, national repentance was required concerning personal immorality, social injustice, personal self-righteousness, religious ritual, and the militant political confrontation with Rome. And in its place an acceptance of him as God's chosen representative and his transformed community as modelled by himself and his disciples. His vision was not of a withdrawn community like the Essenes, nor working within the established religious order to transform it, nor accommodation with the Roman occupiers. Furthermore, Jerusalem and its Temple required cleansing of corruption and lip-service. If this path was not followed then catastrophic destruction would fall on Israel from the Romans. It was not an argument over details of ritual practice or reform of the Temple.[33] The issue was: what constituted God's kingdom? Battle lines were being drawn as Jesus preached. But in this interpretation, this was the threat of *realized eschatology* rather than *cosmic reordering*.

Others would strongly argue that Jesus also considered the latter as imminent too and that we should not detach his teaching from this traditional scriptural vision of the impending world-wide judgment of God. But either way, it did not accommodate with the status quo of first-century society; and the status quo struck back. The message of Jesus had jarred with all the opinion formers of his day: Pharisees, scribes, Sadducees, temple priests. A coalition of the unwilling was forming.

In Galilee this resulted in conflict with the Pharisees. When enacted in Jerusalem it brought conflict with the temple elite. They, more than the Pharisees, had the capability to make conflict deadly. And their opposition to unrest and turbulence was something that the agents of the occupying power – as we shall see in due course – could understand and collaborate with.[34] As the next chapter will explore, conflict – which had never been far from Jesus' ministry – escalated as time went on.

CHAPTER 11

Escalating crisis

We have explored something of the nature of the Jewish religious establishment and their areas of conflict with Jesus. As we read through the Gospel accounts we can see how this tension increased over time and drew in disparate groups who were offended by him and his message. For, alongside the teaching and healing, the gratitude and the astonishment, there is an underlying current of conflict which builds as the story moves closer to the shocking and violent events of Easter. But aspects of it were discernible from the beginning.

"No prophet is accepted in the prophet's home town" (Luke 4:24)

Early on in the Gospel of Luke – right at the start of his Galilean ministry – we gain an insight into an area of conflict in the life of Jesus. It is an event which Luke places much earlier than either Mark or Matthew do in their Gospel accounts (Mark places it in chapter 6, Matthew further on again, in chapter 13). For Luke it sets the scene for what follows in Galilee, whereas the compilers of the other two synoptic accounts place it after Jesus has already established a following and fame (or notoriety, depending on those listening). As a result, we cannot give it a definite chronological position in Jesus' Galilean ministry. But from other clues we can say that negative reactions occurred early on.

Luke briefly says that Jesus has begun preaching in the synagogues after his return from the time of testing in the wilderness and that this results in listeners praising him. But for Luke, this is soon contrasted with negative reactions as Jesus returns to Nazareth and preaches there on the Sabbath. Reading from the Old Testament prophet Isaiah, the passage speaks of one empowered by God's Spirit to preach good news to the poor, liberation to captives, sight to the blind, and freedom for the oppressed. The year of the Lord's favour is declared when Jesus states that this prophecy has been fulfilled as the congregation listens. This claim to personal authority and to be the one through whom the ancient promises are being fulfilled is a hallmark of Jesus' teaching and helps explain something of the reactions to him. These extraordinary claims invite either acceptance or rejection. And the issue centres on whether he is the one with authority to make the claims that he does.

At first it could go either way. Luke records the response that "All spoke well of him and were amazed at the gracious words that came from his mouth" (Luke 4:22). But this is immediately followed by the query: "Is not this Joseph's son?" That this concealed a much more negative response is clear from the wording in the other Gospels. Mark, followed by Matthew, records their surprise, given that this is (just?) the carpenter, or the carpenter's son, and the listeners know his mother and siblings by name. What follows reveals the clear conclusion that they therefore wonder: Who does he think he is? "And they took offence at him" (Mark 6:3).

In Mark and Matthew, Jesus immediately responds to this resentful assessment by making the point that prophets are not honoured in their own town. Whereas Luke records a tradition of words which clearly would have added to the indignation of this critical congregation. After making the point about dishonoured prophets, Jesus gives two examples of Old Testament prophets working miracles for those outside of the Jewish people. One is Elijah whom God sent to a widow near Sidon; the other is Elisha, who healed Naaman the Syrian of his leprosy. These are explosive examples. They suggest more than a prophet not being accepted in his immediate home community, and reveal that God acts beyond the exclusive boundaries of the Jewish people. The suggestion that those within Israel might not be the prime beneficiaries of God's saving actions, causes outrage and those listening attempt to throw him from a cliff – but he walks through them, out of their hands, and away.

This is certainly an extreme reaction and Mark, followed by Matthew, simply say that Jesus worked few miracles there because of their unbelief and they do not state what it was that so offended his one-time neighbours. For Luke this probably presaged the eventual Christian mission to the Gentiles; hence his details and the placing of this at the start of the Galilean ministry. It is as if Luke is asserting that the eventual explosion of the mission out of the boundaries of Judaism was apparent, in implication, at the very start of the ministry. For Mark and Matthew the matter is the simpler suggestion that familiarity with someone they know has made it difficult for these people to accept the claims he makes. Familiarity can breed contempt, as the saying goes.

That there is something in this, is apparent from a tradition known to Mark that as news of his fame spread, consternation gripped his closest relatives. "When his family heard it, they went out to restrain him, for people were saying, 'He has gone out of his mind'" (Mark 3:21). This is the other side of the coin to the records of praise and wonderment. Clearly, some thought his extraordinary behaviour gave cause for concern.

Opposition such as this would have been deeply painful and distressing but – with the exception of the lynch law that swept Nazareth that famous Sabbath – was unlikely to lead to punishment or to official sanctions. Nevertheless, these traditions remind us that Jesus divided people in their assessments regarding his authority and validity. And, if Luke is correct in his placing of the event, this occurred very early on. However, even if the time-location of the Nazareth conflict was actually a little later in the Galilean ministry (as in Mark and Matthew), the response of his family (as recorded in Mark) shows that not all were convinced regarding the nature of his activities – and this occurred fairly early on among some of those very close to him.

Opposition of a more dangerous kind: a sudden escalation?

If rejection by neighbours and family members was painful, a negative response from those who felt their role was policing orthodoxy had the potential to be much more problematic. Enter the scribes and Pharisees, Sadducees and Herodians.

Although Mark may have saved the Nazareth incident to later in his account, he also stresses conflict from a very early period. This occurs after he recounts the return of Jesus from the testing in the wilderness; the arrest of John the Baptist; Jesus proclaiming the imminence of the kingdom of God; the calling of the first disciples; teaching and then an exorcism in Capernaum; healings and exorcisms; a preaching tour in Galilee and more acts of power.

Then, in a block of events (Mark 2:1 – 3:6), Mark presents a series of conflicts between Jesus and the scribes and Pharisees. In the five stories the threat level steadily increases as does the focus of who is opposing him: "scribes"; "scribes of the Pharisees"; undesignated people, literally "they" (it seems, from what follows, either followers of John the Baptist or Pharisees); "Pharisees"; "Pharisees… conspired with the Herodians".

The conflicts are over a number of different actions. Four friends of a paralyzed man break through a roof (so great is the crowd around Jesus) to lower him down for Jesus to heal. To which Jesus responds "Son, your sins are forgiven" (Mark 2:5). The scribes consider this blasphemy on Jesus' part. Jesus perceives their thoughts and declares that he, the Son of Man, has authority to forgive sins and heals the man. The onlookers are amazed and glorify God. The reactions of the scribes are not recorded.

The second incident involves Jesus eating with tax collectors and "sinners", which prompts the Pharisees to criticize his choice of table companions. To which Jesus replies that doctors are for the sick not the well and that he has come to call sinners not the righteous.

The third incident is less conflicted, but there is clearly criticism implied in the question of why Jesus' disciples do not fast as do the followers of John the Baptist and the Pharisees? Describing himself as "the bridegroom" (Mark 2:19–20), Jesus teaches that he has brought something new: new wine that needs new wineskins (Mark 2:22). The implication is not made explicit, but it leaves the listeners to ponder just where this might leave established traditions, structures, and practices.

The fourth incident involves Pharisees criticising Jesus' disciples for plucking and eating grain (in other words, working) on the Sabbath.

Jesus refers to a Davidic precedent and declares: "The Sabbath was made for humankind, and not humankind for the Sabbath" and "the Son of Man is lord even of the Sabbath" (Mark 2:27–28).

The fifth event in this group involves the healing of a man with a withered hand, in a synagogue on the Sabbath. We are told that his opponents watched in order to accuse him but no actual accusation is made since Jesus challenged them with the question: "Is it lawful to do good or to do harm on the sabbath, to save life or to kill?" (Mark 3:4). They remain silent; he is angry at what is described as "their hardness of heart" (Mark 3:5). He heals the man.

This period of conflict concludes with a decision that Jesus must be destroyed. We are told that this decision is the result of collusion between the Pharisees and the Herodians. By "Herodians" is meant the supporters of Herold Antipas, the tetrarch of Galilee who had earlier arrested John the Baptist. They make for unusual allies for the Pharisees to decide to work with.

The recounting gives the impression of a conflict escalating over just a few days, but it is likely that Mark here has telescoped events that occurred over a longer period into "dramatized summaries", which present "quick challenges [to Jesus] and brief and telling replies".[1] Some of these events appear at different places in the accounts presented by Matthew and Luke (grouped according to association with miracles rather than conflicts). Clearly, these events stand at different points because, as we have already stated, "the gospels are not biographies in the modern sense of the word"[2] and these themed-events (termed *pericopes*) were grouped differently depending on the agenda of the individual Gospel compiler(s). This means it is not possible to use these to construct "a day in the life of Jesus" or to provide definite chronological milestones in the emerging story.

In the case of Mark's conflict-collection (in Mark 2:1 – 3:6) – rapidly leading to a plot to kill Jesus – this seems to appear too early in his account (and on the basis of insufficient capital-crime evidence against Jesus at this point). The likelihood is that the conflict grew more slowly than an initial reading of Mark might suggest. Given that Mark then reintroduces the Pharisees and Herodians again later (Mark 12:13),[3] it is possible that his earlier conflict-account (Mark 2:1 – 3:6) had once formed part of a shorter collection of traditions which summed up the life of Jesus with the themes of: "conflict, plot, arrest, execution".[4] And that Mark chose to place these events early in Jesus' ministry.

This view may find further support in the suggestion that none of the areas of conflict seem sufficiently serious to justify a lethal response.[5] The statement of forgiveness is in the passive voice which would usually have the meaning of "God forgives you"; Jesus' disciples are accused of harvesting grain, not Jesus himself, and the offence itself probably would have been punished by nothing more serious than a fine; the healing of the withered hand involved no action that could have been brought before a religious court, although it might be objected that it did not constitute "saving life".

None of the opponents are openly aggressive. The scribes are unhappy "in their hearts"; the Pharisees take no action over the grain incident; they are "silent" when Jesus heals the man with the withered hand.[6]

Some commentators have seen this as reading back into the ministry of Jesus, rejection of the Jewish Law (seen in these cases with regard to Sabbath prohibitions) because this became a feature of the later church and accompanied its expansion into Gentile populations.[7] They would point to Matthew not making the same points as sharply as Mark makes them, and Luke stressing freedom from Sabbath laws, but not referring to food laws which Mark later states were *also* abrogated by Jesus: "(Thus he declared all foods clean)" (Mark 7:19), in a parenthesis on Jesus' later teaching that impurity comes from within (the heart) rather than from externally (from food).

However, more traditional commentators would not accept this conclusion, and would insist that conflicts that later occurred in the Christian community were rooted in earlier events and that these are evidence of that. What is beyond dispute is that conflict occurs as a recurring theme in all three synoptic gospels, even if Mark has placed his first collection of such traditions earlier in his account than we might expect from an overall reading of all three synoptic gospels.

Conflict as a recurring theme

Exorcisms formed a part of Jesus' healing ministry from the start. That these highlighted his spiritual authority in a particularly striking manner meant that they became a matter of sharp conflict for those who did not accept Jesus' spiritual legitimacy.[8] For Mark this surfaced early in his ministry with scribes provocatively claiming that "He has Beelzebul, and by the ruler of the demons he casts out demons" (Mark 3:22). This accusation allowed them to accept that Jesus was performing works of power, while denying he did so with God's authority. It was a highly offensive accusation and prompted Jesus to state that there would be no forgiveness for those who blasphemed against the Holy Spirit (Mark 3:29–30). In Matthew this accompanies a direct counter-challenge by Jesus: "You brood of vipers! How can you speak good things, when you are evil? For out of the abundance of the heart the mouth speaks" (Matthew 12:34). Clearly, battle lines were being drawn. Matthew names Pharisees as responsible for this offensive accusation (Matthew 12:24), whereas Luke only refers to "some of them said" this (Luke 11:15).

This pointed the way toward things to come. Although some commentators would no doubt suggest that Jesus' teaching that his followers would be persecuted in the synagogues and brought before governors and kings (Matthew 10:17–25) reflected the later experience of the early church, it is reasonable to assume that he had predicted such events on the basis of his own experience of opposition. Matthew and Luke also emphasize that Jesus specifically said this would also be accompanied by family discord (Matthew 10:34–36, Luke 12:51–53). This includes the famous statement that "I have not come to bring peace, but a sword" (Matthew 10:34).

As Jesus' fame increased, so people were forced to make decisions about him. It seems that John the Baptist (now in prison) may have had his doubts. He sent a message asking whether Jesus was the one they had expected or should they wait for another? The question implies doubt and raises questions over exactly what kind of messiah John was expecting. We cannot answer that question but it hangs over the event. That Jesus replied by recounting the transforming works of power he was doing and then stating "blessed is anyone who takes no offence at me" (Matthew 11:6), suggests he understood the potentially challenging nature of John's enquiry. We do not know what John made of this because he was soon executed on the orders of Herod Antipas. But it reminds us of the complexity of the challenge posed by Jesus, and the questions he raised, including to those who had once been close to him. It also reminds us that Jesus was being noticed by others who had the power to mount serious opposition.

Shortly after the execution of John the Baptist, Herod became increasingly aware of the new preacher drawing crowds. All three synoptics refer to the news reaching Herod (Mark 6:14–16; Matthew 14:1–2; Luke 9:7–9) with slight variations. Matthew having Herod simply concluding that John the Baptist has been raised from the dead; Mark and Luke adding that some thought Jesus was Elijah or another prophet, as well as that John the Baptist has been raised. What is clear is that it was both inevitable and dangerous that Herod was becoming interested. Political interest was dangerous, as John the Baptist had discovered.

Others, among the Jewish religious elites, would also have been drawing their own conclusions. On a famous occasion Jesus was asked by a scribe what was the most important commandment. Reflecting on the reply,

> The scribe said to him, "You are right, Teacher; you have truly said that 'he [God] is one, and besides him there is no other'; and 'to love him with all the heart, and with all the understanding, and with all the strength', and 'to love one's neighbour as oneself', – this is much more important than all whole burnt-offerings and sacrifices." When Jesus saw that he answered wisely, he said to him, "You are not far from the kingdom of God." After that no one dared to ask him any question.
> **(Mark 12:32–34)**

In one simple moment, the whole Temple system was challenged.[9] The scribe was impressed with Jesus' answer, but the Temple leadership would not have been. They would have read the challenge in his words.[10]

Conflict, as a result of Jesus' words and actions, had hidden depths and nuances that we can miss from a twenty-first-century perspective. Forgiving sin was like an ordinary person "approaching a prisoner in jail [and we might add under sentence of death] and offering him a royal pardon, signed by himself".[11] And it further undermined the whole *raison d'être* of the Temple sacrificial system. It sidestepped all the official channels and the properly regulated priesthood.

So, why do we hear so little of conflict with priests? Perhaps because after the year 70 this debate was no longer on the minds of the early church as the Temple and its priesthood had suddenly been consigned to history through the violent actions of the Romans.[12] Also, Acts 6:7 indicates that priests later converted in large numbers.[13] But in the escalating crisis that led to Jesus' death, the collision with Temple-based power was profound – and lethal.

And there was more to be offended by. If Jesus rejected fasting, then Israel was no longer in spiritual exile. If the Sabbath could be re-envisaged, then the eschatological future "day of rest" had arrived and Israel was no longer separated from the Gentiles. A casual approach to ritual handwashing, a hint that food laws were not the way to personal purity, table-fellowship with "sinners", all transgressed boundaries that defined the unique status of the "Chosen People of Israel". It was as if all these alien "others" were gate-crashing a very exclusive party. And all these things were God-given ordinances which Jesus' actions and teaching indicated had once been necessary *but were needed no longer*. And all because of him.[14] Any one of these things in isolation would have been tolerable, perhaps even open to debate or – if punished – by no more than a fine. But, in combination, they were an assault on what was considered right, proper, and God-ordained. The protectors of Israel's identity and cultural heritage were appalled.

However, not all in the establishment opposed him. We have seen the scribe who was not far from the kingdom of God. And there were others. "One of the Pharisees asked Jesus to eat with him, and he went into the Pharisee's house and took his place at the table" (Luke 7:36); and "some Pharisees came and said to him, 'Get away from here, for Herod wants to kill you'" (Luke 13:31).

This reminds us of the tradition in Mark that Herod Antipas had taken an interest in Jesus (Mark 6:14) and that some thought he might be John the Baptist risen from the dead. It seems to have been this that lay behind the warning given him in Luke 13:31. However, the threat level seems to have been relatively low since we hear nothing more of this dangerous royal interest. Unlike John the Baptist, Jesus did not level direct criticism at Herod, although his view of his ruler is revealingly stated in his response to the threat posed by him:

> He said to them, "Go and tell that fox for me, 'Listen, I am casting out demons and performing cures today and tomorrow, and on the third day I finish my work. Yet today, tomorrow, and the next day I must be on my way, because it is impossible for a prophet to be killed away from Jerusalem'".
> **(Luke 13:32–33)**

Mark has him warn of the danger posed by "the yeast" (the influence?) of the Pharisees and of Herod (Mark 8:15). This is an interesting earlier tradition than that found in Matthew who names the Pharisees and Sadducees (Matthew 16:6); and Luke only names the Pharisees and explains that "yeast" refers to their "hypocrisy" (Luke 12:1). In both Mark and Matthew this occurs after the feeding of the four thousand and attempts to test him by Pharisees (Mark 8:11), accompanied by Sadducees (Matthew 16:1).

Fame was intensifying critical interest. However, it seems that, as long as Jesus was in Galilee, the threat was limited. But this tradition regarding Jesus' response to Herod's interest in him indicates that he knew from where the really lethal threat emanated. Although Luke may have been emphasizing this in the light of what later happened, there is every reason to think that Jesus would have been well aware of where the real danger lay. Religious opponents might frame a charge; but only the political power(s) could execute it – and him.

The road to the ultimate sacrifice

Shortly after this, at Caesarea Philippi (north of the Sea of Galilee),[15] Jesus openly explained to his disciples that ahead lay arrest and execution at the hands of the Jewish elites. It is possible that this movement to an area well to the north of Galilee may have been as a result of conflict with some around the lake (Matthew 16:1–4). A little earlier Jesus had gone as far as the Gentile region of Tyre and Sidon (Matthew 15:21) after conflict with the Pharisees and scribes over his rejection of ritual impurity (Matthew 15:1–20).

Mark and Matthew both have Peter expressing shock at the idea of Jesus being rejected and killed, and rebuking Jesus for saying it. And Jesus, in reply, rebuking Peter (Mark 8:27–33; Matthew 16:13–23). Clearly, Peter did not accept such a view of the career of the Messiah. Conflict was affecting even the core group of followers and worse was yet to come as Jesus turned toward Jerusalem. Other warnings would follow, as Jesus again predicted what lay ahead (see Mark 9:30–32 for example); again to the bewilderment of his disciples.

Before that, though, we have the powerful and arresting account referred to as "The Transfiguration", in which Jesus' inner core of followers (Peter, James, and John) later recorded how they witnessed the transformation of the appearance of Jesus in the company of Moses and Elijah (found in Mark 9, Matthew 17, and Luke 9). For these followers, it was clear proof of his messianic status.

For others this was certainly not the conclusion reached, and the conflicts escalate including more attempts to test him by the Pharisees, culminating in Jesus launching into a comprehensive condemnation of them for greed, wickedness, stressing ritual cleanliness over inner purity, and minute regulations over justice and love for God. And when a lawyer (presumably a scribe) protests that this insults them too, Jesus agrees - and accuses them of burdening people with rules and of being descendants of those who killed the prophets (Luke 11:37 - 12:1). Luke follows this with other healing events on the Sabbath, with predictable condemnation by the leader of a synagogue (Luke 13:14) and lawyers and Pharisees (Luke 14:1–6). And adds that, in contrast to Jesus, the Pharisees were lovers of money and the praise of people (Luke 16:14–15). Just before Jesus left Galilee for the last time, Luke recounts his telling the story of a tax collector and a Pharisee praying at the Temple; the former forgiven by God for his honesty and the latter condemned for his self-righteous legalism. It is a symbolic combination of both Jesus' view of the Pharisees and his turning his face toward Judea and eventually Jerusalem itself. The decisive move out of Galilee appears in both Mark (10:1) and Matthew (19:1) and it was a move that Jesus recognized as momentous:

> See, we are going up to Jerusalem, and the Son of Man will be handed over to the chief priests and the scribes, and they will condemn him to death; then they will hand him over to the Gentiles.
> **(Mark 10:33)**

His prediction of execution – and that on the third day he will rise again – draws back the curtain on the culmination of the conflict that had started in Galilee.[16]

Nevertheless, however we view the nature of the conflict with the Pharisees – deep disagreements over love and compassion versus legalism and ritual, or relatively minor conflicts over application of the Law – it is difficult to imagine it leading to a capital charge and a death sentence. It is in Jerusalem with its priestly theocracy that disagreement becomes lethal.[17] And in this the Pharisees played no significant role. As said before, Mark and Luke assign them no role whatsoever, whereas Matthew mentions them only once in his Jerusalem narrative (Matthew 27:62).

Moreover, as we are about to see, the lengths to which his opponents could go in their efforts to silence him were dependent on the attitude and actions of another – and external – agency, and that was Rome and its coercive force. Just where Rome stood in relation to the preacher and miracle worker from Galilee would be crucial. So we need to, at this point, move our focus to the occupying power. For it would be the actions of this occupying power that would eventually be decisive.

CHAPTER 12

Enter the Romans

Until the momentous events at the end of the life of Jesus, the Romans have "walk-on parts", then they are suddenly rocketed to "centre stage" among those responsible for his death. But what were the representatives of imperial power (the main superpower in the Mediterranean) doing when they are not seen on the "main stage" of the Gospel accounts? And was Jesus on an inevitable collision course with Rome... or not?

What were the representatives of imperial power doing in Judea at the time of Jesus?

Two emperors are mentioned by name in the Gospels. The first was Augustus who ordered the census that took Mary and Joseph to Bethlehem (Luke 2:1). The purpose of this census would have been to assist in accurate taxation. Augustus (also known as Octavian) came to power after the assassination of his great-uncle Julius Caesar, as his heir. Augustus was the first emperor of Rome.[1] He had the army under his direct control and he had ultimate control of Roman territory and relations with client states.[2]

Herod the Great (client-king of Judea), while taking three years to control the people, had firm control thereafter with the help of a vast security apparatus such as informants and garrisons; he also undertook building projects in honour of the emperor.[3] After the death of Herod the Great in 4 BC, revolts erupted in Galilee, Judea, and Transjordan against Roman and Jerusalem rule, but the Romans brutally reconquered, killing and enslaving many in Nazareth and Emmaus, and crucifying leading rebels.[4] Thereafter Jews could continue their beliefs and practices as long as they did not cause any problems for Rome. According to Josephus, in AD 6, after the deposition of Herod Archelaus (son of Herod the Great), Augustus annexed Judea as a province ruled directly by Rome, as part of the province of Syria.

The Roman prefect of Judea at the time of Jesus' ministry and death was Pontius Pilate (Luke 3:1). A single inscription from his time as prefect has survived (the so-called "Pilate stone") along with coins. He alone had the power to inflict capital punishment, and was responsible for collecting tribute and taxes. The prefect shared some civil and religious power with the Jewish Sanhedrin. The primary official residence of the Roman prefect was at the coast in Caesarea Maritima, travelling to Jerusalem for major feasts. The prefect appointed the high priest and controlled the official high priestly vestments in the Antonia Fortress. There could be tensions between the prefect and Herod Antipas in Galilee as revealed in an aside in Luke (23:12). However, generally, Pilate appears to have developed a constructive relationship with the Jerusalem elites.

The Jewish philosopher Philo of Alexandria, writing in around AD 50, paints Pilate in a very poor light. According to Philo's *Embassy to Gaius*,[5] Pilate offended the Jews by bringing golden shields (probably ones inscribed *divi Augusti filius* – son of divine Augustus) into Jerusalem, and displaying them on Herod's palace. The Jewish leaders petitioned him to remove the shields, but he refused. Eventually, according to Philo, the Emperor Tiberius reprimanded Pilate, who then removed the shields. This possibly occurred in AD 31.[6]

This was not his only provocative action. According to Josephus, Pilate offended the Jews by moving military imperial standards into Jerusalem.[7] Because of the images on these, Jews besieged Pilate's headquarters in Caesarea for five days. When Pilate confronted them they refused to back down and he removed the standards. The standards and shields incidents may have been one and the same.

In another, and clearly different, incident Josephus relates that Pilate used the temple treasury to fund a new aqueduct to Jerusalem.[8] Although this was socially useful and must have been done with the agreement of the Jewish Sanhedrin, this use of sacred funds caused a riot while Pilate was visiting Jerusalem. Many died. This occurred possibly between the years 26 and 30 or perhaps in 33, based on Josephus's chronology.[9]

Finally, and in an incident recorded only in Luke's Gospel, we are told that Jesus was informed about "the Galileans whose blood Pilate had mingled with their sacrifices" (Luke 13:1). This probably occurred at Passover, always a tense time in Jerusalem.

The Romans worked in collaboration with a network of client states. As we have already seen, Luke refers to Herod Antipas ruling Galilee; his brother, Philip, ruling Iturea and Trachonitis; and Lysanias (not a Herodian) ruling the small region of Abilene. All ruled as *tetrarchs*, not kings. Herod Antipas continued the building projects of his father and these client rulers reigned under Roman authority; they were loyal to Rome and profited from such loyalty. However, at the time of Jesus' death the Jewish client rulers and Jewish religious leaders could not inflict capital punishment (despite crimes being punishable by death under Jewish Law); only the Roman prefect could.

The second Roman emperor mentioned in the Gospels is Tiberius (the step-son and heir of Augustus). He is in his fifteenth year of rule when John the Baptist starts his ministry (Luke 3:1). We hear no more of him.

With regard to the military, Luke mentions soldiers coming to John the Baptist, but it is unlikely they would have been Roman. Within Palestine there would have been various armed forces: Roman auxiliaries (no Roman citizen legionaries) in Judea; local soldiers in the client states; and para-military police units in the Temple area. There would have been Roman soldiers in Jerusalem, but it is unlikely that Roman soldiers would have been seen on the streets of towns and villages in Judea.

What was the relationship of Jesus with Rome?

Matthew 8:5–13 tells of how a "centurion" comes to Jesus and asks him to heal his servant.[10] It is normally assumed that this man was a Roman officer, however it must be noted that the Greek word translated as "centurion" is used by Josephus to talk of officers in the Roman army, earlier in King David's army, and in his own Jewish army, which has led some to conclude that this "Roman centurion" was actually a Gentile officer in Herod Antipas's army.[11] In support of this interpretation, it is unlikely that Roman soldiers would have been based in Galilee. This may explain the additional information in Luke that "he sent some Jewish elders to him [Jesus]" (Luke 7:3) and they say, "He is worthy of having you do this for him, for he loves our people, and it is he who built our synagogue for us" (Luke 7:4–5). In Matthew's account he goes to Jesus himself.

The Romans had their own pantheon of gods and goddesses, so if this centurion was Roman he clearly believed that Jesus had power over and above the deities of his own culture. He tells Jesus of his paralyzed and ill servant and Jesus says that he will come and cure him. He replies with the famous words:

> Lord, I am not worthy to have you come under my roof; but only speak the word, and my servant will be healed. For I also am a man under authority, with soldiers under me; and I say to one, "Go", and he goes, and to another, "Come", and he comes, and to my slave, "Do this", and the slave does it.
> **(Matthew 8:8–9)**

That Jesus is amazed and comments, "Truly I tell you, in no one in Israel have I found such faith", may support the interpretation that he was a Gentile (though not necessarily a Roman).

This healing demonstrates how Jesus did not discriminate based on ethnicity but would help anyone who had faith in him. If this man was Roman then it demonstrates that there may have been some sympathizers among the occupiers regarding the Galilean preacher, although the most astounding recognition comes from a centurion at the death of Jesus in the synoptics. At the crucifixion it is a centurion (definitely a Roman on this occasion) who declares, "Truly this man was God's Son!" or "a son of God" (Mark 15:39). Luke's version is less confessional: "Certainly this man was innocent" (Luke 23:47).

Another interesting insight into Jesus' relationship with Rome is when Jesus is questioned, by an allied group of Pharisees and Herodians, about whether Jews should pay tribute to Rome. To demonstrate the subjugation of the Jews to the Romans, they had to pay a large amount annually to them. Yet as well as taxes to the Romans, Jews were also required to pay taxes to Herod, and Jewish tithes and offerings to the Temple and priesthood, piling on the economic pressure resulting in impoverishment of many and "the disintegration of village communities". It is these "deteriorating conditions" of "impoverishment, hunger, and debt" that Jesus addresses in his ministry in the Gospels.[12] The question was also spiritually compromising as, according to the Torah, Jews should not possess coins with idolatrous images (here the emperor's face and titles).

This was clearly an explosive subject, as many Jews resented paying the tax, so to approve of such a tax could alienate many, whereas rejecting it risked official sanctions. Asking for a denarius Jesus asks, "'Whose head is this, and whose title?' They answered, 'The emperor's'". He then pronounces "Give to the emperor the things that are the emperor's, and to God the things that are God's" (Mark 12:16–17).

On one hand, this has been read as a dichotomy: an external realm of political obligation and an internal realm of spiritual life. But we should probably read it in a more radical way: this offensively inscribed coin belongs to Caesar, so give it back to him and eschew political rebellion. But, what belongs to God is all humanity (created in the image of God); specifically the Jewish people[13] and their keeping of the Law inscribed on their hearts; and also the Promised Land. "While couched in a clever circumlocution, Jesus' answer was still a blunt declaration of the people's independence of Roman imperial rule/kingdom, since they belonged directly under the rule/kingdom of God."[14] At the very least there "was the strong hint that Caesar's regime was a blasphemous nonsense and that one day God would overthrow it."[15] Jesus' answer thus both wrong-footed those intending to trap him but also laid down a challenge to the oppressive worldly political structures. It called these empires to accountability to God.[16]

So, how much of a challenge was Jesus to Rome?

Would Jesus, if he was believed to be the Messiah, have implied a military challenge to the Roman authorities? Within the Gospels Jesus rarely accepts or declares a messianic title, yet numerous times preaches about the kingdom of heaven or kingdom of God. Within all the synoptic gospels Jesus is asked at his trial whether he is the Messiah by the Jewish authorities, so there was clearly something about his actions and teachings that led them to this conclusion. Within Jewish tradition, the Messiah would lead an army against Israel's enemies (in this case the Romans); rebuild David's kingdom; and restore Israel. For Jesus to be the Messiah and bring in God's kingdom, there could arguably be attached an expectation of a new order of society which would overturn the Roman order.[17] Co-existence of Roman sovereignty with the dominion of God (brought in by the Messiah) would have been impossible as there was no provision for such co-existence of the messianic reign of God with the reign of kings on the earth.[18] It has been argued that "to call oneself the messiah at the time of the Roman occupation was tantamount to declaring war on Rome"[19] however one defined the nature of messianic rule. When a shepherd-boy, named Athronges, with messianic aspirations under Herod Archelaus, placed a crown on his own head and launched an attack against Roman influence it ended in his execution.[20] This could also occur to one with a very different self-awareness to Athronges, when the title Messiah was in the equation.

We have seen how some of Jesus' followers may have harboured apocalyptic political aspirations, most notable Simon the Zealot and Judas Iscariot.[21] However, whether or not these close companions, chosen by Jesus, were members of Roman-hating, rebellion-planning groups, it is clear from Jesus' arrest in the garden of Gethsemane that Jesus did not believe that he had led a violent, military rebellion. "Then Jesus said to them, 'Have you come out with swords and clubs to arrest me as though I were a bandit?'" (Mark 14:48); which can be translated as "Am I leading a rebellion"? He is clearly highlighting the exaggerated response of the authorities to his non-violent ministry. This is particularly poignant given that he is arrested at night in a quiet garden with just a few followers, while praying.

Jesus' non-violent stance is shown through his teachings of forgiveness and peace with God, making it difficult to see how Jesus posed any real military threat to the Romans. Jesus specifically tells his followers not to use weapons: "Blessed are the peacemakers, for they will be called children of God" (Matthew 5:9); and "I say to you, Do not resist an evildoer. But if anyone strikes you on the right cheek, turn the other also" (Matthew 5:39).

Even at his arrest, when the soldiers are armed, he reprimands one of his disciples for using a sword to strike out. "Put your sword back into its place; for all who take the sword will perish by the sword" (Matthew 26:52).

All these central teachings of Jesus demonstrate his emphasis on non-violence. Therefore, although some of his contemporaries might have wanted Jesus to be more radical, his teachings would not have posed a military threat to the Romans.

And yet there is still a challenge to earthly power implicit in his life and preaching. However, it is a challenge which is dependent on God rather than human agency for its fulfilment. From the very beginning of Luke's account the reader is called to see the way that God works through the actions of the (*apparently dominant*) Roman state, in order to work his purpose and to fulfil messianic prophecy (the Bethlehem location). In Luke 2:10–14, when the angels appear to the shepherds, Jesus is announced as "Lord" and "Saviour" and the words "peace" and "good news" are used in association with the news of his birth. Such words were used of Augustus (on declarations, letters, and inscriptions). An inscription from around 9 BC says,

> Augustus... who being sent to us and our descendants as Saviour, has put an end to war and has set all things in order; and [whereas,] having become [god] manifest, Caesar has fulfilled all the hopes of earlier times... in surpassing all the benefactors who preceded him..., and whereas, finally, the birthday of the god [Augustus] has been for the whole world the beginning of good news (euangelion) concerning him [therefore let a *new era begin from his birth*].[22]

To those well-aware of Roman imperial ideology the Gospel references will have challenged exactly these claims made on behalf of the Emperor Augustus (using just these titles and terms). This was highly subversive of Luke, who therefore placed Jesus "in religio-political opposition to the emperor".[23]

Some historians have questioned the significance of this imperial cult, due to the vast numbers of honorific titles, altars, sacred buildings, and rituals surrounding the emperor, begging the question: what should or should not be included in this category due to the volume and diversity of practices?[24] And it has been suggested that political power rather than religious devotion was really the pressing issue.[25] Nevertheless, the ideology of the Roman Empire was anchored in the depiction of the Roman ruler as a god. Nicolaus of Damascus's *Life of Augustus* provides evidence of this deification of Julius Caesar after his death, "no one refrained from tears, seeing him who had lately been honoured like a god".[26] Under Augustus this imperial ideology grew in intensity. The emperor was received with honours that integrated his person at an elevated level into the cosmic hierarchy, with the title *divi filius* (son of the divine).[27] Coinage carried the image of Augustus with the inscription of a deity: CAESAR DIVI F.[28] Although some of this may have been more about a religious veneer over establishing Roman rule in conquered territories,[29] there were many communities where belief in the divinity of the emperor would have been both "obvious and uncontroversial".[30] This constituted what has been termed a "Roman Imperial Theology", an ideology "advertised with poems and inscriptions, coins and images, statues, altars, and structures".[31] It buttressed imperial rule throughout the conquered territories.[32] And, however regarded, it was highly dangerous to challenge it or set up in competition against it.

It can be argued that for many in Galilee and Judea in the first century AD, the loss of (briefly held) independence, the weight of imperial taxation, local royal taxes (in Galilee under Herod Antipas), the compromises involved as a strictly monotheistic religion within a polytheistic empire with an active imperial cult, created an explosive cocktail which combined economic hardship with politico-religious nationalism. It was as if Israel was still in a version of its historic Babylonian exile. Or even of Egyptian slavery and yearning for a new

Passover and a new Exodus. End Time tensions ran high. Jesus' life was lived within this volatile context. In Luke's Gospel in particular we see (even if not always explicitly stated) how "the kingdom of Jesus subverts and overthrows the kingdom of Rome" and its allies.[33] But it was not a subversion that relied on political revolution and earthly power – but humility.[34] We see this in the temptations, where it is the devil who rules "all the kingdoms of the world" (Luke 4:5). However, those who observed Jesus' challenge may have misunderstood the nature of the challenge, or they may have decided that, with popular following in a volatile environment, the risk of allowing him to live was too great.

The miracles and preaching of Jesus drew big crowds which did not go unnoticed. This is most obvious in the Gospels on Palm Sunday when Jesus rides into Jerusalem on a donkey and is met with hundreds of people shouting and singing his praises in messianic terms. Interestingly, in one tradition it was the pressure of a crowd getting out-of-hand that led Pilate to crucify Jesus (Matthew 27:24). The timing of Jesus' arrival would have been significant as it was very near Passover which celebrated the end of Jewish bondage to an imperial power, and therefore heightened Roman fear of rebellion. The prefect would post Roman soldiers on the walls of the Temple courtyard as a visible reminder of Roman domination.[35] The Romans, desperate to put an end to Jewish uprisings, crucified hundreds of people and used military force regularly, taking no chances with individuals or groups who might be rebellious.[36] Jesus would not have been the only man at that time in that area gathering a crowd, but it is unlikely he would have gone unnoticed in Jerusalem.

In the Gospel of John, the chief priests and the Pharisees are clearly worried that Jesus' miracles and following would catch the attention of the Romans, resulting in the destruction of the Jewish community:

> "What are we to do? This man is performing many signs. If we let him go on like this, everyone will believe in him, and the Romans will come and destroy both our holy place and our nation." But one of them, Caiaphas, who was high priest that year, said to them, "You know nothing at all! You do not

> understand that it is better for you to have one man die for the people than to have the whole nation destroyed".
> **(John 11:47–50)**

The proclamation of a "kingdom" (however defined) was politically very risky. To this it might be asserted that it was a kingdom for children (Matthew 18:1–5); the poor in spirit (Matthew 5:3); for tax collectors and prostitutes (Matthew 21:31). Jesus insisted, "The kingdom of God is not coming with things that can be observed; nor will they say, 'Look, here it is!' or 'There it is!' For, in fact, the kingdom of God is among you" (Luke 17:20–21). To Pilate he said that "My kingdom is not from this world" (John 18:36). Despite this, it was still a "kingdom". And that could be construed as a threat, especially if considered to imply the renewal of Israel in opposition to earthly rulers.[37] When crucified, the Gospels all tell of how Jesus was crucified as the "King of the Jews", so this is the crime that Pilate concedes he committed; this is despite finding no case against him following their discussion. This does beg the question: would the Romans have sought to arrest Jesus if it was not for the Jewish authorities? Or was it only a matter of time before Jesus sufficiently annoyed the Romans? Whether or not Pilate actually thought Jesus was a political threat, this was the seed that was planted in his mind, and this seed was a fairly assured way of persuading him to take action against Jesus, resulting in his death.

The simple matter is that Jesus' actions and teachings seemed to threaten the status quo, and this caused his death by an administration well-versed in violent executions.[38] Even if the trigger to start the process was pulled by the Jerusalem elite, any crowd-pulling preacher who talked of a "kingdom" and apocalyptic change (however dependent on the agency of God, not people) was set on a collision course with Roman authority.

CHAPTER 13

"Tell no one..." A secret messiah?

Within Christianity today there are many titles given to Jesus, but we need to examine the Gospel evidence to see where these titles have come from and who used them. Clearly, titles are indications of a person's claim to authority, so it is important to understand the status and significance that Jesus assigned to *himself*, alongside what his contemporaries assigned to him. Was Jesus understood to be a prophet? Did Jesus claim to be the Messiah, and, if so, what kind of messiah? How do we explain the so-called "messianic secret", whereby Jesus tells his followers that his status as Messiah should not be openly discussed? Repeatedly in the Gospels Jesus uses the title "Son of Man" to describe himself, yet what did he mean by this title? Furthermore, the controversial question is: did he claim to be the "Son of God"? What would this have meant in a first-century Jewish context and just how explosive was it? The ultimate question then is: who did Jesus think he was?

Before going any further, the difficulty of understanding a person's mentality when that person operates within a different culture and uses unfamiliar language must be highlighted.[1] How is it that one can uncover an individual's self-consciousness when the original context and form of their sayings is debated? We therefore need to speak of Jesus' expressed self-understanding rather than self-consciousness,[2] and this involves inquiring into his aims, objectives, and motives through observation and interpretation of his words and deeds.[3] This method can give an insight into Jesus' feelings and convictions as to his own significance.[4]

A second question that must be faced is whether later Christological titles (which accord him highly exalted status)[5] have a basis in the life and self-understanding of Jesus himself or whether they are post-Easter interpretations. In the latter case they are then the church's later portrayal of Jesus' self-understanding, with Jesus seen and understood retrospectively, in the new light of the Easter faith.[6] However, even *if* the titles used in the Gospels reflect beliefs of the early church, rather than the explicit claims expressed by Jesus himself (and this would be contested by more conservative scholars), it is not unreasonable to assume that the character of his preaching caused his followers to make such claims.[7]

Jesus the prophet?

Within the Gospels many people at the time clearly thought Jesus was a prophet. At Jesus' triumphal entry into Jerusalem on a donkey, the Sunday before he died on Good Friday, Matthew 21:11 says, "The crowds were saying, 'This is the prophet Jesus from Nazareth in Galilee'". After his resurrection he is identified as having been a prophet, with Luke 24:19 stating early Christian beliefs: "They replied, 'The things about Jesus of Nazareth, who was a prophet mighty in deed and word before God and all the people'". These examples – and there are others – demonstrate how during his lifetime, people clearly thought Jesus was a person who spoke for God (by divine inspiration), guiding his people.

Additionally, within John's Gospel Jesus makes it clear that his message is one that comes from God, thereby fulfilling the role of prophet as a messenger from God: John 7:16 has Jesus saying, "My teaching is not mine but his who sent me". Furthermore, in Matthew 16:21 Jesus displays another aspect of being a prophet which is making predictions concerning the future:

> From that time on, Jesus began to show his disciples that he must go to Jerusalem and undergo great suffering at the hands of the elders and chief priests and scribes, and be killed, and on the third day be raised.

All four Gospels record this prediction as coming to completion. In addition, in Luke 21:20–22 Jesus predicts the later destruction of Jerusalem. Although some modern biblical experts will assert that these predictions reveal the time of writing of the Gospels and their reading back these events into the mouth of Jesus, the Gospels themselves insist that these warnings were, in fact, an integral part of his original proclamation.

Moreover, sayings by Jesus signpost how he understood forthcoming rejection and suffering like the prophets before him.[8] This is portrayed in Luke 13:33 where Jesus accepts not only the role of a prophet but also its fate,

> Yet today, tomorrow, and the next day I must be on my way, because it is impossible for a prophet to be killed away from Jerusalem.

Jesus also suggests he is a prophet in Mark 6:4 when he is rejected in his home town of Nazareth as many took offence at his teachings, "Then Jesus said to them, 'Prophets are not without honour, except in their home town, and among their own kin, and in their own house'". It is reasonable to assume that, in both instances, Jesus was talking about himself in third person to emphasize his point.

However, due to the lack of evidence outside of the Gospels about Jesus as a prophet, it has been suggested that these are constructs of the Gospel writers and therefore Jesus and his earliest followers may not have thought this way.[9] Alternatively, although it might be questioned whether this title fully covers everything that Jesus thought he was, it seems that Jesus believed that at least part of his role was to bring the word of God to people, and this is made clear by the numerous references in the Gospels to Jesus as a prophet. Indeed, given that later Gospel writers had an even more exalted view of him, the presence of these claims in their work suggests these are authentic traditions traceable to Jesus himself. There appears no reason why Jesus would not have believed this, and such a title fits with Jesus' actions and teachings. But does the title "prophet" encompass all that Jesus thought he was?

Jesus the Messiah?

In Luke 24, while identifying Jesus as a prophet, a follower named Cleopas also says how they hoped Jesus would be the one to redeem Israel (Luke 24:21).[10] So did Jesus believe himself to be the Messiah: the promised and expected deliverer of the Jewish people, the awaited Son of David, a saviour and restorer?[11] Within the Jewish tradition, the Messiah was expected to come from the line of David, and Jesus is shown to be a descendent of David in the genealogies of Matthew and Luke. The title "Messiah" (Greek: Christ) in its first century context did not necessarily equate to a divine figure but an agent of God. Therefore, Jesus' teachings of the coming of the new kingdom confirm his desire for the "kingly rule" of God, and his disciples understood this as Jesus' proclamation of himself as the new king who would introduce this rule.[12] The understanding that he acted as God's agent as a prophet would coincide with and be consistent with Jesus' teachings and proclamations heralding God's eschatological (End Time) kingdom.[13]

Yet did the disciples later replace Jesus' original *political* status with that of a more *spiritual* one, a Messiah who forgives sins? Was it only after his death that Jesus' title as Messiah was elevated? The belief in the resurrection could have caused the disciples to re-evaluate the meaning of the crucifixion but it is unlikely it would have led them to state a messianic title had an understanding not already been present within Jesus' ministry.[14]

It is interesting that one of Jesus' rare-recorded assertions of his messiahship is to a Samaritan rather than a Jew, and furthermore to a woman:

> The woman said to him, "I know that Messiah is coming" (who is called Christ). "When he comes, he will proclaim all things to us." Jesus said to her, "I am he, the one who is speaking to you".
> **(John 4:25–26)**

Yet there is a reluctance in the synoptic tradition to ascribe to Jesus explicit declarations (public or private) of such messianic status.[15] So it seems that Jesus had reservations about honorific titles such as "the Coming One" and "Messiah". However, this may have been because of his concern with preconceptions in the minds of his hearers regarding what these titles implied. Given the fevered political context, this would not be surprising.

The recognition of Jesus' messianic status by the disciples is portrayed in Peter's confession in Mark 8:28–30. In this passage Jesus asks the disciples who they say he is, and Peter proclaims that Jesus is the Messiah. He is silenced by Jesus and ordered ("sternly") not to tell anyone. Interestingly, at the beginning of the passage the disciples say to Jesus that people say that he is one of the prophets, and this title gets no reaction from Jesus which juxtaposes with his reaction to the messianic assessment. This points to two possible answers. Either Jesus refused to accept and thus denied the confession as Messiah or he accepted the title but wished to revise the expectations attached to this title. It is unlikely that, due to Jesus' anti-violence attitude, he would have accepted the Davidic messianic hopes of a warrior Messiah liberating Israel from their oppressors (the Romans) without qualification.[16] Therefore, it can be argued that Jesus had a messianic self-understanding but since his view of "Messiah" differed from that of the Jewish people, he did not wish to proclaim this title. Perhaps also, Jesus felt it was too early in his ministry to reveal such a loaded title that would (potentially) lead to great misunderstanding.

What is interesting is that in Matthew there is a similar discussion but with a different outcome.

> Simon Peter answered, "You are the Messiah, the Son of the living God." And Jesus answered him, "Blessed are you, Simon son of Jonah! For flesh and blood has not revealed this to you, but my Father in heaven".
> **(Matthew 16:16–17)**

Yet, we should notice how Peter's answer still proclaims Jesus as Messiah, but qualifies it with "Son of the living God". Therefore, to Matthew's readers this qualification might show a revised messianic understanding and expectation which is more in line with Jesus' thinking, resulting in Jesus' acceptance of the title here. Or this may indicate a later revision of the original conversation as recorded in Mark. The matter is clearly complex.

Consequently, the Gospel material overall indicates that Jesus did view himself as the Messiah leading the kingdom movement; however his revolution would be one of total obedience to God, ruling out violent revolution.[17] Furthermore, Jesus may also have avoided claiming messianic status due to its direct challenge to Herod Antipas, which would have resulted in violent counter-measures. Therefore, this silencing in Mark might be due to Jesus' wish to redefine what it meant to be a Messiah: in Mark he denied the implications attached to Messiah in the Jewish tradition and expectations rather than the title itself.

Another point in the Gospels that reinforces Jesus' messianic status is his trial. How can it be understood that Jesus was crucified as a radical political criminal if those around him did not view him as claiming messianic status? If this view was widely held, then Jesus' actions or words must have promoted this view. During his trial, Jesus openly admits to being the Messiah. The (probably earliest) written account, Mark 14:61–62, says, "Again the high priest asked him, 'Are you the Messiah, the Son of the Blessed One?' Jesus said, 'I am'". It is interesting that Matthew and Luke's parallel accounts retain a more ambiguous reply. Luke 22:67 says, "He [Jesus] replied, 'If I tell you, you will not believe'", whereas Matthew 26:64 states, "Jesus said to him, 'You have said so'". However, it is unlikely this implies a rejection of the title, and the chief priests clearly do not see this as a denial, as Matthew 26:67–68 says, "Then they spat in his face and struck him; and some slapped him, saying, 'Prophesy to us, you Messiah! Who is it that struck you?'". Additionally, if Jesus had not made any messianic statements leading to accusations of being a false-Messiah, then the charge against him as "King of the Jews" cannot be explained. It might be argued, as Rudolf Bultmann did, that Jesus did not understand himself as Messiah, but was unjustly accused and perished because of political misunderstanding, but this seems strained and unlikely.[18]

Overall, it seems reasonable to conclude that, although the lack of messianic proclamations in the Gospels by Jesus is striking, this does not equate to a rejection of the title. What seems more likely is that Jesus did believe himself to be the Messiah and thus died for that title;

in Luke 24:26 the risen Jesus does identify himself as the Messiah who had to suffer to enter into glory. However, we may assume that he wished to revise the role of the Jewish Messiah (not to be a warrior pursuing a violent revolution) so was, therefore, hesitant in using the title due to its potentially unintended response and call to arms.

Jesus the "Son of Man"?

A title which Jesus does use frequently of himself is "Son of Man". There is much debate over what this title meant as Jesus never specifically defines the term. This is the title found on Jesus' own lips throughout the Gospels so, it is clear that this was a title that Jesus was familiar with and identified with.

Some experts argue that the "Son of Man" is a pre-existent, heavenly figure influenced by Daniel 7:13,

> As I watched in the night visions,
> I saw one like a human being
> coming with the clouds of heaven.
> And he came to the Ancient One
> and was presented before him.

"Like a human being" can been translated as "like a son of man". The vision asserts that this righteous one will be exulted by God.[19]

However, it has been argued that evidence is lacking that Jesus identified the "Son of Man" as a heavenly being, as this concept of pre-existence does not seem to clearly emerge in Jewish and Christian theology until the last decades of the first century AD, so could, therefore, be a post-Easter adaptation.[20] Yet, there appears a consensus that the concept, at the very least, represents a figure of the final judgment; so Jesus may have seen himself as this heavenly figure, who was to return in the end times to battle against Israel's enemies.

At his trial in Mark 14:61–62, when Jesus affirms he is the Messiah and "Son of the Blessed One", Jesus adds, "you will see the Son of Man seated at the right hand of the Power", and "coming with the clouds of heaven", emphasizing the eschatological connotations this title carries. This may emphasize what was said earlier, about Jesus revising the messianic expectation as bringing in God's kingdom in the present, through obedience to God, which will come to its ultimate fulfilment in the future. Therefore, perhaps he is not yet the full manifestation of the "Son of Man" but acts as one destined to be this triumphant future figure, during his ministry and suffering.[21] By identifying himself with this figure, Jesus affirms conviction of his vital role in the proclamation of the kingdom of God which would continue until the end of the present age.[22] However, it should be noted that Jesus' use of the title at times does appear to suggest that he is this future-person *here and now*, as well as in the future tense. For example, Matthew 9:6, "But so that you may know that the Son of Man has authority on earth to forgive sins", where Jesus says that he has authority in the *present*, as the Son of Man. In which case, the future hope has broken into the present experience.

Alternatively, some have argued that Jesus' reference to the "Son of Man" was to someone other than himself. However, this is a doubtful interpretation and certainly not representative of the use of the title by Jesus in the Gospels. The title can be best understood when applied to Jesus himself speaking in the third person. The writer of John wishes to make this clear:

> So Jesus said, "When you have lifted up the Son of Man, then you will realise that I am he, and that I do nothing on my own, but I speak these things as the Father instructed me".
> **(John 8:28)**

There is no evidence in the sayings of Jesus that he ever looked for some eschatological redeemer to *follow him*. Jesus appears to believe that he is the end of the line of prophets.

It has been argued that the church created this apocalyptic expectation of Jesus after the crucifixion to explain the apparent failure of Jesus' mission to bring the present age to its close. However, those who separate Jesus from this eschatological title – claiming that this title was a post-Easter church invention – need to argue against the implementation of the kingdom of God being Jesus' main message, which appears almost impossible to do.

A further development of the "Son of Man" debate is to suggest that the title was used in the third person to represent the voice of the church rather than of Jesus himself; another way of speaking of humankind.[23] However, difficulties then arise with sayings concerning the future role.

One can only confidently know how Jesus viewed the notion of "Son of Man" if a clear-cut understanding of his personal definition could be decisively established. Although no answer is conclusive, the best view of Jesus' approach to the title is his own belief in his return at the final judgment to liberate Israel. Consequently, it seems that Jesus took for himself an apocalyptic title encompassing the return of a heavenly figure in the last judgment. If Jesus thought of himself as being such a "Son of Man", this implies that he viewed himself as being a vital component in the completion of God's world-project.[24] This is a highly exalted view. Which brings us to the most contentious title of all.

Jesus the "Son of God"?

Did Jesus believe that he was the "Son of God", the pre-existent second person of the Trinity who is one with God the Father? This is how later Christians came to define the term. Or is the title "Son of God" meant to portray Jesus as a representative of God?

Jesus' use of "*abba*" (Aramaic: father) to address God reveals that he was aware of his intimate relationship with God and indicates dependence. In Mark 14:36 Jesus says, "Abba, Father, for you all things are possible". However, the language of divine sonship and divinity was widespread and varied in use in the ancient world so would have been familiar to contemporaries of Jesus.[25] And "Father" as a title of God was known in first-century Judaism. Therefore, Jesus' usage of *abba* cannot be supposed to be unique and therefore signifying "Son of God" status. Nonetheless, no evidence matches the regularity and consistency with which Jesus uses "Father" in his approach to God, distinguishing Jesus from his contemporaries. Also, Jesus teaching his disciples to address God in this way (Matthew 6:9–15) portrays how

Jesus views their sonship as dependent on himself. Although, the use of the terms *abba* and Father highlights Jesus' intimate relationship with God, it does not identify whether Jesus believed he was coeternal with the Father and therefore one with the Father in the way the later church stated. This address appears to portray dependence, rather than equality of divinity.

A further problem, however, is that Jesus never actually uses the specific title in the Gospels. This has led some to argue that the doctrine of divine sonship played no part in the ministry of Jesus[26] and finds no parallel in the religious environment of the time. Certainly, as later Christians used it, it scandalized contemporary orthodox Jewish believers.

Considering that this title plays such a crucial role and holds so much importance for the Christian church, did Jesus really view himself as the "Son of God" or does this concept (as understood in the later doctrine of the Trinity) belong solely to the early church?

All three synoptic gospels describe the transfiguration of Jesus. Jesus becomes radiantly transformed and his clothes become dazzling white; Elijah and Moses appear talking to Jesus; and a voice comes from a cloud saying, "This is my Son, the Beloved; listen to him!" (Mark 9:7). It may be assumed that the voice was God's, which is made evident in 2 Peter 1:17:

> For he [Jesus] received honour and glory from God the Father when that voice was conveyed to him by the Majestic Glory, saying, "This is my Son, my Beloved, with whom I am well pleased."

Although some argue that the transfiguration was a subjective vision, and others argue it is a misplaced resurrection account, it seems clear that to the Gospel writers it was an actual event in the life of Jesus.[27] Directed to the disciples, God's words confirm Jesus' divine identity and elevate him above both Elijah and Moses (above the prophet and the giver of the Law).[28] There are several interpretations of this event: as the limits of Jesus' humanity being temporarily overcome by the glory of the preincarnate Son of God; as a glimpse of the splendour anticipated at Jesus' resurrection; or as a glimpse of the future glory of the Son of God at his second coming (2 Peter 1:16).[29] The latter interpretation fits with the understanding of Jesus as the messianic "Son of Man" bringing to completion God's kingdom. No historian can provide a definitive answer. But the matter clearly was hugely significant to the later writers of the New Testament.

At his trial this title is brought up by the Jewish leaders when questioning Jesus. In Luke and Matthew's Gospels Jesus does not use the title for himself but is responding to the Jewish leaders who use this title referring to him. Luke records, "All of them asked, 'Are you, then, the Son of God?' He said to them, 'You say that I am'" (Luke 22:70). Jesus' answer is not a clear admission. Yet, for the Jewish priests to have come up with this title and for it to form such a pivotal role in the trial of Jesus, it seems likely that such a title was being used of Jesus even if not specifically said by himself. Furthermore, in Matthew's Gospel, Jesus' response is similar, yet the response of the high priest is to accuse Jesus of blasphemy, and the chief priests conclude that he deserves death (Matthew 26:65–66). In Leviticus 24:10–23 and 1 Kings 21:8–13 the punishment for blasphemy is death by stoning. The precise definition of blasphemy is speaking contemptuously about God, but a broader, less precise definition is any act contrary to the will of God or derogatory to his power.[30] Jesus does not, of course, revile the name of God here, but his response implied to the priests some claim to divine sonship. And sharing in God's power was offensive and a capital offence.

Additionally, in the Gospel of John, Jesus claims "The Father and I are one" (John 10:30), which seems an undeniable claim to oneness with God. The Jews then try to stone him saying, "It is not for a good work that we are going to stone you, but for blasphemy, because you, though only a human being, are making yourself God" (John 10:33).

As mentioned earlier, the trial in Mark is crucial in establishing Jesus' controversial status. "Again the high priest asked him, 'Are you the Messiah, the Son of the Blessed One?' Jesus said, 'I am'" (Mark 14:61–62). In Exodus 3:14, when God is speaking with Moses, he says, "'I AM WHO I AM.' He said further, 'Thus you shall say to the Israelites, "I AM has sent me to you."'" This emphasizes how God is unchanging and self-existent. God as "I am" would have been well known within Judaism. In John 8:58 Jesus says, "Very truly, I tell you, before Abraham was, I am." In the next verse the Jews pick up stones to throw at him and kill him; this angry response implies that these people believed that Jesus was comparing himself to God as described in Exodus 3:14, and therefore making a claim to be – as later Christians would describe the nature – God incarnate. Therefore, it is not unreasonable to assume that Jesus' response in Mark 14 is making a similar bold statement, and the high priest clearly concluded this and condemned him to death for blasphemy (Mark 14:64). It is the claim to divine sonship that results in Jesus' guilty verdict and death. Thus, a combination of a very personal use of "Father", with a messianic understanding of the title "Son of Man", may have meant that this divine sonship was implicit in Jesus' teaching and it may have been this which caused the very question of divine sonship to be asked at his trial. To assume that all this is the invention of the later church, fails to explain why Jesus was regarded as so offensive by the Jewish religious leadership. Clearly, he made claims that they found highly provocative.

In conclusion, Jesus' frequent use of "Son of Man" can be seen as signifying that he believed that he had a crucial role to play in the final judgment. Consequently, it is reasonable to argue that Jesus thought he was an eschatological prophet, the "Son of Man" spreading the word of God; proclaiming his messianic message of the kingdom; and preparing the people for the end times. And that this involved a claim to divine sonship, which burst the boundaries of contemporary Judaism, is a reasonable conclusion.

CHAPTER 14

"O Jerusalem..."

Jerusalem played a crucial role within the religious, cultural, and political life of first-century Judaism. It is, therefore, no surprise that it played a pivotal role in the life and ministry of Jesus. But why was the city so important in Jewish life? And how many times did Jesus go to Jerusalem and why did he go there? In order to answer these questions, we need to explore the role of the great city and its Temple in the life of first-century Judaism and the relationship of Jesus with the city, the Temple, and its powerful elites. We will also need to explore and assess to what extent he represented a challenge to its dominance and that of its religious and social leadership. Was his message designed to support or change the central role of the city and Temple in the life of the nation? Was he always on a collision course with Jerusalem?

The place of Jerusalem within first-century Jewish culture

It is impossible to think of first-century Judaism without thinking of Jerusalem. It was a huge regional centre, with a population in the tens of thousands. It has been estimated that Jerusalem's population stood at about 55,000, but during major feasts, this could rise enormously to somewhere in the region of 180,000.[1] As with so much in population estimates relating to the ancient world, the numbers fluctuate widely in modern assessments. More conservative scholars suggesting a stable population of 20,000; more expansive estimates reach over 100,000.[2]

So, the middle figure of c. 55,000 is a reasonable one and would probably gain general acceptance.

The Roman naturalist and writer Pliny the Elder (lived: AD 23–79) described it as "the most famous city in the East, not just in Judea".[3] It was renowned for its magnificent Temple. We call this the Second Temple and its construction had started in about 515 BC, as a replacement of the Temple earlier destroyed by the Babylonians. This building was then totally renovated and enlarged by Herod the Great (died: 4 BC) in a style which drew architectural inspiration from across the Eastern Mediterranean world of his day. The Temple itself stood on a great white-stone platform. By doubling the size of the Temple Mount area, Herod created the largest temple complex in the entire Roman world. There was simply nowhere else to compare with it.[4] As he reorganized its courts, he also allowed a large area to accommodate Gentile visitors and a special court was established for Jewish women.

The Temple was a pilgrimage site which drew Jewish visitors from across the whole of the Jewish diaspora. It was the only place within Judaism where animal sacrifice was allowed and the massive cult importance of Jerusalem is hard to exaggerate. It was here, in its daily blood sacrifices and huge events of communal worship and holy-day sacrifices, that the Jewish interaction with God occurred at its most profound level.[5] Here it was that personal and national sins were atoned for and the chosen status of the Jewish people was embedded.

As well as being a key religious focus, Jerusalem was also of huge economic importance. Vast numbers of pilgrims and visitors were serviced by a huge range of craftworkers, skilled artisans, and what we would now call the hospitality industry. Their money flowed into the Temple and the city.

The topography of the great city

The city itself was built on and around two hills. The eastern hill was topped with the great Temple complex, accessed by two stone viaducts. The western hill was Mount Zion. Between them, and south of the Temple complex, the narrow unpaved streets and crowded houses of the Lower City stretched down toward the Tyropoeon valley, which ran through the centre of the city. Rising up from here, to the west, was the Upper City (Mount Zion), where the spacious white marble villas and palaces of the elites were located. Two large, arched passageways crossed the Tyropoeon Valley, giving access from the Upper City to the Temple Mount. The city extended to the south, where it included land that, today, lies beyond the walls of the so-called "Old City" (which were constructed in the sixteenth century AD).

The later Jewish historian Josephus wrote that Herod the Great built a theatre in the city, as well as an amphitheatre "on the plain". Modern archaeology locates the latter near the Upper City, some distance from the sacred place of the Temple Mount. In addition, a hippodrome (a horse-racing stadium) existed by the AD 60s.[6] It was located a short distance from the amphitheatre. In this way, Jerusalem experienced the Hellenization that marked out all the cities of the Eastern Mediterranean. Greek influence was wide-reaching. However, unlike other cities of the region it was without the cult statues that accompanied religious devotion everywhere else.[7] And, when Roman prefects attempted to bring in military standards with pagan images, there was trouble. There was nowhere quite like Jerusalem.

Next to the massive Temple complex stood the Fortress of Antonia (named after Mark Antony, one of the benefactors of Herod the Great). The fortress was the centre of Roman military power in the city, as earlier it had been Herod's palace fortress. It stood to the north of the outer wall of the Temple area. A stairway and an underground passageway connected the Fortress of Antonia with the Court of the Gentiles, allowing Roman soldiers easy access in the event of any disturbance or challenge to Roman authority. The high priest's ceremonial robes were kept in one of its four towers. As symbols of his religious authority, their custody allowed the Romans greater control over his activities and they were only released on important religious feast days. This accompanied Roman control of the appointed office of high priest.

The palace of the high priest lay diametrically across the city from the Temple and looked toward that vast structure. When Jesus was arrested, the actual *home* of the high priest was located in a different area of the Upper City. Near the palace of the high priest was Herod's palace, which some experts have suggested was occupied by the Roman prefect when he was present in the city.[8] However, the need to keep a close eye on the Temple may have meant that the *praetorium* (Pilate's headquarters), with the stone pavement of *Gabbatha* mentioned in the Gospel of John in connection with the trial of Jesus, may actually have been in the Fortress of Antonia rather than at Herod's palace.[9] Opinions differ among experts. What is clear is that the outer wall of Herod's palace made up the north-western boundary of the urban area. When Herod Antipas was in Jerusalem, he would have stayed at the Hasmonean palace, which was situated about halfway between Herod's palace and the Temple Mount, and near the Gennath Gate into the city. Outside this gate, in an angle formed by the city walls, a large quarry lay outside the urban defences. At the far end of this quarry was probably the location of Golgotha, where Jesus was crucified. It was in the Hasmonean palace that Jesus was interrogated by Herod Antipas on the morning preceding his crucifixion. These places of elite power – high priest, prefect, and Herod Antipas – were near-neighbours in the same overall quarter of the city.

How many times did Jesus go to Jerusalem?

The simple answer is that we do not know. But we get a clear impression from the Gospels; and that impression differs between the synoptic writers (Mark, Matthew, and Luke), when contrasted with the impression we get from John.

We have placed our exploration of the role of the city at this point in our examination of the life of Jesus for a biographical reason. For, although there are references to the great city and its Temple earlier than this point in his life, it is as crisis escalates, and in the final weeks of conflict, that the city comes fully into view.

If we only had the synoptic Gospels, we would have a very distinctive impression of the life of Jesus and his relationship with the city. A good way to assess this impression is to type "Jerusalem" into a Bible search engine and then narrow the field to the New Testament only.[10] Scrolling down through the references, one quickly gets the overview.

In Matthew, Jesus is born at Bethlehem near Jerusalem. His ministry then takes place in Galilee, but crowds (including Pharisees and scribes) travel from Jerusalem, and Judea generally, to see and hear him. They come "from Galilee, the Decapolis, Jerusalem, Judea, and from beyond the Jordan" (Matthew 4:25). Jesus refers to Jerusalem as being of great significance as "it is the city of the great King [God]" (Matthew 5:35) and it is the place to which he will go to face his final conflict with "the elders and chief priests and scribes" (Matthew 16:21). Twice he makes this point to his disciples *with a specific reference to Jerusalem* as the location of this climactic conflict. These are two of the three times in this Gospel that Jesus predicts his death and resurrection. The third time is as they are journeying to the great city itself. He then enters Jerusalem in triumph on the day now traditionally known as "Palm Sunday", at the beginning of the week that will end with his crucifixion.

Mark begins his account with Jesus in Galilee (there being no account of Jesus' birth or childhood). As in Matthew, crowds and critics come north to him. Then, while "on the road, going up to Jerusalem" (Mark 10:32), Jesus – for the third time – predicts his arrest, death, and resurrection. The connection of these future events with their destination is made clear at the start of this prediction, when he says to his followers: "See, we are going up to Jerusalem" (Mark 10:33). On reaching their destination, there is the triumphal entry into the city, amid the welcoming crowds. And then, the week leading to his execution.

Luke is a little different. We have detailed accounts of Jesus' birth at Bethlehem, near Jerusalem; his presentation at the Temple as a baby; his visit to the Temple (as a twelve-year-old). Then we jump to the Galilean ministry, with the Judeans coming to him. At Luke's account of the transfiguration, Moses and Elijah "appeared in glory and were speaking of his departure, which he was about to accomplish at Jerusalem" (Luke 9:31), which focuses (as in Mark and Matthew) on the coming climactic conflict in the city. We then see an extensive journey to Jerusalem that includes conflict at a Samaritan village, where "they did not receive him, because his face was set towards Jerusalem" (Luke 9:53). Jesus teaches as he travels. Some Pharisees warn Jesus of the threat posed to him by Herod. To this, he replies that, "I must be on my way, because it is impossible for a prophet to be killed away from Jerusalem". And he adds: "Jerusalem, Jerusalem, the city that kills the prophets and stones those who are sent to it!" (Luke 13:33–34). This accompanies what appears to be a cryptic reference to his future resurrection: "on the third day I finish my work" (Luke 13:32). Then there is healing; more predicting of his death; more teaching; then the final entry into Jerusalem.

The impression one gets from these three Gospels (regardless of differences) is that Jesus went to Jerusalem *once* during his ministry and that this resulted in his death. Given that Jewish adults were meant to go to Jerusalem at least once a year and probably three times (on the three main pilgrim festivals of Passover (*Pesach*), Pentecost or Weeks (*Shavuot*), and Booths (*Sukkot*)) this single named-visit can be interpreted as having occurred at *the culmination of a ministry that lasted no longer than one year*. Although Luke recounts a more extensive journey to the city than we find in Mark and Matthew, the overall impression is largely the same. Jesus explodes onto the scene as an adult (aged about thirty according to Luke) and, in the space of (it seems) one year, makes such an impact on those around him that – on his one and only recorded visit to Jerusalem during that year – he is arrested and killed.

This is not the impression that we get from the Gospel of John. Early in John's Gospel we hear of Jesus going up to Jerusalem for Passover (John 2:13). It is then that he cleanses the Temple of "people selling cattle, sheep, and doves, and the money-changers seated at their tables" (John 2:14). This is an event placed at the end of Jesus' life (during the final week) in the synoptic gospels. In John, this action in the Temple is accompanied by an altercation with some of those witnessing it, which results in Jesus telling them, "Destroy this temple, and in three days I will raise it up" (John 2:19); a claim which John says refers to his body but which those facing him take as a reference to the physical destruction of the temple building. It is difficult to exaggerate how provocative the latter scenario would have been to those who heard (and, according to John, misunderstood) him. Later, to a Samaritan woman, he states that a time is coming when both the Samaritan's holy place and the Jerusalem Temple itself will cease to be of significance in the worship of God (John 4:21). As with the previous (misunderstood) comment, this statement would have been highly controversial during the lifetime of Jesus.

Later we learn that "there was a festival of the Jews, and Jesus went up to Jerusalem" (John 5:1). This makes a second visit and the actual occasion is not specified.

A Passover is mentioned – "Now the Passover, the festival of the Jews, was near" (John 6:4) – preceding the feeding of the five thousand in Galilee. However, there is no explicit mention of Jesus going to this festival; although we would naturally assume that he went.

Following time spent in Galilee, we next hear of him going up to Jerusalem during the Festival of Booths or Tabernacles. This follows a disagreement with his brothers (unnamed) who, we are told, did not believe in him and who challenge him to go up to Jerusalem in order to more publically pursue his ministry (John 7:1–9). But Jesus refuses, as it may mean his death and his time has not yet come. However, "after his brothers had gone to the festival, then he also went, not publicly but as it were in secret" (John 7:10). Having done so, he then begins teaching in the Temple, despite attempts to arrest him. There follows more teaching in and near the city (the Mount of Olives), disputes with Jewish opponents, healing, and more teaching.

Then there appears to be a break in the geographical focus (after John 10:21), for the next we hear is that "At that time the festival of the Dedication [*Hannukah*] took place in Jerusalem. It was winter, and Jesus was walking in the temple, in the portico of Solomon" (John 10:22–23). This reads as another visit to Jerusalem, separated from the last by a (short?) period of time. Following a near-stoning for blasphemy, Jesus "escaped from their hands" (John 10:39) and went across the River Jordan to where John the Baptist had once operated.

Jesus finally returns to Jerusalem for the final time (the fifth or sixth time). The disciples recognize the significance of this, given the earlier attempts to arrest and kill Jesus in Jerusalem and "Thomas, who was called the Twin, said to his fellow-disciples, 'Let us also go, that we may die with him'" (John 11:16). On the way, Jesus raises Lazarus from the dead at Bethany. Following this, John tells us that the chief priests and the Pharisees called a meeting of the council in order to plot his death. This is then followed by Jesus being anointed by Mary at Bethany (which prefigures the anointing of his body for burial); then his triumphal entry into Jerusalem and the week leading to his arrest and execution.

What are we to make of this? The first thing we might assert is that this illustrates the point already made, that to treat the Gospels as simple biographies is rather naïve. Rather, their compilers chose and deployed information to make points about the significance of Jesus. Although this occurred within a generally discernible chronological framework, it certainly does not allow us to construct a strict chronology. We have an awareness of the progress of events, rather than a detailed timeline. A case in point – and connected to Jerusalem – is Jesus' assertion "Jerusalem, Jerusalem, the city that kills prophets". In Luke this occurs as Jesus and his disciples are on their long journey to the city (Luke 13:34–35). Whereas in Matthew he says it while he is in the city during the last tumultuous week (Matthew 23:37–39). Given that the culmination of this teaching in both Gospels (Jerusalem will not see him until it says "Blessed is the one who comes in the name of the Lord") is, with slight variations, part of the cries of the crowd on Palm Sunday, it looks as if Luke is correct in placing this statement of Jesus *before* this triumphal entry, whereas Matthew (for his own theological reasons) has placed it *afterward*. Either way, it is a saying which connects Jesus and his status to the response from Jerusalem.[11] And Matthew and Luke have moved the material about differently in their chronology of Jesus and Jerusalem in order to make particular points in their presentation. But the situation remains clear – although Galilee is the prime location of Jesus' ministry, it is the response of Jerusalem that is intimately tied to the culmination of his messianic status.

So, how many times did he visit Jerusalem?[12] On one hand, some would argue that we simply cannot reconcile the synoptics with John. They have their different agendas and ways of deploying information and we have to treat them differently: the synoptics on one hand, and John on the other. That is one of the reasons why much of this biography of Jesus has been based on the synoptics – but supplemented by insights from John. As a generality, it is easier to get an overview of events from the synoptics (particularly from Mark); whereas John provides a greater depth of reflection on certain key events, issues, and themes. And all the evidence suggests that John was written later, with a rather different agenda to the earlier compilers. This shows itself in a number of features, most noticeably in his generic references to "the Jews" (written at a time when Judaism and Christianity had largely parted company) and the ease with which John contemplates a post-Temple faith, given the obliteration of the Jerusalem Temple in AD 70. By the time John was compiled, the Temple and its cult, its sacrifices and its organisation, would have felt like it was part of another – lost – world. It would have been like reflecting on the world of 1939 from the perspective of, perhaps, 1960. That other "world" was still the once-lived experience of older members of the community but was, at the same time, almost unimaginably separated from the present. Jerusalem was destroyed and the Temple was gone. This may have been about to happen, or still a raw event, while the other Gospels were being compiled. It had receded into the past when John was written.

That said, we do not have to simply choose the side of the synoptics for overall chronology and, consequently, assume that everything happened in a year with one climactic visit to Jerusalem. We can equally plausibly argue that John's account of a number of visits to Jerusalem over three years is persuasive and that the earlier three compilers simply sharpened their focus on the last and explosive visit which culminated in Jesus' death – and, as Christians insist, his resurrection. If so, we are back to a ministry lasting three years; a steady ratcheting up of tension; an increasing sense of challenge being felt by the elites of Jerusalem and the Temple; and a final and explosive Passover visit to the city and Temple.

Assuming this explains a number of things that occurred in Galilee, and then in the final week. Judean elite opposition to Jesus, while he was still in Galilee, is easier to understand if they knew him from a number of his visits to the city. This also helps explain their hostility on Palm Sunday. It was clearly not the first time they had encountered this controversial Galilean in the streets of the great city. Secretive arrangements for Palm Sunday – provision of the donkey(s) – and the final Passover – provision of the upper room and guidance to it – are easier to explain if Jesus already had followers and connections in the city. This also helps explain Peter's ability to gain access to the high priest's courtyard on the night of Jesus' arrest.[13]

All in all, it seems reasonable to assume that Jesus visited Jerusalem on at least three Passovers during his ministry; and on a number of other occasions as well. Although Galilee was home territory, Jerusalem was of huge importance in terms of both its national religious significance and its relationship with a person claiming messianic status. Messianic power and the "city of the great King" were deeply interconnected. It was there that such status would be revealed.

This leaves the matter of the cleansing of the Temple. Some biblical commentators suggest that there were two such incidents: one at the start of Jesus' ministry in about the year 30 (as in John) and one at the end in about 33 (as in the synoptics).[14] However, the majority of commentators favour the chronology of the synoptics and conclude that John placed this event at the start of Jesus' ministry in order to make a theological point: the Temple has an exalted role but since it is Jesus' Father's house, Jesus has both a unique relationship with God and with the Temple; Jesus represents a new temple, as seen through his resurrection and the establishment of a new relationship between believers and God; Jesus alone can pronounce on the true nature of the Temple and its use and role (or replacement).[15] In this view, the issue in the Gospel of John was not *when* Jesus cleansed the Temple but that he *did it*.[16] This is the interpretation followed here and we will assume that one dramatic cleansing action took place in the Jerusalem Temple, during the last week, and was the culmination of Jesus' conflict with the religious elites. It is difficult to imagine that he would have lived to do that twice.

The significance of Jerusalem in the life of Jesus

When one says "Jerusalem" one means "Temple". That is the crux of the matter and that is the way to understand Jesus' relationship with this central place within Judaism in his lifetime. With regard to this there are a number of possible positions.

The first, is that, in the lifetime of Jesus himself, his new teaching offered a completely new spiritual *alternative* to the Temple. External ritualism would be replaced by heartfelt religious belief.[17] In short, the Temple was being made redundant. This has, in many ways, become a traditional Christian understanding of his relationship with contemporary Jewish religious practice, including that of the Jerusalem Temple. This teaching would have been totally unacceptable within contemporary Judaism.

The second, is that Jesus presented himself as the apocalyptic Messiah who claimed that he would *destroy* the current Temple and institute a new one. It was the later church, it has been suggested, which toned down this radicalism in favour of a concept of purification (as revealed in the Gospels).[18] This is allied to a similar interpretation that he saw the imminent *destruction* of all existing society, due to the End Time action of God to transform the world and cosmic order.[19]

The third, is that he demanded *purification* of the existing Temple in order to make it acceptable to God in its practices. In this he shared a view of the corruption of the Jerusalem elites that was also held by members of the Qumran sect, and later by Josephus and the Zealots.[20] For the Jewish peasantry the Jerusalem Temple elites and the Romans were virtually one as bad as the other.[21] What was needed was the institution (restoration) of an "egalitarian theocracy".[22] It was this that underlay the egalitarian parables and social experiments of Jesus and his followers.

The fourth, is that Jesus declared that existing Jewish nationalism was on a road to conflict with Rome which would itself destroy community, city, and Temple in the resulting conflagration. Politically radical Judaism, fixated on revolutionary nationalist fervour, would not win. It had set its sights on national liberation which would actually lead to death and destruction; rather than the community transformation which would come from embracing the good news being promulgated by Jesus.[23]

What is common to the first three interpretations is that each sets Jesus on a collision course with those who held power within the city. Zealous love for a purified Temple, or personal conviction that he was its replacement as mediator with God, challenged the religious powerbrokers who considered themselves to be the gatekeepers to the relationship between the Jewish people and their heavenly Lord. As Jesus and his followers drew closer to the city for that springtime festival of Passover, we should not be surprised that it turned out to be his last. He himself had said that it was "impossible for a prophet to be killed away from Jerusalem" and now he was drawing closer to the great city, and his final conflict, with every step…

CHAPTER 15

From Palm Sunday to the Last Supper

The last week of Jesus' life is packed with action, drama, teaching, and accelerating conflict. In later Christian tradition it became known as "Holy Week" or "Passion Week". In this chapter we will examine how we can reconcile the presentation of that final week, as found in the different Gospels. We also ask what perspective on events do we find in the very different style, content, and approach found in the Gospel of John (where, of 21 chapters, chapters 12–21 occur in this one week)? We also assess whether this was a week spiralling out of control, an inevitable consequence of events, or a deliberate strategy employed by Jesus.

The Gospel accounts are not always in agreement regarding the exact order of the events which occurred in the last week of the life of Jesus. This can sometimes be missed due to the fact that over the centuries certain traditional observances have developed which are connected to the specific days of this tumultuous week. This makes the chronology appear very solid when, in fact, there are some complexities. Nevertheless, we can be confident regarding the basic chronology of the core events which occurred over the five days from Jesus' triumphant entry into Jerusalem, on what we call "Palm Sunday", and the late-night arrest that occurred in the garden of Gethsemane over Thursday to Friday night (the days traditionally called by English-speaking Christians "Maundy Thursday" and "Good Friday").

What is clear is that these events occurred in the run-up to that year's celebration of the Jewish festival of Passover. As we have seen, there are debates over the length of Jesus' ministry but we conclude that the traditional calculation of about three years is the most persuasive. As a result – and looking for a Friday (Jewish *Shishi*) that fell on Passover[1] – we are left with the most persuasive date for his execution being: Friday 3 April 33; or *Nisan* 14 in the official Jewish calendar.[2]

Sunday: the triumphal entry into Jerusalem

The dramatic events of Jesus' triumphant entry into Jerusalem occurred at the start of the busy working week. With *Shabbat* having occupied the previous day (Saturday), Jerusalem woke up on *Rishon* (Sunday) to begin the week that led up to the great celebration of Passover.[3]

It should be remembered that in Judaism, then as now, the day begins after sunset (traditionally after three stars come out) and not at sunrise. This means that the Jewish day is the period of time between one evening and the next. Rather than midnight (or sunrise) starting a day, the new day starts at that point of three stars appearing. So, what we would call the late evening of one day is, in Judaism, the start of the next day. For simplicity, though, we will use the non-Jewish day-divisions so it is clear to which day we are referring. But it should be remembered that when we speak of the events that occurred late on a Thursday (*Chamishi*) evening, Jesus and his followers would have considered these as occurring in the early part of Friday (*Shishi*).

The events of that day of riding into Jerusalem appear in all four Gospels. It clearly was a defining moment in the life of Jesus and in that final week. We have already seen that, although the inner core of followers – "The Twelve" – predominate in our view of Jesus' disciples, there are others – unnamed and out of the main focus – who play their part too. Here we see this at work, although it is easy to miss it. Two disciples are sent on ahead to arrange Jesus' mount for the entry into the city. If anyone asks what is going on, they are to respond with a pre-arranged pass-phrase. Then the donkey (and colt too in Matthew's account) will be readily released. The prepared-donkey, the exchange of challenge and pass-phrase, the release of the donkey, comes out particularly clearly in Mark's account. Jesus then enters the city, while "A very large crowd [or "most of the crowd"] spread their cloaks on the road, and others cut branches from the trees and spread them on the road" (Matthew 21:8).

The gentle humility of Jesus is emphasized by Matthew, quoting Zechariah 9:9, “Look, your king is coming to you, humble, and mounted on a donkey” (Matthew 21:5). Yet this should not obscure the radicalism of the event or its potentially explosive character. For this entry is full of controversial significance. It is freighted with meaning and Jesus would have known it. Matthew reminds us how the circumstances fulfilled an Old Testament messianic passage. The cloaks and branches on the road are extravagant displays of excited devotion. The shouts of “*Hosanna*” (meaning “Save now!”) are both cries of praise – and also declarations of expectation. That there were messianic expectations seem clear from the association of this with the crowd’s declaration that Jesus is “Son of David” and “comes in the name of the Lord!” (Matthew 21:9).

In Roman-administered Judea, proclaiming Davidic kingship and shouting out verses from the Old Testament that probably had messianic characteristics – Matthew has the crowd quoting Psalm 118 – was going to lead to trouble. Mark has the crowd crying out the explicitly provocative: “Blessed is the coming kingdom of our ancestor David!” (Mark 11:10). Roman military intelligence (no doubt assisted by local agents and translators) will have been listening to the cries on the streets with growing interest.

It is no surprise that Matthew tells us that, “When he entered Jerusalem, the whole city was in turmoil, asking, ‘Who is this?’” (Matthew 21:10). Luke adds that, “Some of the Pharisees in the crowd said to him, ‘Teacher, order your disciples to stop.’” To which Jesus replies, “I tell you, if these were silent, the stones would shout out” (Luke 19:39–40). The Pharisees know exactly what is going on and they do not like it! They read between the lines – and it didn’t take much analysis – and saw the exalted claims being made for (and we suggest by) Jesus.

But matters of messianic theology were not the only things on the minds of the religious authorities. The population of the city was massively increased by the arrival of pilgrims and Passover offered an opportunity for political protests involving the great numbers of people who crowded into Jerusalem for its celebration. The Jewish historian Josephus, writing later in the first century, gives several examples where the festival turned violent. The event itself was of high political significance and potentially explosive, as the anniversary of the deliverance of the Jewish people out of Egyptian slavery into freedom, a fact emphasized by Josephus each time he mentions the holiday. Passover was the perfect time to attempt a new deliverance – this time from Rome. The city was tinder dry. All it took was a spark. And the Jerusalem religious authorities knew it.

It is often assumed that the only reason that John the Baptist lost, first his freedom, and then his life, was because he criticized the marriage of Herod Antipas with Herodias. But, as we saw in an earlier chapter, Josephus suggests that the underlying reason was that he attracted large crowds. Crowds were unpredictable, volatile, dangerous. They might be manipulated. They could become a threat. According to Josephus, once John became a crowd-pulling figure, his days were numbered. On Palm Sunday the crowds are there and noisy. Romans and the Jewish religious leaders watch with mounting concern. The ingredients are there for trouble. Someone is going to get hurt.

That evening, according to Mark, Jesus withdrew to Bethany, almost certainly to the home of his friends, Mary, Martha, and Lazarus.

Monday: the cleansing of the Temple

We have briefly seen, in the last chapter, that the dramatic cleansing of the Temple occurs near the end of the synoptic gospels (at Matthew 21:12–17, Mark 11:15–18, and Luke 19:45–46) *but* near the start in the Gospel of John (at John 2:13–16). Whether we view this as two separate events or one event that John moved to the start of his Gospel, all three synoptic writers describe it as a defining event at the start of the final week of the life of Jesus. Even if John is correct that two such events occurred, the one described in the synoptics sets the tone for this final week: conflict.

Although the wording in Matthew (Matthew 21:12–17) and in Luke (Luke 19:45–46) would seem to imply that the event followed on immediately from the triumphal entry (and so on Sunday), Mark explicitly says that on that Sunday evening, Jesus and his disciples withdrew to Bethany after *only looking at the temple*. Consequently, Mark places the temple-cleansing event the next day – *Sheni*

(Monday). This seems more likely, as Mark precedes it with the account of Jesus cursing a fig tree that fails to provide fruit (Mark 11:12–14) as he returns to the city. This seems a fitting backdrop to Jesus' anger at the failure of those in the Temple (Mark 11:15–18) to live up to the holiness of the place. Unfruitfulness seems a fitting image in preparation for this. This seems more convincing than Matthew's placing of the fig tree event (although also on the Monday morning) *after* the cleansing of the temple that has taken place *on the previous afternoon*. Interestingly, Matthew (Matthew 21:18–22) asserts that the fig tree immediately withered, whereas Mark (Mark 11:20–25) says that this was seen to be the case the next morning (that is on *Shlishi* (Tuesday)), as Jesus and his disciples once more returned to the city. That this was discovered the morning after the cleansing of the Temple seems to be particularly appropriate: the fig tree's fate is the result of failing to meet Jesus' demands, just as on the previous day those who were behaving inappropriately in the Temple were driven out by him.

It should be noted that there is no mention of the cursing of the fig tree, and its subsequent withering, in the Gospel of Luke.

For Mark – and followed here – the Monday of that week was dominated by the cleansing of the Temple which culminates in the Temple elites conspiring to kill Jesus (Mark 11:18). Then, after a tumultuous day, Jesus and his followers once more leave the city. We assume, from the previous information in Mark, that they once more retire to their base at Bethany.

Tuesday: teaching with attitude

On *Shlishi* (Tuesday) morning, Jesus and his disciples return to Jerusalem. According to Mark it is only then that they pass the now-withered fig tree on their way. This is followed by an intense day of conflict. Again, the discovery of the withered fig tree at this point seems a fitting bridge from the previous day's cleansing, to the conflict of this Tuesday.

Once in the city, Jesus is challenged over the authority of his teaching (Mark 11:27–33). This is followed by him telling the parable of the tenants (Mark 12:1–12) which, with its story of the dispossession of rebellious tenants, was clearly a warning of coming judgment on Israel by God. Those opposing him clearly get the point and are outraged.

This is followed by a range of teaching themes in the latter part of Mark chapter 12 and in chapter 13: the challenge of the legitimacy of paying taxes to Rome (clearly posed to try to compromise Jesus); the matter of whether marriage will exist in the future heavenly state; the nature of the greatest commandment in the Law; the nature of the Messiah's authority; Jesus warning against the teachers of the Law; a poor widow's offering counting above the ostentatious giving of the wealthy; the approaching destruction of the Temple in an impending apocalyptic End Time event.

For Mark this all occurs in an intense Tuesday in the city. The escalating conflict is clear in the attempts to trap Jesus and the questioning of his understanding; the exalted nature of the Messiah being asserted by Jesus; Jesus challenging the self-assuredness of the rich and his declaration of the impending destruction of the Temple itself. Here we see the End Time Messiah in head-on collision with the leaders of Judaism as embodied in the Jerusalem elite.

This is followed (it seems on that very evening), by Jesus being anointed in Bethany by "a woman" (Mark 14:1–9) in an event that presages his death and preparation for burial. That things are clearly moving in that direction is made clear in what follows. It is then that Judas joins the plot to betray Jesus (Mark 14:10). Things are spiralling toward an explosive confrontation.

It should be noted that Mark does not name the woman who anointed Jesus. He simply says that "a woman came with an alabaster jar of very costly ointment of nard" and that it occurred at the home of "Simon the Leper" (Mark 14:3). Matthew follows this (Matthew 26:6–7). However, in John's Gospel she is named as Mary the sister of Lazarus – whom Jesus had raised from the dead – and the event is located at their home (John 12:1–8). John places this "Six days before the Passover" (John 12:1) and before the triumphal entry of Palm Sunday. As with the cleansing of the Temple, we either assume two similar events or that it has been differently located in order to make a particular point in two different traditions. That the actual location differs (the house of Simon the Leper or the home of Mary, Martha, and Lazarus) sounds like two different events, but the similarity in content suggests one event, differently told. We cannot definitively decide between these options. What is clear in Mark is that the action causes anger among some of those present, who object to what they consider a waste of money, since the perfume could have been sold and the money given to the poor. Perhaps we see here a brewing conflict between social radicals among Jesus' followers and those (exemplified by the woman) who have an exalted view of Jesus as a person. For the former, as personified by Judas in the 1970s musical *Jesus Christ Superstar*, Jesus had begun to matter more than the things he said.[4] Once more, Jesus and his status was at the centre of controversy.

In the Gospel of Matthew we find a similar mixture of conflict-orientated teaching but – without a Monday cleansing of the Temple – this all appears to have occurred on that Monday (rather than on the Tuesday of Mark). Mark's earlier account seems a rather more convincing chronology. These are, though, minor differences in a chronology across the different synoptic Gospels that is generally consistent in its component parts, the overall direction of these events, and in the intensifying conflict.

We find in Matthew detailed End Time teaching which has a recurring theme of the apocalyptic judgment of God. That Matthew has Jesus say at the culmination of this: "after two days the Passover is coming – and the Son of Man will be handed over to be crucified" (Matthew 26:2) may suggest that, in his grouping of these dramatic teachings, Matthew has overflowed Monday into Tuesday, without this division being apparent in his narrative. If so, Matthew like Mark has that Tuesday end with the emergence of a plot to kill Jesus. "Then the chief priests and the elders of the people gathered in the palace of the high priest" and there they plan a secretive arrest and death to eliminate Jesus without causing unrest in the city (Matthew 26:3–5). Separated from this by the anointing at Bethany, is Judas' decision to betray Jesus for thirty pieces of silver. As in Mark, there is no indication of day, but Wednesday was probably in mind as it comes immediately before the account of the events of that Thursday.

Much has been made regarding alternative motivations of Judas – even Jesus being complicit in his own betrayal – as found in "alternative gospel" accounts. A Coptic-language document, known as the *Codex Tchacos* (first identified in the 1970s near Beni Masar, in Egypt), includes the self-identified *Gospel of Judas* (*Euangelion Ioudas*), which was written in the third or fourth century, but contains text that appears to date from a late-second-century original. This suggested earlier manuscript may have been written in Greek, given the presence of particular dialect forms and Greek loan-words in the Coptic document. The *Gospel of Judas* relates the story of Jesus' death from the viewpoint of Judas. In contrast to the betrayal of Jesus for money, depicted in the canonical Gospels, this later work portrays Judas as acting on instructions given by Jesus, since Judas (alone of the disciples) belonged to a "holy generation" (a status which differentiated him from other followers). The work is late, has no historical validity, and bears all the hallmarks of Gnostic belief in a "true (that is, hidden) Gospel" and secret knowledge denied to mainline Christians. Whatever were the inner workings of Judas' mind, we have no early document which competes with the (very limited) explanations given in the canonical Gospels.[5]

Luke's account of the last few days is even less day-specific than the account in Matthew and it is possible to read through his recounting of teaching, conflict and End Time warnings without gaining any impression regarding on which days these occurred. The account is anchored on Palm Sunday at the beginning, and the day of Unleavened Bread (Maundy Thursday) at the end, without anything in the text identifying the days on which other events and teaching occurred. All we are told of this time is that "Every day he was teaching in the temple, and at night he would go out and spend the night on the Mount of Olives" (Luke 21:37). There is no mention of his base at Bethany. But, like the other Gospel writers it is clear where this is heading. "When the scribes and chief priests realized that he had told this parable [tenants expelled from a vineyard] against them, they wanted to lay hands on him at that very hour, but they feared the people" (Luke 20:19). It is this, according to Luke, that leads to the use of "spies who pretended to be honest, in order to trap him by what he said, so as to hand him over to the jurisdiction and authority of the governor" (Luke 20:20).

All of this is clear evidence that Jesus was driving forward both the narrative and the confrontation with contemporary authorities.

He was not adrift in a torrent of events that he did not understand. However, this has led some to assert that Jesus assumed the end times were imminent but was caught out when the apocalypse did not occur in his favour. As Albert Schweitzer once shockingly put it,

> In the knowledge that he is the coming Son of Man [Jesus] lays hold of the wheel of the world to set it moving on that last revolution which is to bring all ordinary history to a close. It refuses to turn, and He throws himself upon it. Then it does turn; and crushes Him. Instead of bringing in the eschatological conditions, He has destroyed them.[6]

This is certainly not how the Gospel writers and traditional Christianity view his relationship with eschatology. Although the End Time cosmic transformation – as early Christians clearly anticipated it – did not occur, the mainstream traditional interpretation has been that Jesus clearly looked toward an apocalyptic future event, but that his mission was not dependent on it occurring as the culmination of his ministry. But at this point we begin to move from biography into areas of faith.

An unquiet Wednesday: the plot to kill Jesus

There is no tradition in the Gospels regarding what Jesus did on the *Revi'i* (Wednesday) of Holy Week. Some New Testament experts have suggested that, after two exhausting days in Jerusalem, accompanied by conflict with the elites, Jesus and his disciples spent that Wednesday resting among allies in Bethany. They were also, undoubtedly, preparing for the great celebration of Passover which occurred at the end of the week.

Mark's account places Judas's decision to betray Jesus immediately after the anointing at Bethany: "Then Judas Iscariot, who was one of the twelve, went to the chief priests in order to betray him to them" (Mark 14:10). He probably could not have done so on the evening of the anointing since it was already late and the company were staying at Bethany outside the city. It is reasonable to assume that he did so on Wednesday. He could have covered this by a number of reasons for going into the city. This may have included preparations for the Passover itself.

What this means is that, although there is no firm Christian tradition for what occurred on that Wednesday, we may assume that it was one of feverish activity in the palace of the high priest, as high ranking members of the high priestly family and other members of the Sanhedrin finalized their plans. These were assisted by the unexpected arrival of Judas who offered to provide inside knowledge, which would assist in an arrest that took place out of the public gaze, due to a city that was highly volatile at this time of year.

Thursday: the Last Supper

And so began *Chamishi* (Thursday), which later Christians in the English-speaking world know as Maundy Thursday, the day of the Last Supper.

There has long been an awareness that there are some difficulties in reconciling the Gospel accounts with regard to the way the events of this evening meal dove-tailed with the great Jewish feast of Passover in the year of Jesus' arrest and execution. This is because there is a difference between the synoptic gospels and the Gospel of John. In the synoptics, the wording is clear that the meal was a Passover meal and that it occurred on the first day of the Festival of Unleavened Bread as one would expect (Mark 14:12–16; Matthew 26:17–19; Luke 22:7–13). Mark specifically adds "when the Passover lamb is sacrificed" (Mark 14:12) and this detail is also found in Luke's account.

John, though, has a number of points of difference which read as if he has located the meal one day earlier than the start of Passover. First, he states that the final time together occurred "before the festival of the Passover" (John 13:1). Second, nothing in John's account suggests that what occurred was a Passover meal (John 13:2 – 16:33). Thirdly, on the Friday morning (the morning after the arrest of Jesus the previous night) the Jewish leaders are reluctant to enter the spiritually polluting pagan environment of the residence of the Roman governor (the prefect Pilate) "so as to avoid ritual defilement and to be able to eat the Passover" (John 18:28). The implication is that the Passover meal was due to be eaten later that day, in the evening. Finally, John explicitly says that the day of Jesus' trial before Pilate and his execution was "the day of Preparation for the Passover" (John 19:14). He takes a tradition known in Mark that this trial and execution occurred on "the day before the Sabbath" (Mark 15:42) and words it as "that Sabbath was a day of great solemnity" (John 19:31) which would be consistent with his suggestion that Passover that year coincided with the Sabbath day (that is, was on a Saturday).[7]

Various solutions have been suggested for this difference: different groups within contemporary Judaism may have kept Passover on different days; there may have been different views concerning when a day started and ended; it is possible that any meal taken during "Passover week" counted as "Passover". However, there may be a theological explanation. John may have *combined* the day of Jesus' death *and* the sacrifice of the Passover lamb in order to have both of them occur on the same day. This would have given added emphasis to the later Christian belief that Jesus' death was the means by which people escaped the slavery of sin and death in a new kind of exodus, and fulfilled and completed the Old Testament; while beginning a new era in the relationship between God and all people (not only the "Chosen People of Israel", who had earlier been liberated from Egyptian slavery).[8] We have already seen that it is possible that John chronologically relocated the cleansing of the Temple in his Gospel for a similar reason: in order to make a theological point.

On balance, from the earlier evidence in the synoptic gospels, it seems most likely that Jesus shared a Passover meal with his disciples on that Thursday and based what he said and taught that evening on that symbolic meal which celebrated God's liberation of the Jewish people from bondage under Pharaoh.

The events that led up to this meal are revealing. Mark tells us that:

> He [Jesus] sent two of his disciples, saying to them, "Go into the city, and a man carrying a jar of water will meet you; follow him and wherever he enters, say to the owner of the house, 'The Teacher asks, Where is my guest room where I may eat the Passover with my disciples?' He will show you a large room upstairs,

> furnished and ready. Make preparations for us there".
> **(Mark 14:13–15)**

This they do, find things exactly as described, and prepare the Passover meal. Luke has the same tradition, with its curious details of the man carrying the water jar (a task usually associated with women). Matthew simply has, "Go into the city to a certain man, and say to him, 'The Teacher says, My time is near; I will keep the Passover at your house with my disciples'" (Matthew 26:18). All, though, point to prearranged signals and arrangements and remind us of the existence of followers of Jesus' beyond those who play the most prominent parts in the Gospel accounts. They also indicate that Jerusalem – though far from home territory in Galilee – was still a place where Jesus had an established network of friends and supporters.

The meal itself was clearly of huge significance to Jesus and his followers and commemorating it became a focal point within the meetings of early Christians in the years that followed. Although modern Christians may differ in their theology concerning this meal, it remains a shared experience across all Christian groups, with the exception of The Salvation Army. All others still meet at or around what is termed "the Lord's Table". When we look at the message and symbolism of this original event we can see why it remains a crucial part of Christian experience.

Our earliest written record of what occurred and the core of the experience of that evening can probably be found in 1 Corinthians, a letter written by the apostle Paul in about AD 55.[9] This would put its writing at least a decade before the likely date of composition of the earliest of the Gospels (Mark c. 70). In that letter Paul recounts a tradition that says:

> For I received from the Lord what I also handed on to you, that the Lord Jesus on the night when he was betrayed took a loaf of bread, and when he had given thanks, he broke it and said, "This is my body that is for you. Do this in remembrance of me." In the same way he took the cup also, after supper, saying, "This cup is the new covenant in my blood. Do this,

> as often as you drink it, in remembrance of me." For as often as you eat this bread and drink the cup, you proclaim the Lord's death until he comes.
> **(1 Corinthians 11:23–26)**

This short, simple, but tremendously profound wording clearly records the early Christian community's memory of what occurred that Thursday evening. And it connects past events with a future (eschatological) hope. These are also examples of *agrapha* – sayings of Jesus independent of the Gospels.

Attention is sometimes drawn to differences between the accounts of this last meal as recorded in the synoptic gospels.[10] But these are minor, compared to the overwhelming similarity in these accounts and in their general agreement with the (earlier) tradition as recorded by Paul. Nobody reading these accounts will come away with any other message than that Jesus built his dramatic final teaching on Passover symbols of sacrifice and liberation; he took bread and wine and presented them as symbols of his body and blood; this symbolized a new relationship ("covenant") with God achieved through him; his approaching sacrifice is clearly stated. Matthew explicitly states that the pouring out of Jesus' blood (as symbolized in the cup of wine) is "for the forgiveness of sins" (Matthew 26:28). But the implication is clear in Mark and Luke too. Furthermore, Luke (like Paul) states that this symbolic meal is to continue as a remembrance. In addition, Jesus predicts his betrayal by one of his close companions. Peter's denial is also predicted.

These actions were clearly vivid within the early community of Christians as they recalled these events. What the accounts have in common massively outweighs differences in order or detail. We may be confident that the Last Supper, with its powerful symbolic use of bread and wine, occurred as recounted in the synoptics.

What is more puzzling is why the tradition of the bread and wine was (apparently) not known to the compiler(s) of the Gospel of John. If we only had John, there would be no Eucharistic celebration as Christians have celebrated it for two millennia. On the other hand, if we did not have John we would not have the tradition of the detailed teaching – often referred to as the "farewell discourses" – that we find there, since there is simply nothing like this in the synoptic gospels. Since John must have been aware of the Eucharistic rite universally practiced by Christians (and its origins),[11] the absence is striking.

Some have argued that John explores the tradition (but relocated to the Galilean ministry) in his recounting of Jesus' teaching of being the "bread from heaven" and the "bread of life" in John chapter 6. This includes the words: "Those who eat my flesh and drink my blood have eternal life, and I will raise them up on the last day" (John 6:54).[12] This is possible, but it is more likely that he was more interested in the inner meaning of the events rather than their concrete and specific form. Significance was more important to him than ceremony and rite, as these were forming in the early churches. In this sense, universal principles outweighed specific examples. This was something that may have been reinforced by John's knowledge that Christian communities were already very familiar with these practices through the traditions exemplified in the synoptic gospels.[13]

What is certainly clear, is that as the shadows lengthened on that Thursday evening, the dramatic events of that turbulent week were about to reach their explosive climax.

CHAPTER 16

Messiah on trial...

As we explore this momentous event we will examine the motivations of Judas Iscariot for handing Jesus over to the chief priests, along with how he was later remembered and presented in the early church. We will explore what the arrest and trials(s) of Jesus reveal about the complex power politics that reached a climax on that Thursday night and Friday morning. In exploring the trial(s) before the Sanhedrin, Pilate, and the role of Herod Antipas, we will assess the charges levelled against Jesus, the interactions of the religious and secular authorities, and the events leading to a guilty verdict. But guilty of what?

The role of Judas Iscariot

Within all the synoptic gospels, as soon as Judas is introduced (as Jesus chooses his disciples) the writers set the scene for what Judas will later do in the story. Mark 3:19 and Matthew 10:4 identify Judas as "who betrayed him", whereas Luke 6:16 suggests a process: "who became a traitor". The writers, using hindsight, are painting a picture for the reader of Judas' character. Although John's Gospel does not have this listing of disciples, the writer(s) is still intent on making it clear to the reader that his distinguishing feature is his disloyalty to Jesus. In John 6:70–71 Jesus says, "'Did I not choose you, the twelve? Yet one of you is a devil.' He was speaking of Judas son of Simon Iscariot, for he, though one of the twelve, was going to betray him." Furthermore, in John 13:10–11, after Jesus has washed his disciples' feet, he says, "'And you are clean, though not all of you.' For he knew who was to betray him; for this reason he said, 'Not all of you are clean.'" Even today the word Judas is synonymous with "back-stabber", and he has become "the poster child for treachery and cowardice".[1] So, what part did Judas play in the arrest of Jesus?

Controversially, it has been claimed that as the early church spread and developed, moving away from Judaism, it fabricated the actions and disloyalty of Judas (with Judas stereotyped as the typical Jewish traitor, leading the way for the church's increasingly anti-Jewish stance). In this interpretation, John, thought to be the latest of the Gospels written, demonized Judas the most.[2] This interpretation argues that Judas did nothing until he was told to by Jesus, and that the Greek word which is often translated as "betrayed" (demonstrating the church's aim to portray Judas in a negative light) should actually be translated as "handed over".[3] So did Judas want the Jewish authorities and Jesus to work out their differences by being brought together?[4] The sources we have that were written closest to the time are the Gospels, so first we need to explore what they say.

All four Gospels detail how Judas led the Jewish chief priests to Jesus on the Thursday night (the night of the Last Supper) before he was executed on the Friday. At the Last Supper Jesus reveals to the disciples that one among them will betray him (Mark 14:18–21; Matthew 26:20–25; Luke 22:21–23; John 13:18–26). In Mark's and Matthew's accounts Jesus says that it would have been better for the one who would betray him to have not been born. In Matthew 26:25 Judas responds to Jesus' announcement: "'Surely not I, Rabbi?' He [Jesus] replied, 'You have said so.'" In John 13:26 Jesus makes it clear to the disciples it is Judas, "Jesus answered, 'It is the one to whom I give this piece of bread when I have dipped it in the dish' So when he had dipped the piece of bread, he gave it to Judas son of Simon Iscariot." John 13:18 states that this was to fulfil scripture: "The one who ate my bread has lifted his heel against me." All the Gospels then tell of how Judas led a crowd from the Jewish authorities to Jesus, who had gone outside the city to the garden of Gethsemane.

So why did Judas do it? Obviously, without a testimony from Judas any answer is speculation. The only sources we have are the Gospels which express their beliefs about why he did it, rather than

Judas' personal expression of motivation. There is speculation about whether Judas was part of a revolutionary, terrorist group, the *Sicarii*, who wanted an end to Roman rule. So, did Judas hand Jesus over to the authorities to force him to declare himself as the Messiah? Or was Judas disillusioned by Jesus' peaceful approach, wanting a more violent and revolutionary messiah to be rid of the Romans? It seems ironic that *Sicarii* means "dagger-men" and Judas, as traditionally explained, metaphorically stabbed Jesus in the back. Yet there is no mention of Judas' membership of this group in the Gospels, and the group is thought to have been active only after the death of Jesus.[5]

Perhaps money was a motivating factor? In John 12:4–6 Judas passes judgment on a woman who used perfume to anoint Jesus, "Why was this perfume not sold for three hundred denarii and the money given to the poor?" The Gospel writer then adds the aside: "He said this not because he cared about the poor, but because he was a thief; he kept the common purse and used to steal what was put into it." Mark 14:3–9 does not specify Judas as the one doing the scolding, but in Mark 14:10 he immediately goes to the chief priests in order to betray Jesus, which implies that he may have been annoyed by the woman's actions. Perhaps Judas was angry at being rebuked by Jesus in public regarding his challenge to the woman. Or perhaps he considered the whole episode revealed lack of social radicalism on Jesus' part and too great an emphasis on his own person.

Mark 14:11 and Matthew 26:14–16 present money as being a key motivator. Matthew 26:15 specifies that it was thirty pieces of silver (the price of a slave in Exodus). Estimates of value range from $90 to $3,000 in modern coinage.[6] Either way, not a huge sum of money to pay for an abandonment of allegiance.

Two Gospel compilers state that the devil entered Judas (John 13:2; 13:27; and Luke 22:3–4); so horrified are they at the betrayal. Though, as we have seen, John also emphasizes Judas' dishonesty (John 12:6).[7]

Modern speculations include the suggestion that Judas was worried by the large groups that Jesus was attracting and thought this could lead to the destruction of the Jewish people at the hands of the Romans, so decided to hand Jesus in before it was too late.[8]

Later Christians saw the actions of Judas as having been predicted in Psalm 41:9, "Even my bosom friend in whom I trusted, who ate of my bread, has lifted the heel against me." This idea of prophecy fulfilled appears in John 17:12, "Not one of them was lost except the one destined to be lost, so that the scripture might be fulfilled". In this view, Judas's actions were pre-known, perhaps pre-determined. In which case, his personal agency was not speculated on.

So, what becomes of Judas? Matthew 27:3–10 tells of how Judas, having seen that Jesus was condemned, repented and tried to give back the thirty pieces of silver to the chief priests and elders, saying, "I have sinned by betraying innocent blood." Perhaps he had not realized that Jesus would be sent to Pilate. Yet the chief priests and elders refuse to engage. Judas then throws down the pieces of silver in the Temple, and leaves. He then hangs himself, seemingly overcome by the guilt of what he had done.

It is clear from this passage that the thirty pieces of silver constituted blood money, which meant that it was not lawful for the chief priests to put it in the treasury. So, with the money they bought the Potter's Field (to the early church, fulfilling a prophecy from Jeremiah) in which to bury foreigners and it became known as the Field of Blood. There is a hint in Matthew that perhaps Judas did not expect Jesus to be condemned. Perhaps he hoped Jesus' arrest might trigger apocalyptic events.

Interestingly, the death of Judas was remembered differently by members of the early church, as demonstrated in Acts (traditionally written by the Gospel writer Luke):

> Now this man acquired a field with the reward of his wickedness; and falling headlong, he burst open in the middle and all his bowels gushed out. This became known to all the residents of Jerusalem, so that the field was called in their language Hakeldama, that is, Field of Blood.
> **(Acts 1:18–19)**

It is presented as an authorial aside, within a speech recorded as being made by Peter. This detailing of Judas's death in Acts is different to Matthew's account, so his dramatic death here seems more like an act of God rather than suicide. This sense of prophetic destiny is emphasized by Peter, concluding regarding the death (Acts 1:20):

> For it is written in the book of Psalms, "Let his homestead become desolate, and let there be no one to live in it" [Psalm 69:25]; and "Let another take his position of overseer" [Psalm 109:8].

Clearly, it was believed by the other disciples, from their reflection on the Psalms, that Judas's disloyalty had been prophesied by King David. Matthias then replaced Judas as the twelfth disciple.

The arrest

The synoptic gospels all agree that, following the meal with his disciples, Jesus led them out of the city to the Mount of Olives. This limestone ridge lies east of the city and is separated from it by the Kidron Valley. John specifically refers to them crossing this geographical feature (John 18:1) but does not actually refer to the Mount of Olives by name. He adds that the group made their way to a garden there, which Matthew and Mark name as Gethsemane (without specifying the kind of place that it was). Information in Luke indicates that it was a place well known to them (Luke 22:39). John adds something similar (John 18:2). We can assume it was valued as a secluded place for private prayer. This night, though, that quiet privacy would be shattered.

In the darkness of the garden, Jesus agonized over what was to come. Although John moves swiftly to the arrest that occurred there, the synoptics record a dramatic tradition of Jesus praying to be spared what is to follow, but subjecting himself to the will of God. It is telling that the only time the hybrid Aramaic-Greek phrase "*Abba*, Father" appears in the Gospels (in Mark 14:36) is at this time of deeply intimate prayer. While Jesus prays, the tired disciples fall asleep.

Luke alone adds the tradition that Jesus was comforted by an angel during this time of agonizing prayer and that sweat fell from him "like great drops of blood" (Luke 22:44). This information is missing from a number of the surviving manuscripts of the Gospel of Luke. This has led to a suggestion that they represent a tradition that was added to the earlier and original text of the Gospel. It is difficult to decide, but their picture of the deeply stressed humanity of Jesus may indicate that they were part of the original account.

Then Judas led an armed group of the temple police and guards into the dark garden and Jesus is identified by a kiss (a point made in all three synoptic gospels). All four Gospels say that one of the disciples (John names him as Simon Peter) drew a sword and struck one of those sent by the high priest. In Matthew, Luke, and John he is rebuked by Jesus for the action.

The disciples scatter and Jesus is led away as a prisoner.

The role of the Sanhedrin

It was the Jewish authorities who arrested Jesus. Luke makes it clear that Jesus needed to be arrested when no crowd was present – the Jewish authorities wanted to avoid a riot and feared the reaction of Jesus' followers (Luke 22:6). Just days earlier Jesus had been welcomed and praised by a huge crowd as he entered Jerusalem. Jesus was clearly aware of their strategy, saying to his accusers, "Day after day I was with you in the temple teaching, and you did not arrest me" (in Mark 14:49). The fact that Jesus was arrested at night and was not surrounded by all his disciples would have made this a prime opportunity. By the time his followers knew what was occurring, it was too late. Jesus is then brought before the Sanhedrin, the supreme Jewish council and highest court of justice in Jerusalem, for a night trial. These members of the Jerusalem and temple elite had the most to lose if their relationship with Rome deteriorated due to perceived loss of control. The removal of the privileges accorded to their religion may have occurred.[9]

It has been argued that much of the evidence surrounding Jesus' death has been driven by a long history of Christian anti-Judaism; the Gospel stories of "the Jews" (especially in John's Gospel)[10] having condemned Jesus and demanding his execution before Pilate having played a key role.[11] The synoptics, though, focus on the role of the elites, and the responsibility of some individuals – who acted within a specific time-frame – cannot be taken from these accounts as attributing blame to an entire religious group.

In Matthew and Mark the Sanhedrin broke the Jewish Law about when an arrest and trial for the death penalty could take place: it is not allowed to happen at night.[12] Later Jewish traditions record: "Let a capital offence be tried during the day, but suspend it at night."[13] And *Maimonides Sanhedrin III* says with greater detail,

> As oral tradition says, the examination of such a charge is like the diagnosing of a wound – in either case a more thorough and searching examination can be made by daylight.[14]

Due to the trial happening at a forbidden time, the court had no jurisdiction and therefore did not pronounce a valid verdict, even by their own legal standards.[15] In Matthew the next morning, "all the chief priests and the elders of the people conferred together against Jesus in order to bring about his death" (Matthew 27:1) and Luke concurs (Luke 22:66). This implies there were two meetings of the Sanhedrin, one at night and one in the morning (perhaps to legitimize the council that met at night), before Jesus was sent to Pilate, the Roman prefect.

This raises the question of what happened during this trial? Matthew and Mark say how false witnesses made accusations against Jesus (with Mark also saying that their testimonies did not agree). This is a bold claim, as according to Deuteronomy 19:16–19 false witness was a serious crime – the punishment being equal to the punishment of the falsely accused. But in this case the elites instigated the events. Matthew says,

> Now the chief priests and the whole council were looking for false testimony against Jesus so that they might put him to death, but they found none, though many false witnesses came forward. At last two came forward and said, "This fellow said, 'I am able to destroy the temple of God and to build it in three days'".
> **(Matthew 26:59–61)**

In John, Jesus says, "Destroy this temple, and in three days I will raise it up" (John 2:19). Yet John 2:21–22 makes it clear that Jesus was foreshadowing his death and resurrection rather than voicing a violent threat to the Temple. This raises the distinct possibility that – however Jesus originally framed this statement – he was perceived as a threat to the Temple and so to Jewish national identity.

Jesus' silence during these false accusations echoes Isaiah 53:7, "yet he did not open his mouth" – the usual interpretation of this silence is that Jesus believed he was submitting to God's will.

The misunderstanding that Jesus conflicted with the Temple led to a belief he was in conflict with Judaism itself as the Temple was central to Palestinian Judaism.[16] As the Temple played no role for the Roman authorities, this directly attacked the interests of the Sanhedrin who became a source of hostility.[17] However, criticism of the Temple was ground for antagonism not execution. On the other hand, if the prophecy could be explained as false prophecy and leading people astray, capital punishment could have ensued (Deuteronomy 13:1–10; 18:20). On balance, the main reason for arresting Jesus seems to have been his actions in the Temple and his prophesying its destruction. However, his accusers accompanied this with a charge of blasphemy as the most effective strategy for securing his death.[18]

The Jewish authorities were worried Jesus was leading people astray; a monumental aspect in this charge was Jesus' messianic character. In the synoptic gospels Jesus is asked whether he is the Messiah and the Son of God. The response of Jesus varies though. In Luke, "He replied, 'If I tell you, you will not believe; and if I question you, you will not answer. But from now on the Son of Man will be seated at the right hand of the power of God'" (Luke 22:67–69). The messianic claim was obvious. But Luke raises the heat further by having them then ask: "'Are you, then, the Son of God?' He said to them, 'You say that I am.'" (Luke 22:70). Some would suggest that this reads as if seen through the lens of later church Christology, but others would argue that it reflects an authentic claim to divinity that is, otherwise, rare within the synoptic gospels. The latter seems clear from the evidence.

In Matthew, to the question (on oath) of whether he is the Messiah, the Son of God, Jesus answers, "You have said so. But I tell you, From now on you will see the Son of Man seated at the right hand of Power and coming on the clouds of heaven" (Matthew 26:63–64). It is interesting that this refocuses the attention on messianic End Time action rather than on divine status. However, the earlier tradition in Mark states explicitly, in response to this charge: "I am; and 'you will see the Son of Man seated at the right hand of the Power', and 'coming with the clouds of heaven'" (Mark 14:62). This early tradition therefore insists that combined divine and messianic status (rooted in a reference to the prophet Daniel) are thus declared by Jesus at this point in his trial.

Jesus' response of "I am" in Mark may have been interpreted as a claim to divinity, mirroring the name God uses for himself in Exodus 3:14. This certainly stands out and is comparable to the more explicit "I am" language attributed to Jesus in the later Gospel of John (John 18:6 for example).

Mark (14:63–64) and Matthew (26:65–66) make it clear that the high priest concludes from Jesus' response that he has committed the crime of blasphemy and the Sanhedrin declares he deserves death. According to Leviticus 24:10–23 and 1 Kings 21:8–13 blasphemy, under Jewish Law, was punishable by death by stoning. The definition of blasphemy is not specified in the Old Testament. The broader, and less precise definition, of blasphemy is to act contrary to God's will or to act in a way that is derogatory to God's power, whereas the more precise definition of blasphemy is to speak contemptuously about God so reviling or cursing God's name.[19] However, there "is not one single instance [other than Jesus] of a person ever being accused of blasphemy and sentenced to death by the Jewish authorities because he claimed to be the 'Messiah'".[20] Since much of the questioning of Jesus by the Sanhedrin was centred around these messianic claims it must be assumed that this was a significant, punishable offence as far as they were concerned. This must have been because Jesus expressed messianic claims in a very distinct form. From "Messiah" and "Son of God" follows the charge of "King of the Jews" as Jesus is presented to Pilate.

The immediate cause of Jesus' arrest was the "physical demonstration against the Temple by one who had a noticeable following".[21] Although Jesus' messianic entrance into Jerusalem would have worried the high priests, it was his Temple prophecy and demonstration that would have sealed his fate;[22] especially when combined with claims of divine authority. So, Jesus, with his large following, controversial teachings that were construed as blasphemous, and open criticism of the teachers of the Jewish Law, was considered highly dangerous.[23] As we have seen (in Chapter 15), Passover was the prime time for "trouble-makers" to pose the greatest threat to the political and religious elites.

Yet, as the Jews were occupied by the Romans, although they could condemn someone to death, they could not carry out the death penalty. Hence their dependence on Pontius Pilate, the Roman prefect, to whom Jesus was sent next.[24] The religious had become political.

Pilate: "Take one"

In all four Gospels the Jewish authorities accuse Jesus in front of Pilate and Pilate asks Jesus if he is the "King of the Jews". Clearly the claim (as a charge) must have first been made by the Jewish authorities.[25] This is specified in Luke as they tell Pilate that Jesus told them to not pay taxes and that he was saying he was the Messiah, a king. This title of king – one that made no appearance during the Jewish trial(s) – emphasizes the political threat a messianic claim could carry with it. As Pilate's role was to keep order and make sure taxes were collected, Jesus was presented as a direct challenge to him carrying out his duties. In both Luke and John, when Pilate seems disinterested, the Jewish authorities seem insistent on Pilate taking on Jesus. They know only this route can lead to execution.

In John, Pilate emphasizes how Jesus' own nation has handed him over which leads Jesus to answer,

> My kingdom is not from this world. If my kingdom were from this world, my followers would be fighting to keep me from being handed over to the Jews. But as it is, my kingdom is not from here.
> **(John 18:36)**

A Western twenty-first-century interpretation would say that Jesus seems to be talking of a spiritual rather than earthly realm, therefore being no threat to earthly rule. However, although politics and religion are usually very much separated in Western democracies, at the time of Jesus they were integrated and the spiritual claim was more of a threat than first appears.[26] Later, Jesus makes it clear that he believes the Romans would not be in power if it were not for the power of God, "Jesus answered him, 'You would have no power over me unless it had been given you from above'" (John 19:11). Again, this suggests a very different kind of kingship to the one in the charge against him. But Jesus could very easily have been misunderstood by authorities who believed that he was proclaiming a kingdom of this world which would attack Rome.[27] And they may have feared that, whatever he believed, others could manipulate the situation.

However, if they believed that Jesus was planning a revolutionary coup, why were the disciples not also arrested? Mysteries remain. Either way, at this point Pilate is reluctant to have Jesus killed, so this title "King of the Jews" does not instantly persuade him to execute Jesus. In John 18:38 Pilate specifically says he finds no case against Jesus. Pilate was renowned for being a brutal man, so this appears out of character. Perhaps Pilate did not think there was enough evidence or that Jesus' meek demeanour did not present a political threat. It is surely too reductionist to simply assume that this revealed the early church attempting to gain imperial favour by absolving the key imperial actor, at the expense of the Jewish authorities. It looks like Pilate was wrong-footed and did not act as expected.

Herod Antipas

In Luke's Gospel, when Pilate finds out that Jesus is from Galilee, rather than Jerusalem – so was under the jurisdiction of Herod (the client ruler there) – he sent him to Herod. Pilate, it seems, was trying to end his involvement.

Jesus was questioned at length by Herod, and the chief priests and scribes accused him, but Jesus did not answer. Herod and his soldiers mocked Jesus, they put a robe on him, but then sent him back to Pilate. The tradition states that Pilate and Herod became friends on that day (they had been enemies previously), so perhaps Pilate appreciated this act of royal brutality. We gain no further insight.

Pilate: "Take two"

In Luke's Gospel Pilate then calls the Jewish leaders and people and tells them how both he and Herod have not found Jesus guilty of any of their charges, so says he will flog Jesus but not put him to death. All the Gospels show a discourse between Pilate and the Jewish crowd where the Jewish crowd (in some Gospels roused by the Jewish priestly authorities) insist that the notorious prisoner Barabbas be released and Jesus be crucified. We are told that there was a custom that on Passover the Romans would release one Jewish prisoner (one method for appeasing the occupied Jews). We know nothing more about such a custom.

In Matthew (27:19), Pilate's wife tells him to have nothing to do with this innocent man as she has suffered because of a dream she has had about Jesus. This is again consistent with the early church belief that Pilate was not the main operator in the eventual execution. We are told that Pilate is overwhelmed by the crowd and wishes to satisfy them. This reference to the Jewish crowd could be identified as an example of shifting the blame to the Jews generally or it could be a genuine reflection of hostility toward Jesus amongst some of the people in Jerusalem. In John, the crowds wish to present Jesus as a direct challenge to the emperor, playing on an insecurity of Pilate as his role was to quash any form of rebellion or threat to Rome.

> From then on Pilate tried to release him, but the Jews cried out, "If you release this man, you are no friend of the emperor. Everyone who claims to be a king sets himself against the emperor".
> **(John 19:12)**

> Pilate asked them, "Shall I crucify your King?" The chief priests answered, "We have no king but the emperor".
> **(John 19:15)**

We have no other evidence regarding the motivations of Pilate, nor of the dynamics of this critical event. The New Testament depicts things slipping out of Pilate's control. And so Pilate hands Jesus over to be crucified. He would not have wanted to have failed to punish a possible rebel; nor for allowing a riot by the Jerusalem crowd; and he definitely did not want to be accused of not being a friend of the emperor. Matthew's Gospel says,

> He took some water and washed his hands before the crowd, saying, "I am innocent of this man's blood; see to it yourselves." Then the people as a whole answered, "His blood be on us and on our children!". **(Matthew 27:24–25)**

Jesus was given the punishment of crucifixion: a penalty for taking part in treasonable activity. So, although the Jewish authorities may have arrested Jesus because of his teaching and, most significantly, his perceived threat to the Temple – they handed him over to Pilate as *politically* dangerous.[28] Jesus' influence over the people and accusations of him leading people astray would have been seen by both parties as a danger. Jesus, the religious elite clearly argued, needed to die to ensure that the Romans did not intervene resulting in imprisonment and deportation of many.[29] Furthermore, the final catalyst was the unrest at Jesus' trial on the Friday morning which could have turned into a riot, reflecting badly on Pilate as if he had no control over his region. The later Roman writer Suetonius (writing c. 120) records a garbled tradition that, in his day, Jesus (whom he misnames *Chrestus* and thought was actually present in the 40s when Jews were expelled from Rome on account of unrest connected to Christians) was considered an agitator (*impulsore*).[30]

Overall then, the religious and political grounds leading to Jesus' execution cannot be separated. What modern historians think of as religion was embedded within political-economic dimensions of first-century life.[31] Therefore, it is too simplistic to talk of sharply contrasting reasons why the Jewish leaders or Romans wanted Jesus dead. There was close collaboration between Jewish and Roman authorities over matters of social unrest. Therefore, although the Romans finalized the death of Jesus, it was instigated by the Sanhedrin with the original arrest. The threat to the religious way of life in Jerusalem would have caused the Sanhedrin, and possibly some of the people, to want Jesus eliminated. Pilate appears to have feared this unrest and was under pressure from the high priests and other groups within Jerusalem society, so concluded the trial with Jesus' death, executing him as the "King of the Jews". This was regardless of how Jesus viewed his kingship. Political expediency and religious anger dictated the same outcome: death.

CHAPTER 17

The death of Jesus

The death of Jesus is perhaps the most famous death in history. We will explore how and where it occurred; how his death is presented by the Gospels; and how Jesus' death was perceived by the early church. For, although many at the time would have considered it a humiliating and catastrophic end to his mission, Christians declared it was actually an integral part of a victorious culmination of his life. They still do.

A humiliating and brutal form of execution

Crucifixion was an ancient, and harsh, method of execution designed to disgrace and degrade. Most modern people, when they imagine a crucifixion, envisage someone being nailed to a wooden cross in some way. However, the evidence reveals that when a person was crucified, although they might, indeed, be nailed to the cross, they may in some cases have been simply tied on. Roman writings refer to both practices.

Jesus was crucified during Roman occupation in the first century AD. However, there are recordings of crucifixion as a punishment taking place well before this time. According to the Greek historian Herodotus, in the sixth century BC, Darius I of Persia used crucifixion as a punishment for political opponents. Such a form of execution is also believed to have been used by the Macedonian king, Alexander the Great, and also by the Carthaginians of North Africa. The use of crucifixion was then adopted by the Roman Republic and the later Roman Empire as a demeaning and brutal punishment for those (citizens, non-citizens, or slaves) found guilty of treason. It was considered to be an exemplary cruel punishment, fit for the enemies of Rome.

A striking example of the Roman usage of crucifixion as a punishment for rebellion occurred in the first century BC. In 71 BC the slave revolt led by the gladiator Spartacus was defeated. It was the last of three slave rebellions that the Romans crushed. As retribution, the Roman general, Crassus, crucified 6,000 prisoners from the army of ex-slaves. The avenue of the dead and dying lined the Appian Way from Rome to Capua. It sent a clear message to all those who looked on it of what the Romans would do to those who tried to rise up against them.

One might assume that crucifixion kills the victim through loss of blood, if nails are used. However this is not the case. The main cause of death is asphyxia, as the full weight of the victim hung from the arms, with death usually occurring within two or three hours. As the victim grew weaker it would prove harder for them to pull themselves up on their arms to breathe. However, if the body was supported in some way, then the time to death could last as long as three days. The Romans sometimes added a small seat, or a ledge to rest the feet, to add support. This way the death took longer and the pain was prolonged. Whether the victim was nailed or bound to the cross, the result was the same: suffocation. It was a savage form of execution.

A shocking archaeological discovery was made in 1968, when the first (and currently only) evidence of the use of crucifixion was found. This discovery corroborated the written sources which said that the Romans used crucifixion as a punishment in Judea. This discovery was made by the Israeli Department of Antiquities when they were excavating a series of tombs, north of the walled-city of Jerusalem, at Giv'at ha-Mivtar. There they found a stone box (an ossuary), containing human bones. Within the ossuary was a heel-bone, with an iron nail driven through it, as well as the bones of a three- or four-year-old child. It seems that the nail in the adult's foot bent as it hit a knot in the wood – a piece of olive wood was found on the tip of the nail – which meant that the bent nail was difficult to remove after death. So, what seems to have happened is that the whole foot was cut off, although kept with the body. Another small piece of wood survived between the bone and the nail-head; probably designed to prevent the foot ripping apart and free of the nail.

Studying the bones, initial suggestions were that both legs would have been twisted to one side, with knees bent, and then a large single nail would have gone through both heel bones to attach them to the cross. The victim would then have been in a semi-sitting position, body twisted to one side. It seems as though the man's legs were finally brutally broken, in order to accelerate death, with the full weight of the body hanging from the arms.[1] This is what the Gospel of John describes as happening to the two criminals crucified with Jesus (John 19:31–32). Due to a scratch found on a bone on the right forearm, it seems that the person's arms would have been nailed to the horizontal bar, with the nail driven in just above the wrist.

Some of these conclusions, regarding the evidence from Giv'at ha-Mivtar, have been challenged. Some experts later argued that the heels were nailed separately to either side of the upright post and questioned whether the arms were nailed and the legs broken.[2] The arms may have been tied – instead of nailed – to the cross-beam. Both methods are attested and one piece of graffito from Pompeii, Italy, reads: "May you be *nailed* to the cross!", whereas another says: "Get *hung*!"[3] From this we can conclude that there was variety in how this punishment was carried out. Clearly there was no one way to crucify. However, one thing is certain: the death was agonizing and humiliating.

Returning to the archaeological discovery at Giv'at ha-Mivtar, on the outside of the ossuary the words "Yehohanan, son of Hagakol" were carved into the side. Some believe that "Hagakol" was not a personal name but was actually a term which meant "crucified". If this was the case then the writing should be read as: "Yehohanan, son of the Crucified One". If so, Yehohanan was the child's name.[4] But the matter remains open to debate.

What is not debated is that at the time of Jesus, the Romans crucified large numbers of people. In AD 7 a rebellion occurred in Judea following the death of King Herod. After its suppression, the Roman Legate of Syria, Quintilius Varus, crucified 2,000 Jews in Jerusalem. In AD 70 the Roman general, Titus, crucified somewhere in the region of 500 Jews a day, over a period of several months, during the siege of Jerusalem. This followed a widespread revolt against Roman rule.

Consequently, whereas Jesus' crucifixion is now extremely famous and associated with one man and one event, the mode of execution would have been very familiar to those at the time.

Not only was the death itself degrading and brutal, before the crucifixion itself Jesus was flogged. Often this bloody aspect is forgotten, and we think of paintings of a bloodless, intact muscular body of Jesus on the cross. The reality would have been far from this oddly serene image. A bloody and helpless body struggling for breath would have been the actual experience.

As seen in the previous chapter, the role of the Jerusalem Jewish authorities in the arrest of Jesus is pivotal, yet without the Romans the crucifixion would never have happened. The Jews, under Roman occupation, could not put anyone to death so the elites needed the Romans to carry out this ultimate penalty. And crucifixion was clearly a form of execution favoured by the Romans. Tacitus, a Roman historian writing about eighty-five years after the death of Jesus, records that Jesus was crucified by Pontius Pilate, as recorded by the Gospels: "Christ [*Christus*], had been executed in the reign of Tiberius by the procurator Pontius Pilate."[5] Although Tacitus describes Pilate as *procurator*, this title for a governor was not introduced until 41 and, at the time, Pilate would have been titled *prefect*. It is also interesting to note that Tacitus clearly thought that *Christus* was a personal name, which it is not. There is every reason to conclude that this was a piece of information found in Tacitus's original text, and is not an interpolation by later Christian scribes.[6] Here we find direct (and possibly unique) early corroboration of the New Testament account of the death of Jesus at the hands of the Romans. However, Tacitus does not describe the method of execution.

There is a similar statement concerning Pilate, but with the added information "condemned him [Jesus] to the cross", in the writings of the Jewish historian Josephus. There has been debate concerning whether this particular information in Josephus was in the original or is due to later Christian interpolation. On balance, it is reasonable to assume that it was in the original and offers further corroboration of the Gospel accounts.[7]

The death of Jesus in the Gospels

Matthew and Mark mention the flogging of Jesus before he was handed over to be crucified. They both then tell of how the soldiers publicly mocked Jesus, putting a robe on him and placing a crown of thorns on his head, as they knelt down to him and said, "Hail, King of the Jews!" (Matthew 27:29, Mark 15:18). They further struck him and spat on him. This emphasizes that the whole process, and not just the act of execution itself, was designed to humiliate. John records similar details but in John's Gospel this happens as Pilate is presenting Jesus to the Jewish crowd.

Furthermore, although John's Gospel tells of how Jesus carried his own cross, all three synoptics tell of how Simon of Cyrene was pulled from the crowd to carry Jesus' cross. This implies that Jesus was so exhausted from the flogging that he had insufficient strength left to carry his cross. This contrasts with the author(s) of John who seems to want to show Jesus without such human weakness. Luke also mentions that, among the great numbers following Jesus, were women "beating their breasts and wailing for him" (Luke 23:27). In his Gospel Luke tends to emphasize the marginalized in society, of which women would have been a significant group. During his ministry Jesus had made a point of spending time with women, as well as men. This is probably why Luke pauses to emphasize the women who were publicly demonstrating their grief and distress. These women were unafraid and unashamed to be associated with Jesus even now – as he had once so publicly stood by them. But where is mention of the male disciples of Jesus? Their absence is striking.

All four Gospels mention that Jesus was crucified at a place called Golgotha, meaning the "place of the skull". It is disputed where the exact location of Golgotha was, but it was most likely outside the city walls. John 19:20 says that Jesus was crucified "near the city" (implying outside but close). Furthermore, due to Jewish custom, executions would not have taken place in Jerusalem itself. Therefore, it was probably on a routeway into Jerusalem, travelled by many, so that people would be deterred from opposing the Romans. Matthew 27:39 and Mark 15:29 record how passers-by mocked and derided Jesus when he was hanging on the cross, emphasizing that this place was on a route with much footfall. Some modern experts accept that Helena (the mother of Roman emperor Constantine) correctly identified the location of Golgotha and, accordingly, the Church of the Holy Sepulchre was built there in the fourth century. And although it is inside the city walls in present day Jerusalem, the site would have been outside the walls of Jerusalem originally. Others prefer the idea of a hill now called "Gordon's Calvary", north of the Damascus Gate. There is also dispute about why it was called the "place of the skull". Some favour the idea that it was called this because the hill was shaped like a skull; but a more likely view is that, as a place of execution, the bones and skulls of criminals were present there. In Jewish outlook it would have been a ritually unclean place.

The Gospels do not go into detail about how Jesus was crucified, they simply say he was. However, when recording the resurrection appearances in John 20:27, Jesus says to his disciple Thomas, "Put your finger here and see my hands", and in Luke 24:39 Jesus says, "Look at my hands and my feet; see that it is I myself." Therefore, the Gospels indicate his hands and feet were nailed. However, the Greek word used in the New Testament could describe the *wrists* as well as the *hands*; and Jesus' arms may have been both tied to give support to the body and nailed (through either wrists or hands).[8] The same word translated as "hands" in John is translated as "wrists" when later describing where chains were fixed on the apostle Peter.[9] This, along with the fact that the New Testament never describes the cross in detail, or exactly how Jesus was placed on it, means that over two thousand years it has been artistically represented in a number of ways.

According to Matthew and Mark, Jesus was offered a wine mixture to drink (perhaps to numb the pain) but he did not take it. John says he took a little sour wine. The soldiers divided Jesus' clothes among them by casting lots. Luke 23:34 tells of how Jesus says, "Father, forgive them; for they do not know what they are doing" as the author clearly wished to show that, even in his death, Jesus was compassionate and forgiving. Later Christians would also interpret it as meaning that the Roman guards did not know they were complicit in the death of the Son of God.

Jesus was not crucified alone but with two other criminals, Matthew and Mark calling them "bandits". Yet, although Matthew and Mark say that both of these men taunted Jesus, Luke says that only one of the crucified criminals mocked Jesus, whereas the other repented and acknowledged the innocence and status of Jesus. Some have attempted to reconcile this difference by saying that both criminals *started* taunting Jesus, mimicking the scoffing of the chief priests, and then one of the criminals later changed his mind and repented.

All the Gospels tell of how an inscription regarding Jesus' charge was put over his head: "The King of the Jews". This emphasizes the alleged political challenge Jesus presented to the Romans. John further emphasizes that the sign was written in Hebrew, Latin, and Greek, so all would be able to read it and be warned. John also tells how the chief priests objected to the sign, as they said it made it seem like he was the "King of the Jews" rather than "This man said, I am King of the Jews", yet Pilate (we are told) ignored them (John 19:19–22). Furthermore, all three synoptics tell of the brutal mocking and criticism Jesus faced while on the cross, from onlookers.

Mark records that Jesus was crucified at nine in the morning, and then all the synoptics say darkness covered the land until three in the afternoon when Jesus died. The Greek historian Thallos (writing c. 55) refers to an eclipse of the sun, in a way postulated to be a possible response to early Christian claims about this event.[10]

In contrast with regard to timing, John (19:14) says it was about noon when Jesus was handed over to be crucified. On the cross, Mark 15:34 and Matthew 27:46 have Jesus cry out, "My God, my God, why have you forsaken me?" The bystanders misunderstand what Jesus is saying and believe he is calling on Elijah to save him. Then both Mark and Matthew say that Jesus cried out with a loud voice and breathed his last. Yet neither say the words Jesus uttered when he cried out. In Luke, on the other hand, the only utterance recorded is,

> Then Jesus, crying with a loud voice, said, "Father, into your hands I commend my spirit." Having said this, he breathed his last.
> **(Luke 23:46)**

It is possible that Luke was filling in a gap left by the account in Matthew and Mark. Overall, these accounts point to Jesus experiencing despair and horror of separation from God,[11] and then, just before he dies, is at peace. In John 19:30 Jesus seems in complete control of his death, calling out: "'It is finished.' Then he bowed his head and gave up his spirit." In John, Jesus is, throughout, the triumphant and defiant divine victor on the cross.

At the death of Jesus, the synoptics tell of how the curtain of the Temple tore in two. This curtain cut off the entrance into the Holy of Holies where God's presence was believed to be in the Temple. Only the high priest could walk through this curtain and only once a year. Therefore, whether this tearing actually happened or whether it was symbolic, it was meant to demonstrate to the readers that any barrier between God and humans was destroyed by the death of Jesus. Matthew and Mark emphasize the curtain was torn from top to bottom, implying God was the cause.

Matthew 27:51–52 alone says how at the death of Jesus the earth shook, rocks split, and tombs were opened and many bodies of holy people were raised. Matthew, mentioning the earthquake, seems to be providing a reason for how the veil tore in two and implies it was an act of God. One reading of the tombs re-opening and the "bodies of the saints" being raised is that through, "the death and resurrection of Jesus the saints of the Old Israel, the prophets who foretold His coming, became united in close fellowship with the believers of the new".[12] Another reading is that these events "show that the death of Jesus was an act of God… the effect of this act will be life for the dead".[13] Instances in the Old Testament, such as Judges 5:4 and 2 Samuel 22:8, demonstrate how earthquakes were regarded as evidence of God's action.[14]

The synoptics then all turn their attention to the Roman centurion watching. In Luke 23:47 the centurion proclaims, "Certainly this man was innocent", whereas Matthew 27:54 and Mark 15:39 have stronger acclamations of "Truly this man was God's Son!" It is not entirely clear in these accounts what led to this epiphany, but the writers seem to think it obvious that in his death his innocence was recognized.

John seems intent on stressing how Jesus' death fulfilled Scripture. On numerous occasions he says how events during Jesus' death happened so that Scripture could be fulfilled. First, when the soldiers were dividing his clothing and casting lots for it (John 19:24). Second,

Jesus saying he was thirsty on the cross (John 19:28) so was given sour wine to drink. Third, none of his bones being broken (John 19:36) as the Jewish authorities had asked that the legs of the crucified men would be broken so that they would die more swiftly, so that their bodies might be removed from the cross before the Sabbath. Yet Jesus was already dead, so this did not happen to him. Instead, the guards – to check he was really dead – pierced Jesus' side, and blood and water came out confirming his death. Again, Jesus being pierced is stated to echo Scripture in this account (John 19:37).

Luke mentions that all Jesus' acquaintances, including women, stood at a distance watching. Matthew and Mark just mention female followers of Jesus being there. This does not necessarily contradict Luke and mean that the male disciples were not there, but clearly for the writers of Matthew and Mark it is the presence of the women that is of significance. Both mention Mary Magdalene and Mary the mother of James and Joseph/Joses. Mark also mentions Salome and Matthew also mentions the mother of the sons of Zebedee (very probably these, apparently, two women were actually the same person). These female followers were clearly dedicated, although afraid as they looked on from a distance. On the other hand, John mentions a different group of women (Jesus' mother, Jesus' mother's sister, Mary the wife of Clopas, and Mary Magdalene). Yet they are standing near the cross throughout the crucifixion so John is presenting them as being bolder in their support.

All four Gospels tell how Joseph of Arimathea asked for Pilate's permission for the body of Jesus, which was granted. Jesus' body was removed from the cross, wrapped in linen cloth, and laid in a new tomb before the Sabbath. The synoptics say that the tomb was carved in the rock, and John says that the new tomb was in a garden; clearly near the place where Jesus was crucified. Matthew and Mark record that a great stone was rolled over the entrance of the tomb.

Despite some differences between the Gospel accounts, where all Gospels agree is "the massive attention they give to the passion narrative and the way they aim their Gospels toward the cross as the climax to the story of Jesus".[15] For later Christians, Jesus' life and ministry culminates in his death (with the resurrection to follow). At the time, it must simply have been devastating.

The crucifixion of Jesus as perceived by the early church

The crucifixion of Jesus was hugely humiliating and needed explaining to early Christians and their neighbours. The earliest surviving known image of the crucifixion dates from about the year 200 and was found on the Palatine Hill, in Rome. It might be a surprise to know that this picture was not made by a Christian. Instead, it was an offensive graffito mocking Christians and their God. The graffito shows a human figure raising a hand in worship to a figure naked on a cross; the crucified figure is depicted with the head of a donkey. Below the crude sketch are scratched Greek words that read: "*Alexamenos sebete theon*",[16] which, despite some complications in the hastily written Greek, is most convincingly translated as, "Alexamenos worships [his] God".[17]

Given the highly negative Roman view of crucifixion as a punishment for common criminals the contempt is predictable. Lucian of Samosata in the second century AD similarly mocked early Christians for "worshipping that crucified sophist".[18] His repetition of "crucified" in his references to Christ emphasizes the shameful origins of Christianity in his opinion.[19] Jews too viewed crucifixion with disdain. The Old Testament said that "anyone hung on a tree is under God's curse" (Deuteronomy 21:23). Arguably this does not refer to crucifixion, since the reference implies that the criminal was already dead. And "hung on a tree" suggests the display of a dead body not the nailing of a body to wood. Despite this, when Greek and Roman rulers introduced crucifixion to the Jewish communities, its shame and humiliation resonated with an existing mind-set regarding a body "on a tree". For Jewish people the Messiah would not have had such a shameful death.

Consequently, the early Christians had an uphill battle explaining the significance of Jesus' death and why they believed the Son of God could die such a degrading death. Paul's letters to the first churches were written within twenty-five years of the death of Jesus and Paul clearly made a high priority of explaining the meaning of the cross and Jesus' death.

This disparity between Christians and non-Christians regarding the crucifixion of Jesus is highlighted in 1 Corinthians 1:18 and 23 as Paul writes,

> For the message about the cross is foolishness to those who are perishing, but to us who are being saved it is the power of God... but we proclaim Christ crucified, a stumbling-block to Jews and foolishness to Gentiles.

Clearly, non-Christians (Jews, Greeks, Romans, and others) of the first and second centuries AD would not have understood the idea of crucifixion as an honourable religious symbol or as the defining feature of a saving deity. The teachings of the early church were scandalous. Furthermore, Paul responds directly to the Deuteronomy 21:23 text,

> For all who rely on the works of the law are under a curse... Christ redeemed us from the curse of the law by becoming a curse for us – for it is written, "Cursed is everyone who hangs on a tree" – in order that in Christ Jesus the blessing of Abraham might come to the Gentiles, so that we might receive the promise of the Spirit through faith.
> **(Galatians 3:10, 13–14)**

Paul is arguing here that Jesus took on humanity's curse through his death so that sinners might be saved. So, it was not that his death was shameful, but he took on people's shame in his death. The letter to the Hebrews echoes the idea that Jesus' death was salvific,

> Therefore, my friends, since we have confidence to enter the sanctuary by the blood of Jesus, by the new and living way that he opened for us through the curtain (that is, through his flesh).
> **(Hebrews 10:19–20)**

The anonymous writer is saying that through Jesus' death, believers have their relationship with God restored. Furthermore 1 Corinthians 15:3 specifically states that "Christ died for our sins". Not only that but he humbled himself through his death, "he humbled himself and became obedient to the point of death – even death on a cross"

(Philippians 2:8). For Paul and other early Christians, Jesus' death was a sign of his humility and love for humanity; a love and humility that should be replicated by his followers.[20] Despite contemporary negative understandings of crucifixion, the view held by the church would come to be that it was a symbol of God's love, of salvation, and of the defeat of sin. What began as a humiliation would be presented as a triumph. And that was firmly rooted in what early believers insisted happened three days later...

CHAPTER 18

"On the third day"

If the death of Jesus has provoked controversy, the claims about what occurred on the Sunday after have divided people for two millennia. In order to assess the nature of this controversy we will explore the different presentations in the four Gospels; the significance of the abrupt ending of the Gospel of Mark; and the early church claims regarding post-resurrection appearances (from the garden tomb, via the road to Emmaus and the upper room, to Galilee).

The third day?

The *Nicene Creed* – framed in the late fourth century and based on the *Creed of Nicaea*, that had been formulated at the earlier First Council of Nicaea (the first ecumenical council of the church) – states that Jesus rose again on the third day:

> For our sake he was crucified under Pontius Pilate;
> he suffered death and was buried.
> On the third day he rose again
> in accordance with the Scriptures[1]

From the Gospels, Jesus was crucified on the Friday (now known as Good Friday) and was removed from the cross before the Jewish holy day, the Sabbath, which is a Saturday. One can understand that Jesus' followers wanted him off the cross before the Sabbath started (if they had any opportunity to influence events) because Deuteronomy 21:23 says, "his corpse must not remain all night upon the tree; you shall bury him that same day". Furthermore, the body could not be buried on the Sabbath, so it was done quickly as Friday drew to a close; and then the women returned on the Sunday morning to anoint the body.

As previously mentioned, Jewish days start at nightfall and last until the next nightfall – rather than the day starting at midnight and lasting until 11.59pm. So, Sabbath starts on Friday evening and lasts until Saturday evening. It was imperative that Jesus' body be off the cross before nightfall. In terms of that phrase "On the third day", Christians do not believe that Jesus was resurrected 72 hours after his crucifixion. Rather, he was crucified on the Friday (day one); in the tomb all of the Sabbath (day two) and then rose at some point early on Sunday morning (day three). Sunday being the first day of the working week.

What do the Gospels say?

Matthew 27:62–66 tells how the chief priests and Pharisees went to Pilate and asked for Jesus' tomb to be made secure – sealed by the stone and guarded by soldiers until the third day – so that the disciples would not steal the body. They state that Jesus had said he would rise again on the third day, and they did not want the disciples to be able to make false claims of this happening.

The Gospels then record how after the Sabbath (on the first day of the week) some women came to the tomb. Matthew 28:1 says, "After the sabbath, as the first day of the week was dawning", which could be read as meaning they went in the dark after nightfall which marked the end of the Saturday or very early on Sunday (the usual assumption). John 20:1 says it was still dark. But Mark 16:2 says, "Very early on the first day of the week, when the sun had risen, they went to the tomb" and Luke 24:1 corroborates this: "But on the first day of the week, at early dawn, they came to the tomb". Therefore, although there is slight uncertainty over exactly when they arrived at the tomb, what is clear is that it was remembered as occurring just before or about dawn on the Sunday – before anyone else was around. These women (or woman) wanted to get to the tomb as soon as possible. Mark 16:1 and Luke 24:1 state that they brought spices with them, and Mark specifies that this was to anoint the body of Jesus.

Mark mentions Mary Magdalene, Mary the mother of James, and Salome. Whereas Matthew mentions Mary Magdalene and "the other Mary". Luke 24:10 says it was Mary Magdalene, Joanna, Mary the mother of James, and other women. In John it was just Mary Magdalene that went to the tomb and saw that the stone had been removed. Yet in John 20:2, when she is telling two of the male disciples what happened she says, "They have taken the Lord out of the tomb, and *we* do not know where they have laid him" (emphasis added). The fact that she says "we" implies she was not alone. The author may have only named her because she was known to the readers or significant to the author. The use of "we" might also demonstrate the author(s) knowledge and use of the synoptic tradition. What is the same in all accounts is that it is not men who make the first discovery.

Women were not deemed reliable witnesses in court. So, it is interesting that here women are witnesses to such a monumental event in Christianity, as surely the account would have seemed more credible to first-century listeners if men were the first witnesses. Therefore, this consistency among the authors of women playing the main role(s) at this event is important.[2] Moreover, each account makes a similar claim, despite naming different variations of women present. Perhaps all the women mentioned by each Gospel were there at the tomb, but each chose which woman/women to name in their account based on their own personal perspective, purpose, and audience.[3] As J. Warner (a homicide detective) has commented:

> In my experience as a cold case detective, no two eyewitness accounts ever agree on every detail or every emphasis. This doesn't shake me as an investigator and it's never inhibited an investigation. It's just the nature of eyewitness testimony. Related to the number and identity of the women at the tomb of Jesus, the four Gospel accounts demonstrate the same variation I've seen in my professional work.[4]

Moving on, Matthew 28:2–4 mentions an earthquake; an angel of the Lord rolling back the stone and sitting on it; and the guards shaking out of fear and becoming like dead men. This exact sequence of events is not mentioned in any other Gospel (in the same way that the earthquake at the death of Jesus was only mentioned in Matthew). Some have argued that this was historically what happened and offers an explanation for how the stone was rolled away; others have argued that this earthquake and angelic appearance was symbolic of Jesus' resurrection being an act of God (as seen in Old Testament examples, as in Chapter 17).

When the women get to the tomb all the synoptics speak of the stone having been rolled away from the entrance of the tomb and they mention angelic figures. Mark 16:5 says, "As they entered the tomb, they saw a young man, dressed in a white robe, sitting on the right side; and they were alarmed", and Luke 24:4 says something similar, "While they were perplexed about this, suddenly two men in dazzling clothes stood beside them." The white robe in Mark and the dazzling clothes in Luke seem to match Matthew's description of the angel: "His appearance was like lightning, and his clothing white as snow" (Matthew 28:3). Matthew seems to want to make it explicit to his readers that this was an angel. Later on, Luke 24:23 states that the women told people they had seen angels. In John 20:12 Mary Magdalene sees two figures, described as angels (similar to Luke's account), dressed in white and sitting where Jesus' body had been lying. John's Gospel records the angelic vision as taking place during what seems to be Mary's second visit to the tomb. Whether there was one angel or two, there is a supernatural presence in all the accounts. The women were, unsurprisingly, afraid.

The discourse of this angelic figure is very similar in Matthew and Mark. He tells the women not to be afraid, and that Jesus, who was crucified, is not here but has been raised. He then tells them to tell the disciples that Jesus is going ahead to Galilee and they will see him there. The "men" in Luke say something slightly different, "Why do you look for the living among the dead? He is not here, but has risen" (Luke 24:5). They then remind the women that Jesus told them he would be crucified and raised on the third day; they then remembered his words (Luke 24:6–8).

The reactions of the women to this news differs across the synoptic gospels. Mark's Gospel ends abruptly, "So they went out and fled from the tomb, for terror and amazement had seized them; and they said nothing to anyone, for they were afraid" (Mark 16:8). In Matthew they ran to tell the disciples and Luke makes it clear they told the disciples what happened. Mark's account does not necessarily contradict the other two. He simply records the immediate raw response.

In John's Gospel – as the angels appear later in his account – when Mary Magdalene first appears he simply says that she came to the tomb (while it was dark) and saw that the stone had been rolled away. Then Mary tells some of the disciples what she has seen at the tomb.

Luke 24:11–12 recounts how the disciples did not believe what the women said at first. But Peter ran to the tomb and saw that only the linen cloths remained, leading him to be "amazed". In John 20:2–10 Peter, as well as the disciple whom Jesus loved, are told the news and they then go to the empty tomb and see the grave clothes:

> Then the other disciple, who reached the tomb first, also went in, and he saw and believed; for as yet they did not understand the scripture, that he must rise from the dead.
> **(John 20:8–9)**

The addition of another disciple with Peter, in John's Gospel, fits with what is said later on in Luke 24:24 that others went to the tomb and found it as the women said but did not see Jesus. So, it is probable that more people than Peter went to the tomb, but as the lead disciple Luke just mentions him. There is speculation as to whether the disciple "whom Jesus loved" was the author of John, and he gave himself that title. So perhaps he explicitly records himself in his account, as he wants to make it clear that he too was witness to the empty tomb.

Taking all the Gospel accounts together, a woman or group of women went to the tomb early on Sunday and found the empty tomb and an angel(s) speaks to her/them. They were amazed and afraid but at some point they told the disciples, some of whom went to the tomb and saw for themselves. The accounts all insist on the key details. For some, the variations among the accounts will reduce their persuasiveness, whereas others would argue that it might be expected to find "some degree of resolvable variation in true, reliable eyewitness accounts".[5] Furthermore, there is a strong argument that differences in the accounts reflect "differing theological perspectives and pastoral emphases of each author" and do not allow for sequencing and harmonizing of these different authorial voices.[6]

With regard to what was claimed about these encounters we enter an area of faith, rather than what can be verified according to normal historical enquiry. What is undeniable and irreducible is that the Gospel traditions insist that something quite extraordinary happened and that it radically changed their lives. Readers must make up their own minds.

Alternative explanations for the resurrection?

Various alternative explanations have been offered for why the tomb was empty on that Sunday morning; below are some but this is not an exhaustive examination.

First, it has been argued that Jesus was not actually dead but unconscious when he was taken off the cross. He then awoke in the tomb and rolled the stone away. This, of course, conflicts with John's account of Jesus' side being pierced and blood and water pouring out confirming his death. Yet this is not mentioned in the synoptics, so perhaps the detail was later added to promote the belief that Jesus really was dead. Nevertheless, in the synoptics Jesus was so exhausted from the flogging that he was not able to carry his cross, which might lead one to question if he would have had the strength to roll away the tomb stone even if he was alive. In Mark 16:3 the women, on the way to the tomb of Jesus, were discussing who would roll away the stone for them, implying it would be too heavy for women; therefore one might assume that if it was too heavy for women, it would be too heavy for a man, who was weak from the ordeal of crucifixion. Furthermore, Matthew 27:66 states that the stone was sealed. Or did Matthew add that in to dismiss the notion that anyone (except divine intervention) could have moved the stone?

Another explanation offered is that perhaps the body had been stolen. Yet if that was the case why would robbers leave the most expensive linen cloth (Luke 24:12)? John also says that the cloth was still there (John 20:7). It would seem odd for robbers to be so tidy as to fold up some of the linen cloth. Did then the Romans or Jewish authorities steal the body to stop Jesus' tomb becoming a shrine? However, it seems unlikely that these two groups (who wanted an end to Jesus' following once and for all) would have not then produced the body to prove Jesus was in fact dead, when rumours started to circulate that Jesus had risen from the dead. Perhaps the disciples stole the body? The Gospel of Matthew is keen to dispel this idea as Matthew 28:11–15 tells how some of the guards went to the Jewish authorities and told them what happened, so they bribed the soldiers and told them to say the disciples stole the body at night while they were asleep. Matthew 28:15 says, "So they took the money and did as they were directed. And this story is still told among the Jews to this day." It is up to the reader to decide what came first: the accusation that the disciples took the body so it would look like Jesus was raised or Matthew's explanation for this accusation.[7]

Perhaps, it has been suggested, on the Sunday morning the women went to the wrong tomb. In their grief they were not thinking straight and went to the wrong place. To this it could be countered that they were present at the burial of Jesus and witnessed its location.

Finally, it has been suggested that post-traumatic-stress-disorder triggered hallucinatory experiences among Jesus' followers and that his presence among them was a spiritual rather than a physical experience. This, it is sometimes argued, is a reason why Paul's letters (written before the Gospels) do not explicitly refer to an empty tomb.[8]

Traditional Christianity, of course, would counter that the Gospels are correct, and that Jesus did rise from the dead, regardless of the complexities in the accounts. A Christian claim that is as extraordinary then as now. The resurrection is where history gives way to faith. That a scattered and demoralized group of followers rapidly rebounded from apparent disaster with such energy and dynamism is certainly beyond dispute.

Two additional endings to Mark's Gospel?

The oldest manuscripts of Mark end the Gospel at verse 8, where the women are afraid, so do not say anything to anyone. But there is also an *additional shorter* – and *an additional longer* – ending of Mark in some manuscripts.[9]

Some modern commentators consider that the author meant to end the Gospel at verse 8; others that the original ending after 16:8 was lost so editors added new endings due to the abruptness; or others that the original ending was intentionally removed.[10] The abrupt ending might explain why Mark (although thought to be the oldest Gospel) is not the first Gospel in the New Testament collection. Yet, if Mark was written before the year 70 (the consensus of most scholars), we must conclude that "the *first generation of Jesus' followers* were perfectly fine with a Gospel account that recounted *no appearances of Jesus*".[11]

A small number of manuscripts end the Gospel with the shorter ending,

> And all that had been commanded them they told briefly to those around Peter. And afterwards Jesus himself sent out through them, from east to west, the sacred and imperishable proclamation of eternal salvation.

This shorter ending contradicts the sentence before and is not in the oldest manuscripts, so most believe this was a later addition.

The longer ending, verses 9–20, contains a list of resurrection appearances of Jesus to different people: to Mary Magdalene; to two followers walking into the country; and to the eleven disciples. Some scholars, though, do believe that these verses were part of the earliest manuscripts, and some English translations of the Bible (such as the 1611 King James Version) include verses 9–20 as if they were the original ending without footnoting it as a longer ending. On the other hand, many modern translations state that these verses were not included in the earliest surviving manuscripts. Generally, New Testament scholars believe this was a late addition and was not written by the original author of Mark, but someone perhaps influenced by the resurrection appearances in the other Gospels. This is because these twelve verses give a series of bare facts, unlike anything else in Mark. Also, there are numerous Greek words and expressions used here that are not found in the rest of Mark. Finally, verse 9 is not continuous with the previous narrative but seems abrupt.[12] Revealingly, an Armenian manuscript, dated 986, was discovered at the end of the nineteenth century which ascribes the long ending of Mark to "Elder Aristion", although the accuracy of this attribution is open to question.[13]

In conclusion, it seems clear that Mark did not originally end with the appearance of the risen Jesus. However, the implication seems clear – and the shock palpable – that "Jesus is out, on the loose...".[14]

Early church claims regarding post-resurrection appearances

There is, it seems, no mention in the original version of Mark of any of the resurrection appearances in Jerusalem that appear in the other Gospels. We might ask: did Matthew, Luke, and John add in resurrection appearances to make up for this deficiency? However, it is interesting that both Mark and Matthew (Mark 16:7 and Matthew 28:7) refer to future appearances that will occur in Galilee. Matthew also has Jesus himself appearing to the women (on their way to tell the disciples what they have seen and heard) telling them, "Do not be afraid; go and tell my brothers to go to Galilee; there they will see me" (Matthew 28:10). The Galilee appearances form the climax of Matthew's Gospel. It is clearly significant that the geographical focus moves away from Jerusalem to the place where Jesus was most active. Galilee comes back into sharp focus, after the events in Jerusalem which have dominated the narrative in the closing sections of all four Gospels. There the disciples see and worship Jesus; their faith strengthened in seeing him. But even then, some doubted. Nevertheless, he then commissions them (Matthew 28:16–20).

This juxtaposition of amazement but also doubt is seen in other resurrection appearances. In Luke 24:36–49, Jesus appears to the disciples in Jerusalem (there is no Galilee narrative in Luke). Their initial reaction is to be terrified, and believe they are seeing a ghost.

Jesus then shows them his hands and his feet to prove his identity and invites them to touch him to show he is not a ghost. But "in their joy they were disbelieving and still wondering" (Luke 24:41). As in Matthew 28:17 there is both amazement and doubt. Was this a fear on their part of experiencing disappointment based on false joy.[15] The resurrection is clearly disconcerting.

In Luke, the risen Jesus eats with the disciples and helps them to understand the prophetic scriptures. This Lukan passage is followed by the ascension (Luke 24:50–53), where Jesus returns to heaven. It is at this point they worship him and express great joy. John (21:1–14) also has an account of Jesus eating fish with some of his disciples, but in John this is the third appearance of Jesus to his disciples and it occurs in Galilee.

John 20:19–23 also has an account of Jesus appearing to the disciples the evening of the first day of the week (the day the empty tomb was discovered) in the room where they were hiding. In John's account the disciples rejoice, and there is no mention of disbelief. However, Thomas was not with them and did not believe what they told him. So, a week later Jesus appears again (even though the doors are locked). Thomas responds, "My Lord and my God!" (John 20:28). So, in John's Gospel it is the character of Thomas who displays the juxtaposition of doubt and worship. Thomas's statement of faith is the climax of this particular Gospel.

In other accounts of Jesus appearing to his followers, they do not recognize him straight away. Jesus appears to Mary Magdalene in John (20:11–18) at the tomb. She is crying and sees Jesus standing there, but she does not know who he is and mistakes him for the gardener, asking him if he knows where her Lord has been taken. As soon as Jesus says her name (tellingly, in its Aramaic form), she recognizes him, and he says to her,

> Do not hold on to me, because I have not yet ascended to the Father. But go to my brothers and say to them, "I am ascending to my Father and your Father, to my God and your God".
> **(John 20:17)**

In Luke 24:13–35 two of Jesus' followers are travelling to Emmaus (seven miles from Jerusalem) and Jesus walks and talks with them, interpreting the things about himself in the Scriptures. Only when evening comes and Jesus blesses and breaks the bread, an action he did at the Last Supper, do they recognize him. He then vanishes. They then return to Jerusalem and tell the disciples. This characteristic of Jesus raised (but transformed) and alive (but not as before) is striking.[16]

There are three common themes in these different accounts: not recognizing Jesus initially; doubt about whether it is him; joy and worship of Jesus as they see him for who he is. Though complex and mysterious, all these accounts insist that he has been raised from the dead.[17]

The same insistence, though expressed in various ways, appears in other (almost certainly earlier) Christian accounts. It has long been asserted that the evangelistic speeches attributed to Peter in the book of Acts, represent the original faith statements of the Aramaic-speaking Jerusalem community and long pre-date the writing of Acts itself.[18] This is described as the "Petrine *kerygma*" (proclamation). In this, the claim that Jesus has been raised and exalted to the right hand of God is foundational. This is presented as God's vindication of Jesus and proof of his messianic status. His message and his (humiliating and shocking) death are understood – and the latter completely transformed – through this belief. Viewed through the lens of the resurrection, "Jesus has become the content of the message; the proclaimer has become the proclaimed".[19] The same can be said about the preaching of Paul as presented in Acts.[20] Just as Peter had declared on the Day of Pentecost that "God raised him [Jesus] up, having freed him from death, because it was impossible for him to be held in its power" (Acts 2:24); so Paul proclaims, at Antioch of Pisidia, that "God raised him from the dead; and for many days he appeared to those who came up with him from Galilee to Jerusalem" (Acts 13:30–31).

For early Christians, Jesus' death *and* resurrection have become inseparable and the latter transforms understanding of the former; the resurrection is the non-negotiable and essential lens through which the life, teaching, actions, and significance of Jesus is understood. For these early believers it is faith in this – and through these climactic Easter events – that forgiveness of sins is achieved, eternal life entered into, and the future renewal of all things (made contingent on Jesus' return) made possible. The earliest evidence for this Easter faith appears in the Pauline letter known as 1 Corinthians.[21] Paul writes: "If Christ has not been raised, your faith is futile and you are still in your sins" (1 Corinthians 15:17).

It is at this point that the exploration of the life and ministry of Jesus transitions into the study of faith in him as the Christ.[22] This was a matter which involved vast amounts of debate among early Christians concerning his nature and significance. For some modern scholars it was the nature of that ensuing debate (concerning "the Christ of faith") that decided, even distorted, the way that the man Jesus ("the Jesus of history") was presented in the Gospel sources. For early believers (as for mainstream Christians since) the contrary case would be, and is still, asserted: that it was the nature and actions of the man Jesus that underpins all that came later in expressing understanding concerning him.

Perhaps it is best to end on the question that Jesus himself posed to his closest companions, in the vicinity of Caesarea Philippi: "Who do people say that I am?" (Mark 8:27). We will leave readers to decide for themselves…

About the authors

Esther Whittock read Theology and Religious Studies at Jesus College, University of Cambridge, where she graduated with a First Class degree. She specialized in Christianity and biblical studies, focusing in her third year on Christology in the New Testament, the theology and composition of the Gospel of John, and the way that Christ and the Bible is understood in Indian and African cultures. She also has an MA in Educational Leadership.

She is currently a secondary school teacher of Religious Studies at Heart of England School in the West Midlands; and previously she taught in an inner city secondary school in Birmingham.

She is the co-author of *Christ: The First 2000 Years* (2016), *The Story of the Cross* (2021), and *Daughters of Eve* (2021); all with Lion Hudson.

Martyn Whittock graduated in Politics from Bristol University in 1980. He taught history for thirty-five years and latterly was curriculum leader for Spiritual, Moral, Social, and Cultural education at a Wiltshire secondary school. He is a Licensed Lay Minister in the Church of England. He has acted as a historical consultant to the National Trust and English Heritage. He retired from teaching in 2016 to devote more time to writing.

He is the author or co-author of fifty-two books, including school history textbooks and adult history books. The latter include: *A Brief History Of Life in the Middle Ages* (2009), *A Brief History of the Third Reich* (2011), *A Brief Guide To Celtic Myths and Legends* (2013), *The Viking Blitzkrieg AD 789–1098* (2013), *The Anglo-Saxon Avon Valley Frontier* (2014), *1016 and 1066: Why The Vikings Caused The Norman Conquest* (2016), *Norse Myths and Legends* (2017), *When God Was King* (2018), *The Vikings: from Odin to Christ* (2018), *Mayflower Lives* (2019), *Trump and the Puritans* (2020), and *The Secret History of Soviet Russia's Police State* (2020).

Also co-written with his daughter, Esther, are *Christ: The First 2000 Years*, *The Story of the Cross*, and *Daughters of Eve*.

References

Chapter 1. A conversation of many "voices"

1 All dates are given in the AD system of Christian dating, which attempts to date events from the birth of Jesus, unless differentiated by BC after the number. Whether this dating system is accurate we will explore in Chapter 3.

2 For more on this see Metzger, B., *The Canon Of The New Testament: Its Origin, Significance & Development* (Oxford: Clarendon Press, 1987); Hill, C. E., "The Debate Over the Muratorian Fragment and the Development of the Canon", *Westminster Theological Journal*, 57:2, Autumn 1995, pp. 437–52.

3 Hixson, E., "Despite Disappointing Some, New Mark Manuscript Is Earliest Yet", *Christianity Today*, 30 May 2018; Wallace, D. B., "The Textual Basis of New Testament Translation", *The Evangelical Parallel New Testament* (Oxford: Oxford University Press, 2003), p. xxiii, gives 5,600 extant Greek manuscripts.

4 See https://www.library.manchester.ac.uk/search-resources/special-collections/guide-to-special-collections/st-john-fragment/what-is-the-significance/ (accessed October 2019). Recent research has suggested a date a little later, toward 200.

5 See http://www.csntm.org/About/Projects/Chester-Beatty-Library (accessed October 2019).

6 Koester, H., *History and Literature of Early Christianity*, vol. 2, second ed. (Berlin: Walter de Gruyter, 2000), p. 7.

7 Goodacre M., "Gospel Dates", *Bible Odyssey*, http://www.bibleodyssey.com/tools/video-gallery/g/gospel-dates (accessed November 2019). Bible Odyssey provides an accessible online academic resource, with contributions by scholars from across the theological spectrum, geared to the student and the general user. It is produced by the Society of Biblical Literature, which promotes the academic study of the Bible and of sacred texts generally.

8 Murphy, F. J., *An Introduction to Jesus and the Gospels* (Nashville TE: Abingdon Press, 2005), p. 292.

9 Murphy, F. J., *An Introduction to Jesus and the Gospels*, p. 292.

10 Eusebius, *Hist. Eccl.*, 3.39.16.

11 For example: Koester, H., *Ancient Christian Gospels: Their History and Development* (London: Bloomsbury, 1990), pp. 316–17. See also Koester, H., *History and Literature of Early Christianity*, p. 207. This rejection of a Hebrew origin for the Gospel of Matthew is widespread among modern experts.

12 Whittock, M., Whittock, E., *Christ: The First 2000 Years* (Oxford: Lion Hudson, 2016), pp. 40–55.

13 Mournet, T. C., *Oral Tradition and Literary Dependency: Variability and Stability in the Synoptic Tradition and Q* (Heidelberg: Mohr Siebeck, 2005), p. 119.

14 All Bible quotations, unless otherwise stated, are from *The Holy Bible, New Revised Standard Version (Anglicised Edition)*, published by Oxford University Press, 1995. Where quotations refer to, for example, John 1:1 this means John, chapter 1, verse 1. An excellent online way to access this and other translations can be found at https://www.biblegateway.com/ which we have found very useful.

15 Other examples in Paul's writings include: 1 Corinthians 7:10, "the wife should not separate from her husband", and 1 Corinthians 9:14, "those who proclaim the gospel should get their living by the gospel".

16 Heine, R.E., *Reading the Old Testament with the Ancient Church* (Grand Rapids MI: Baker Academic, 2007), p. 34.

17 Nelson, R., "The Beginner's Guide to the Gnostic Gospels", https://overviewbible.com/gnostic-gospels/ provides a succinct and accessible overview (accessed November 2019).

18 Van Voorst, R., *Jesus Outside the New Testament: An Introduction to the Ancient Evidence* (Grand Rapids MI: Wm. B. Eerdmans Publishing, 2000), p. 189.

19 Gospel of Thomas, 82, quoted in Van Voorst, R., *Jesus Outside the New Testament: An Introduction to the Ancient Evidence*, p. 182.

20 A brief overview of this "Gospel" and its issues can be found at: Skinner, M., "Why Isn't the Gospel of Thomas in the Bible?" http://www.enterthebible.org/blog.aspx?m=3783&post=779 (accessed November 2019).

21 Tuckett, C., *The Gospel of Mary* (Oxford: Oxford University Press, 2007). A controversial translation and presentation of this manuscript (which is rejected by mainline Christians) is: Leloup, J. Y., *The Gospel of Mary Magdalene* (London: Simon and Schuster, 2002).

22 *The Greatest Story Ever Told* being the title of a 1965 US film about Jesus of Nazareth, produced and directed by George Stevens and distributed by United Artists.

Chapter 2. Back-story...

1 See https://www.vox.com/a/maps-explain-the-middle-east (accessed November 2019).

2 The name Israel was used to describe the tribes descended from the

patriarch Jacob (who was also known as Israel) and then the kingdom of Israel which emerged, uniting them. This kingdom name came to be synonymous with the name Judah, before eventually being replaced by it. In the modern era the area name Israel was first used widely during the British Mandate. The official name in English was "Mandate for Palestine". However, on official documents, written in Hebrew, the name also included the initials for *Eretz Yisrael*.

3 It is sometimes used in a wider geographical sense, which also incorporates the whole eastern Mediterranean running from Greece to Cyrenaica in eastern Libya.

4 Ajami, F., *The Struggle for Mastery in the Fertile Crescent* (Stanford CA: Hoover Institution Press, 2014).

5 The name first appears in the fifth-century BC writings of the Greek historian Herodotus to describe the coastal area of the Levant. The Romans later applied it to a much larger area following the defeat of the Bar Kokhba Revolt (AD 132).

6 Pritchard, J. B. (ed.), *The Times Atlas of the Bible* (London: Times Books, 1987), p. 135.

7 Josephus, *Antiquities of the Jews*, 13.9.1. This account was written in the later first century AD.

8 According to the Roman historian Cassius Dio, *Roman History*, book 49.

9 According to the Roman historian Plutarch, in his *Life of Antony*; and the Jewish historian Josephus in *Antiquities of the Jews*, 15.1:2 (8–9).

10 Esbus, Herod took by force from the Nabateans.

11 Hippus and Gadara, east of the Sea of Galilee.

12 Eyal, R., *The Hasmoneans: Ideology, Archaeology, Identity* (Göttingen: Vandenhoeck & Ruprecht, 2013), p. 190.

13 Eyal, R., *The Hasmoneans: Ideology, Archaeology, Identity*, p. 190.

14 Pritchard, J. B. (ed.), *The Times Atlas of the Bible*, p. 148.

15 Cult, here and elsewhere in this book is used in its technical sense of a system of religious belief and practice.

16 Doudna, G., in D. Stacey, G. Doudna, *Qumran Revisited: A Reassessment of the Archaeology of the Site and its Texts, BAR international series, 2520* (Oxford: Archaeopress, 2013), pp. 95–107.

17 For an overview of Qumran and some of the issues relating to its interpretation (not necessarily in agreement with the overview here) see Magness, J., *The Archaeology of Qumran and the Dead Sea Scrolls* (Grand Rapids MI: Wm. B. Eerdmans, 2003).

18 For example: Mishnah, *Ma'aser Sheni* 5:15 and *Sotah* 9:10; Babylonian Talmud, *Berakhot* 29a; Jerusalem Talmud, *Ma'aser Sheni* 5:5. The Talmud is an edited and abbreviated record of rabbinic discussion that occurred over a period of around 300 years (starting c. AD 200) discussing the edited version of the Mishnah. This itself was a record produced during earlier discussions (that had occurred over around 200 years) concerning how to follow the Torah in practice. As a result, both documents (as they now survive) contain older and later material concerning Jewish traditional teaching and commentary.

Chapter 3. "O little town of Bethlehem"

1 Aramaic *Miriam* or *Miryam*, Joseph's name would have been *Yosef*.

2 It is possible that we now underestimate the potential rivalry between emerging Christianity and the "John the Baptist movement" which ran on into the middle of the first century and beyond. Acts 18:25 and 19:1–7 refer to disciples of John active long after his death and the third-century documents known as the *Pseudo-Clementine Recognitions* and *Pseudo-Clementine Homilies* record garbled traditions suggesting the continuation of, what is termed, a sect of "daily baptizers" after the death of John the Baptist. It may also explain the emphasis in John 3:30 on "He [Jesus] must increase, but I [John the Baptist] must decrease" in a Gospel written perhaps as late as the 90s and conscious of continued competition between the two groups of followers. See Kelly, J. F., *The Birth of Jesus According to the Gospels* (Collegeville MN: Liturgical Press, 2008), pp. 16–17.

3 The Gospel of John recounts perhaps four adult visits by Jesus to Jerusalem.

4 Kelly, J. F., *The Birth of Jesus According to the Gospels*, p. 43, briefly outlines some of the questions raised by these two contrasting birth narratives in Matthew and Luke.

5 A point well made by Kelly, J.F., *The Birth of Jesus According to the Gospels*, p. 5. He, revealingly, quotes the experience of the Irish biblical scholar Wilfrid Harrington in this respect.

6 AH being used in the West from the Latin: *Anno Hegirae* (in the year of the *Hijra*). Dates before this being identified as BH (Before the *Hijra*). In Muslim countries, it is sometimes denoted simply as 'H'.

7 Szalay, J., "Who Invented Zero?", *Live Science*, 18 September 2017, https://www.livescience.com/27853-who-invented-zero.html (accessed December 2019).

8 Josephus, *Antiquities of the Jews*, 18.26. See also Dąbrowa, E., "The Date of the Census of Quirinius and the Chronology of the Governors of the Province of Syria", *Zeitschrift für Papyrologie und Epigraphik*, 178, (Bonn:

Dr. Rudolf Habelt Ltd, 2011), pp. 137–142.

9 Kelly, J. F., *The Birth of Jesus According to the Gospels*, p. 83.

10 Kidger, M., *The Star of Bethlehem* (Princeton NJ: Princeton University Press, 1999), p. 54.

11 McClymond, M. J., *Familiar Stranger: An Introduction to Jesus of Nazareth* (Grand Rapids MI: Wm. B. Eerdmans, 2004), p. 155, note 7.

12 A matter made more complex by the apparent appearance of a year-long ministry in the synoptic gospels and a three-year-long one in John's Gospel.

13 A succinct and accessible discussion of this can be found at Gilad, E., "If You Think Jesus Was Born in the Year 0 You're Dead Wrong", *Haaretz*, 23 December 2016, https://www.haaretz.com/science-and-health/.premium-if-you-think-jesus-was-born-in-the-year-0-you-re-dead-wrong-1.5477068 (accessed December 2019).

14 Though missing from some manuscripts of Mark, this statement is present in the best attested of them.

15 Gooding, D., *According to Luke* (Leicester: IVP, 1987), pp. 38–39.

16 Allen, G. V., Akagi, K., Sloan, P., Nevader, M. (eds.), *Son of God: Divine Sonship in Jewish and Christian Antiquity* (University Park, PA: Pennsylvania State University Press, 2019).

17 Kelly, J. F., *The Birth of Jesus According to the Gospels*, pp. 30–32.

18 Schäfer, P., *Jesus in the Talmud* (Princeton NJ: Princeton University Press, 2007), p. 10.

19 Schäfer, P., *Jesus in the Talmud*, p. 123.

20 Schäfer, P., *Jesus in the Talmud*, p. 24.

21 Morris, L., *Tyndale New Testament Commentaries: Luke* (Leicester: IVP, 1974), p. 67.

22 1 Samuel 16:1.

23 Read-Heimerdinger, J., Rius-Camps, J., *Luke's Demonstration to Theophilus: The Gospel and the Acts of the Apostles According to Codex Bezae* (London: Bloomsbury T&T Clark, 2015), p. 336, note 20.

24 Justin Martyr, *Dialogue with Trypho*, 78.

25 Singman, J. L., *Daily Life in Medieval Europe* (Westport CT: Greenwood, 1999), p. 21.

26 Morris, L., *Tyndale New Testament Commentaries: Luke*, pp. 84–85.

27 Read-Heimerdinger, J., Rius-Camps, J., *Luke's Demonstration to Theophilus: The Gospel and the Acts of the Apostles According to Codex Bezae*, p. 336, notes 18, 20.

28 Molnar, M. R., "The Historical Basis for the Star of Bethlehem", in van Kooten, G. H., Barthel, P. (eds.), *The Star of Bethlehem and the Magi: Interdisciplinary Perspectives from Experts on the Ancient Near East, the Greco-Roman World, and Modern Astronomy* (Leiden: Brill, 2015), pp. 19, 23, figure 2.2.

29 Lawrence, P., *The Lion Concise Atlas of Bible History* (Oxford: Lion Hudson, 2012), p. 134.

30 Fenton, J. C., *Saint Matthew* (Harmondsworth: Penguin Books, 1963), pp. 44–45.

31 Molnar, M. R., "The Historical Basis for the Star of Bethlehem", p. 30.

32 Fenton, J. C., *Saint Matthew*, p. 46.

33 Molnar, M. R., *The Star of Bethlehem: The Legacy of the Magi* (New Brunswick NJ: Rutgers University Press, 1999).

34 Moore, P., "December 25, The Star of Bethlehem", *The Observer's Year: 366 Nights in the Universe* (London: Springer, 2005), p. 345.

35 Lawrence, P., *The Lion Concise Atlas of Bible History*, p. 135.

36 Though by the Roman era we do not know if contemporary magi still followed the tenets of Zoroastrianism.

37 Kelly, J. F., *The Birth of Jesus According to the Gospels*, p. 49.

38 Ptolemy, *Tetrabiblos*, 2.6.

39 Geminus, *Introduction to the Phenomena*, Manitius, C. (trans.) (Leipzig: Teubner, 1898).

40 Collins, D., *The Star of Bethlehem* (Stroud: Amberley, 2012).

41 Dąbrowa, E., "The Date of the Census of Quirinius and the Chronology of the Governors of the Province of Syria", pp. 137–42.

Chapter 4. Growing up in "Galilee of the Gentiles"

1 Howell Toy, C., Torrey, C. C., "Judith, Book of", http://jewishencyclopedia.com/articles/9073-judith-book-of (accessed January 2020).

2 Flavius Josephus, *Life of Josephus*, trans. Mason, S. (Leiden: Brill, 2003), Appendix A.

3 See https://www.etymonline.com/word/galilee (accessed January 2020).

4 Flavius Josephus, *Life of Josephus*, p. 235. Explored in detail in Flavius Josephus, *Life of Josephus*, trans. Mason, S., p. 181.

5 Flavius Josephus, *Life of Josephus*, p. 181.

6 For more on this controversial possibility see Crossan, J. D., Reed, J. L.,

Excavating Jesus: Beneath the Stones, Beneath the Texts (San Francisco CA: HarperSanFrancisco, 2001).

7 Josephus, *Antiquities of the Jews*, 18.2.1; *The Jewish War*, 2.9.1, 4.10.7; *The Life of Josephus*, 72.

8 See https://www.bibleplaces.com/sepphoris/ (accessed January 2020).

9 An accessible overview of the evidence from Sepphoris can be found at: Strange, J. F., "Sepphoris was the 'ornament of all Galilee'", September 2001, https://www.bibleinterp.com/articles/sepphoris.shtml (accessed January 2020).

10 Levick, B., "Messages on the Roman Coinage", in Paul, G. M., Ierardi, M. (eds.), *Roman Coins and Public Life Under the Empire: E. Togo Salmon Papers II* (Ann Arbor MI: University of Michigan Press, 1999), pp. 49–50.

11 Strange, J. F., "Sepphoris was the 'ornament of all Galilee'".

12 Taylor, J., "7 Differences Between Galilee and Judea in the Time of Jesus", 17 August 2011, outlining points made by Professor R. T. France, in his commentary on *The Gospel of Matthew* (Grand Rapids MI: Wm. B. Eerdmans, 2007), https://www.thegospelcoalition.org/blogs/justin-taylor/7-differences-between-galilee-and-judea-in-the-time-of-jesus/ (accessed January 2020).

13 Strange, J. F., "Sepphoris was the 'ornament of all Galilee'".

14 Flavius Josephus, *Life of Josephus*, p. 199. See also Charlesworth, J. H., Aviam, M., "Reconstructing First-Century Galilee: Reflections on Ten Major Problems", in Charlesworth, J. H. and Rhea. B. (eds.), *Jesus Research: New Methodologies and Perceptions – The Second Princeton-Prague Symposium on Jesus Research, Princeton 2007* (Grand Rapids MI: Wm. B. Eerdmans, 2014), pp. 130–31, on the strong case for the deep Jewishness of Galilee and of Jesus and his mission.

15 Flavius Josephus, *Life of Josephus*, p. 199.

16 For this suggestion see Cromhout, M., "Were the Galileans 'religious Jews' or 'ethnic Judeans'?", *Hervormde Teologiese Studies* 64/3 (2008), pp. 1279–297.

17 For an overview of these arguments see Deines, R., "Jesus the Galilean: Questioning the Function of Galilee in Recent Jesus Research", in Ochs, C., Watts, P. (eds.), *Acts of God in History: Studies Towards Recovering a Theological Historiography* (Tübingen: Mohr Siebeck, 2013), p. 63.

18 Wallace, D. H., "Nazarene," in Bromiley, G. W. (gen. ed.), *The International Standard Bible Encyclopedia, volume III: K–P* (Grand Rapids MI: Wm. B. Eerdmans, 1986) (revised ed.), pp. 499–500.

19 Eusebius, *Church History*, 1.7.14.

20 Wallace, D. H., "Nazarene", p. 500.

21 Tertullian, *Against Marcion*, 4.8.

22 Krauss, S., "NAZARENES", http://www.jewishencyclopedia.com/articles/11393-nazarenes (accessed January 2020).

23 Wallace, D. H., "Nazarene", p. 500.

24 Abdul-Raof, H., T*ext Linguistics of Qur'anic Discourse: An Analysis*, (London: Routledge, 2018).

25 Butler, T. C., "NAZARETH, NAZARENE – Place name meaning, 'branch'", *Holman Bible Dictionary* (Nashville TN, Broadman & Holman, reprint ed.,1991).

26 Monette, G., *The Wrong Jesus: Fact, Belief, Legend, Truth… Making Sense of What You've Heard* (Carol Stream IL: NavPress & Tyndale House, 2014), pp. 99–100.

27 Huyck, J., *From Home to Home, Finding Meaning in Mobility* (Little Rock, AR: Liturgical Press, 2018), p. 30.

28 Monette, G., *The Wrong Jesus: Fact, Belief, Legend, Truth… Making Sense of What You've Heard*, p. 100.

29 Charlesworth, J. H, Aviam, M., "Reconstructing First-Century Galilee: Reflections on Ten Major Problems", pp. 115–16.

30 Douglas, J. D., Hillyer, N., Bruce, F. F., *New Bible Dictionary* (Leicester: Inter-Varsity Press, 1990), p. 746.

31 Smith, A. W., "'And Did Those Feet...?': The 'Legend' of Christ's Visit to Britain", *Folklore*, 100.1 (1989), pp. 63–83.

32 Lane, W. L., *The Gospel of Mark* (Grand Rapids MI: Wm. B. Eerdmans, 1974), pp. 201–02.

33 Nineham, D. E., *Saint Mark* (Harmondsworth: Penguin, 1969), p. 166.

34 Lane, W. L., *The Gospel of Mark*, p. 202.

35 Isbouts, J.-P., "How Jesus's childhood influenced the Gospels", *National Geographic*, https://www.nationalgeographic.com/culture/people-in-the-bible/jesus-precocious-childhood-influenced-gospel/ (accessed January 2020).

36 See https://www.bibleodyssey.org/en/people/main-articles/infancy-gospel-of-thomas (accessed January 2020).

Chapter 5. "A voice crying in the wilderness"

1 Article on "Mandaeans", O*xford Dictionary of the Christian Church* (Oxford: Oxford University Press, 2005).

2 Kelly, J. F., *The Birth of Jesus According to the Gospels*, pp. 16–17.

3 A Christian pilgrim (the German archdeacon Theodosius, in *De situ terrae sanctae*), who visited the Holy Land c. 518–530, noted the belief that the family home was five miles from Jerusalem, which would fit the traditional location at Ein Karem.

4 Kazmierski, C. R., *John the Baptist: Prophet and Evangelist* (Collegeville MN: Liturgical Press, 1996), p. 31.

5 Brown, R. E., *The Virginal Conception and Bodily Resurrection of Jesus* (Mahwah NJ: Paulist Press, 1973), p. 54

6 Vermes, G., *The Nativity: History & Legend* (London: Penguin, 2006), p. 143.

7 Freed, E. D., *The Stories of Jesus' Birth: A Critical Introduction* (London & New York: Continuum International, 2001), pp. 87–90.

8 Wink, W., "John the Baptist" in Metzger, B. M., Coogan, M. D. (eds.), *The Oxford Companion to the Bible* (Oxford: Oxford University Press, 1993), p. 371.

9 Ngo, R., "Baptismal Site 'Bethany Beyond the Jordan' Added to UNESCO World Heritage List", 29 September 2018, https://www.biblicalarchaeology.org/daily/news/baptismal-site-bethany-beyond-the-jordan-added-to-unesco-world-heritage-list/ (accessed February 2020).

10 Although, it should be noted, for Qumran the wilderness was the location for doing the preparation, whereas for John the wilderness was only the place from which the "voice" would cry out. There is no hint in his teaching of a wilderness location for the community of those striving to escape the impending judgment coming on the world.

11 Wink, W., "John the Baptist", p. 372.

12 Which may not even have occurred in the first century AD. See Wink, W., "John the Baptist", p. 372.

13 Charlesworth, J. H., "John the Baptizer and Qumran", https://www.bibleodyssey.org/en/passages/related-articles/john-the-baptizer-and-qumran (accessed February 2020).

14 *Sanhedrin* 29c.

15 Walsh, M., *Roots of Christianity* (London: Grafton Books, 1986), p. 46.

16 Although it should be noted that he is referred to ninety times in the New Testament. The number of references, to anyone other than Jesus himself, is exceeded only by references to Peter and Paul.

17 Joseph, S, J., *Jesus, Q, and the Dead Sea Scrolls: A Judaic Approach to Q* (Tübingen: Mohr Siebeck, 2012), p. 147.

18 Walsh, M., *Roots of Christianity*, p. 46.

19 Crossan, J. D., *God and Empire* (London: HarperCollins, 2007), p. 117 ff.

Chapter 6. "The kingdom of heaven is at hand"

1 Köstenberger, A. J., Kellum, L. S., Quarles, C. L., *The Cradle, the Cross, and the Crown: An Introduction to the New Testament* (Nashville TN: B&H Academic, 2009), p. 140; Maier, P. L., "The Date of the Nativity and Chronology of Jesus" in Vardaman, J., Yamauchi, E. M. (eds.), *Chronos, Kairos, Christos: Nativity and Chronological Studies Presented to Jack Finegan* (Winona Lake IN: Eisenbrauns, 1989), pp. 113–29.

2 The three synoptic gospels refer to just one Passover, specifically the Passover at the end of Jesus' ministry when he is crucified. The Gospel of John refers to two actual Passovers, one at the beginning of Jesus' ministry and the second at the end of his ministry. There is a third reference to Passover that many claim is a third actual festival, but may be a forecasting of the second Passover. This third reference to a Passover in the Gospel of John is why many suggest that Jesus' ministry was a period of about three years. See Köstenberger, A. J., Kellum, L. S., Quarles, C. L., *The Cradle, the Cross, and the Crown*, pp. 141–43; Blomberg, C. L., *Jesus and the Gospels: An Introduction and Survey* (Nashville TN: B&H Academic, 2009), pp. 224–29.

3 Sloyan, G. S., *John* (Louisville KY: Westminster John Knox Press, 2009), p. 11

4 Josephus, *Antiquities of the Jews*, 18, 5.2.

5 Throckmorton, B. H. (ed.), *Gospel Parallels: A Comparison of the Synoptic Gospels* (Nashville TN: Thomas Nelson, 1992), p. 14.

6 Justin Martyr, *Dialogue with Trypho*, 88, 3.

7 Morris, L., *Tyndale New Testament Commentaries: Luke* (Leicester: IVP, 1974), p. 99.

8 Nineham, D. E., *Saint Mark* (Harmondsworth: Penguin, 1969), p. 61.

9 Morris, L., *Tyndale New Testament Commentaries: Luke*, p. 99.

10 Justin Martyr, *Dialogue with Trypho*, 88, 103.

11 Rodgers, P. R., *Text and Story: Narrative Studies in New Testament Textual Criticism* (Eugene OR: Pickwick Publications, 2011), p. 24.

12 Ehrman, B. D., *Misquoting Jesus: The Story Behind Who Changed the Bible and Why* (London: Harper Collins, 2005), pp. 158–61. The wide ranging and challenging approach found in this particular book is not followed in this study, but we accept that the evidence regarding these particular verses provokes some debate as to the original form.

13 Ehrman, B. D., *The Orthodox Corruption of Scripture: The Effect of Early Christological Controversies on the Text of the New Testament* (Oxford: Oxford University Press, 2011), pp. 62–67, note 12.

14 Rodgers, P. R., *Text and Story*, pp. 22–30, on this verse in particular, as well as the issue generally.

15 Mark 9:7; Matthew 17:5; Luke 9:35.

16 Rodgers, P. R., *Text and Story*, p. 27.

17 Ellis, E. E., "How the New Testament Uses the Old", in Marshall, I. H. (ed.), *New Testament Interpretation* (Eugene OR: Wipf & Stock, 2006 [reprint]), pp. 199–219.

18 Rodgers, P. R., *Text and Story*, p. 28.

19 Pennington, J., "Why Did Jesus Need to Be Baptized?", *The Gospel Coalition*, Bible & Theology, May 2019, https://www.thegospelcoalition.org/article/jesus-need-baptized/ (accessed February 2020).

20 Marsh, J., *Saint John* (Harmondsworth: Penguin, 1968), p. 193. Some other commentators have gone so far as suggesting that the episode in John 3:22–30 could be placed at a different point earlier in John's Gospel (placed after 2:12 has been suggested). But the better explanation regarding chronology is probably that it was not a pressing issue to the compiler(s) of John's Gospel.

21 Barrett, C. K, *The Gospel According to John* (London: SPCK, 1978), p. 230.

22 Chilton, B. D., "Kingdom of God", in *The Oxford Companion to the Bible* (Oxford: Oxford University Press, 1993), p. 408.

23 Chilton, B. D., "Kingdom of God", p. 409.

24 Vine, W. E., Unger, M. F., White, W. (eds.), *Vine's Complete Expository Dictionary of Old and New Testament Words* (Nashville TN, Camden, New York: Thomas Nelson, 1985), p. 525.

25 Reed, J. L., *Archaeology and the Galilean Jesus: A Reexamination of the Evidence* (Harrisburg PA: Trinity Press International, 2000), p. 152.

26 Laughlin, J. C. H., "Capernaum: From Jesus' Time and After", *Biblical Archaeology Review* 19:5, September/October 1993, https://www.baslibrary.org/biblical-archaeology-review/19/5/10 (accessed February 2020).

Chapter 7. A band of brothers

1 For a detailed study of the relationship between Jesus and his disciples in the Gospel of John, see Köstenberger, A. J., *The Missions of Jesus and the Disciples According to the Fourth Gospel: With Implications for the Fourth Gospel's Purpose and the Mission of the Contemporary Church* (Grand Rapids MI: Wm. B. Eerdmans, 1998).

2 Overman, J. A., "Disciple", in *The Oxford Companion to the Bible* (Oxford: Oxford University Press, 1993), p. 168.

3 Overman, J. A., "Disciple", pp. 168–69.

4 See footnote b, https://www.biblegateway.com/passage/?search=Luke+9%3A51-6&version=NRSVA (accessed February 2020).

5 Meier, J. P., *Marginal Jew* (London: Doubleday, 1994).

6 Under Roman rule, direct forms of taxes were added to existing local ones. So, the tax burden in Roman-administered Judea is likely to have been even heavier than the situation in Galilee. See Udoh, F. E., *To Caesar What Is Caesar's: Tribute, Taxes, and Imperial Administration in Early Roman Palestine (63 B.C.E. – 70 C.E.)* (Providence RI: Brown Judaic Studies, 2005).

7 Root, B. W., *First Century Galilee: A Fresh Examination of the Sources* (Tübingen: Mohr Siebeck, 2014), p. 22. For an overview of the matter see pp. 22–25.

8 Josephus, *Antiquities of the Jews*, 17.205. This refers to taxation in Judea under Herod Archelaus, but it is likely that similar taxes were levied in Galilee under Herod Antipas.

9 Root, B. W., *First Century Galilee: A Fresh Examination of the Sources*, p. 24.

10 English, D., *The Message of Mark* (Leicester: Inter-Varsity Press, 1992), regarding Mark 6:30–44.

11 English, D., *The Message of Mark*.

12 Betz, O., "Apostle", in *The Oxford Companion to the Bible* (Oxford: Oxford University Press, 1993), p. 42.

13 Betz, O., "Apostle", p. 42.

14 France, R. T., *The Gospel According to Matthew: An Introduction and Commentary* (Grand Rapids MI: Wm. B. Eerdmans, 1985), p. 177.

15 Betz, O., "Apostle", p. 42.

16 MacArthur, J. F., *The MacArthur Bible Commentary* (Nashville TN: Thomas Nelson, 2005), p. 1206, provides a useful table of the different order of the Twelve (eleven in Acts) and name variants found in the synoptic gospels and in Acts.

17 France, R. T., *The Gospel According to Matthew: An Introduction and Commentary*, p. 177.

18 Carrington, P., *The Early Christian Church: Volume 1, The First Christian Church* (Cambridge: Cambridge University Press, 2011), p. 77.

19 Carrington, P., *The Early Christian Church*, p. 33.

Chapter 8. A band of... sisters

1 Bailey, K. E., "Women in the New Testament: A Middle Eastern Cultural View", *Theology Matters*, Jan/Feb 2000.

2 Stott, J. R. W., *The Message of Romans* (Leicester: Inter-Varsity Press, 1994), p. 396.

3 Morris, M., *The Epistle to the Romans* (Grand Rapids MI: Wm. B. Eerdmans & Leicester: Inter-Varsity Press, 1988), p. 533.

4 Morris, M., *The Epistle to the Romans*, p. 534. See also Stott, J. R. W., *The Message of Romans*, p. 396.

5 Stagg, F., Stagg, E., *Woman in the World of Jesus* (Louisville KN: Westminster John Knox Press, 1978).

6 Bilezikian, G., *Beyond Sex Roles: What the Bible Says about a Woman's Place in Church and Family* (Grand Rapids MI: Baker, 1989), p. 82.

7 Freedman, D. N. (ed.), *Eerdmans Dictionary of the Bible* (Grand Rapids MI: Wm. B. Eerdmans, 2000), p. 865.

8 Freedman, D. N. (ed.), *Eerdmans Dictionary of the Bible*, p. 864.

9 See also Mark 14:1–9 and Matthew 26:6–13 (who do not name her, but the host is named as "Simon the Leper"). In all these accounts, the disciples/some present/Judas, criticize her for her extravagance.

10 See a version of this passage in: *The Gospel According to Philip* (Oregon House CA: The Petrarch Press, 2006). For other structuring of these quotes see the same passage quoted in: Swidler, L. J., *Jesus was a Feminist: What the Gospels Reveal about His Revolutionary Perspective* (Lanham MD: Rowman & Littlefield, 2007), p. 93.

11 See http://www.biblewise.com/bible_study/apocrypha/gospel-philip.php (accessed February 2018).

12 Jones, K. J., *The Women in the Gospel of John: the Divine Feminine* (Atlanta GA: Chalice Press), 2008.

13 *Gospel of Thomas*, 114:2–3, https://www.biblicalarchaeology.org/daily/biblical-topics/bible-versions-and-translations/the-gospel-of-thomas-114-sayings-of-jesus/ (accessed March 2020).

14 For more on this document see Wiener, N., "A 'Gospel of Jesus' Wife' on a Coptic Papyrus", *Biblical Archaeology*, 19 September 2012, https://www.biblicalarchaeology.org/daily/news/a-gospel-of-jesus-wife-on-a-coptic-papyrus/ (accessed March 2020).

15 *The Gospel of Mary*, see the excerpt at https://www.pbs.org/wgbh/pages/frontline/shows/religion/maps/primary/mary.html (accessed March 2020).

16 For an accessible introduction to this text see http://www.earlychristianwritings.com/pistis.html (accessed March 2020).

17 Professor Joan Taylor, from King's College London, in conversation with Michael Collett, "The story of Jesus has been told by men for men – but it's not just about men", 9 September 2019, https://www.abc.net.au/news/2019-09-10/the-story-of-jesus-isnt-just-about-men/11481632 (accessed March 2020). Professor Taylor is co-host with Professor Helen Bond of the documentary *Jesus' Female Disciples: The New Evidence*, Minerva Media, Channel Four, 8 April 2018. For more information see CSCO, New College, University of Edinburgh, https://www.christianorigins.div.ed.ac.uk/2018/04/08/jesus-female-disciples-the-new-evidence-minerva-media-channel-four/ (accessed August 2020).

18 For an exploration of this conundrum see Munro, M., "Women disciples in Mark?", *The Catholic Biblical Quarterly*, vol. 44, no. 2 (April 1982), pp. 225–41.

19 Professor Joan Taylor, in conversation with Michael Collett, "The story of Jesus has been told by men for men – but it's not just about men".

Chapter 9. The "good news": what exactly was it?

1 Wright, N. T., *Jesus and the Victory of God* (London: SPCK, 1996 [reissued 2015]), p. 147.

2 The visible remains at the most famous of these, at Capernaum, almost certainly date from the second to third century or later. However, excavation under the prayer hall of the synagogue has uncovered structures (including a well-paved floor and the basalt foundation of the western wall) which date from the time of Jesus. "Capernaum-City of Jesus and its Jewish Synagogue", 26 November 2003, *Israeli Ministry of Foreign Affairs*, https://mfa.gov.il/mfa/israelexperience/history/pages/capernaum%20-%20city%20of%20jesus%20and%20its%20jewish%20synagogue.aspx (accessed August 2020).

3 Wright, N. T., *Jesus and the Victory of God*, pp. 166–67.

4 Wright, N. T., *Jesus and the Victory of God*, p. 162.

5 Safrai, S., "Religion in Everday Life", in Safrai, S., Stern, M. (eds.), *The Jewish People in the First Century*, vol. 2 (Philadelphia: Fortress Press, 1976), p. 800 f.

6 Each time this appears in the New Testament it is accompanied by the Greek for "father", hence "Abba Father": Mark 14:36; Romans 8:15; Galatians 4:6.

7 Wright, N. T., *Jesus and the Victory of God*, p. 149, note 9.

8 Barr, J., "Abba isn't 'Daddy'", *Journal of Theological Studies*, vol. 39, 1988, pp. 28–47.

9 Jeremias, J., *New Testament Theology*, Bowden, J. (trans.) (London: SCM Press, 1971), p. 67.

10 Schelbert, G., *ABBA Vater* (Göttingen: Vandenhoeck & Ruprecht, 2011); Vermes, G., *Jesus and the World of Judaism* (Philadelphia PA: Fortress Press, 1983), p. 42; Barr, J., "Abba isn't 'Daddy'", pp. 28–47, note 8.

11 For an accessible overview of the debate see Stanton, G. T., "FactChecker: Does 'Abba' Mean 'Daddy'?" *The Gospel Coalition*, Bible & Theology, 13 May 2013, https://www.thegospelcoalition.org/article/factchecker-does-abba-mean-daddy/ (accessed April 2020).

12 Good, D., "Jesus and Abba", *Episcopal Café*, 27 October 2011, https://www.episcopalcafe.com/jesus_and_abba/ (accessed April 2020).

13 Barr, J., "Abba isn't 'Daddy'", p. 46.

14 Babylonian Talmud.

15 Van Voorst, R., *Jesus Outside the New Testament: An Introduction to the Ancient Evidence* (Grand Rapids MI: Wm. B. Eerdmans Publishing, 2000), pp. 93–95. The passage in question is: *Antiquities of the Jews* 18.3.3. It is sometimes called the *Testimonium Flavianum*.

16 Wright, N. T., *Jesus and the Victory of God*, p. 149.

17 Luke's version of this statement, or a similar one, is even sharper: "Whoever comes to me and does not hate father and mother, wife and children, brothers and sisters, yes, and even life itself, cannot be my disciple" (Luke 14:26).

18 This would accelerate from the second century AD onward, following the destruction of the Temple, the failure of nationalist uprisings, and the increasing prominence of rabbinic promulgation of Torah-piety.

19 Webb, R. L., *John the Baptizer and Prophet: A Socio-Historical Study*, JSNTSS vol. 62 (Sheffield: Sheffield Academic Press, 1991), chapter 9.

20 Josephus, *Antiquities of the Jews*, 20.97–98, 169–72; *The Jewish War*, 2.261–63, 6.286–8, 300–09.

Chapter 10. "Broods of vipers" or "stalwarts of national life"?

1 Josephus, *Antiquities of the Jews*, 17.42.

2 Freeman, T., "What Is Torah? A Comprehensive Overview", *Chabad*, https://www.chabad.org/library/article_cdo/aid/1426382/jewish/Torah.htm (accessed April 2020).

3 "The Torah", https://www.myjewishlearning.com/article/the-torah/ (accessed April 2020).

4 Surviving as the Jerusalem Talmud and the Babylonian Talmud.

5 As appearing in the New Revised Standard Version.

6 Sanders, E. P., *Judaism: Practice and Belief, 63BCE – 66CE* (London: SCM, 1992), modified his earlier thoughts on this. See also Davies, W. D., Allison, D. C., *A Critical and Exegetical Commentary on the Gospel According to Saint Matthew*, 2 vols. (Edinburgh: T&T Clark, 1988–1991).

7 Riches, J. K., *Jesus and the Transformation of Judaism* (London: Darton, Longman & Todd, 1980), pp. 130–35, 142–44, 166 f.

8 Riches, J. K., *Jesus and the Transformation of Judaism*, p. 133.

9 Riches, J. K., *Jesus and the Transformation of Judaism*, p. 187.

10 Borg, M. J., *Conflict, Holiness and Politics in the Teachings of Jesus* (New York/Toronto: The Edwin Mellen Press), 1984.

11 See b. *Sanhedrin* 107b and b. *Sotah* 47a in Van Voorst, R. E., *Jesus Outside the New Testament* (Grand Rapids MI: Wm B. Eerdmans, 2000), p. 112.

12 Wright, N. T., *Jesus and the Victory of God*, pp. 376–77.

13 Wright, N. T., *Jesus and the Victory of God*, pp. 376–77.

14 Borg, M. J., *Conflict, Holiness and Politics in the Teachings of Jesus*; N. T. Wright, *Jesus and the Victory of God*, p. 93.

15 Rivkin, E., *What Crucified Jesus?* (London: SCM, 1984), pp. 96–99.

16 Rivkin, E., *What Crucified Jesus?*, p. 44.

17 *Sanhedrin*, 17b.

18 See https://www.jewishvirtuallibrary.org/scribe, source: *Encyclopaedia Judaica*, 2008, The Gale Group (accessed April 2020).

19 "Scribes and Pharisees", Britannica, https://www.britannica.com/biography/Jesus/Scribes-and-Pharisees (accessed April 2020).

20 As with the Pharisees, the five that are not found in the Gospels appear in the Acts of the Apostles.

21 Josephus, *Antiquities of the Jews*, 13.10.5–6.

22 Satlow, M. L., "Who Were the Sadducees?", Bible Odyssey, https://www.bibleodyssey.org/en/people/related-articles/sadducees.aspx (accessed April 2020)

23 Josephus, *The Antiquities of the Jews*, 13.297, (trans. William Whiston, 1737), Lexundria, https://lexundria.com/j_aj/13.297/wst (accessed April 2020).

24 Josephus, *The Jewish War*, 2.427.

25 Wright, N. T., *Jesus and the Victory of God*, p. 435.

26 Leviticus 21:1–3 forbade contact with corpses except those of close family.

27 Stökl, J., "Priests and Levites in the First Century C.E.", Bibleo Odyssey, https://www.bibleodyssey.org/passages/related-articles/priests-and-levites-in-the-first-century-ce (accessed April 2020).

28 Josephus, *Against Apion*, 2.108.

29 Sanders, E. P., *The Historical Figure of Jesus* (London: Allen Lane, 1993), p. 41.

30 Sanders, E. P., *The Historical Figure of Jesus*, p. 42.

31 Sanders, E. P., *Jesus and Judaism* (Philadelphia PA: Fortress Press), 1985, pp. 309–18.

32 Wright, N. T., *Jesus and the Victory of God*, p. 94.

33 Wright, N. T., *Jesus and the Victory of God*, p. 317.

34 Wright, N. T., *Jesus and the Victory of God*, p. 132.

Chapter 11. Escalating crisis

1 Sanders, E. P., *The Historical Figure of Jesus* (London: Allen Lane, 1993), p. 130.

2 Sanders, E. P., *The Historical Figure of Jesus*, p. 130.

3 Gundry, R., *Mark: A Commentary on His Apology for the Cross, Chapters 9–16* (Grand Rapids MI: Wm. B. Eerdmans, 2000), p. 696, on this "reintroduction".

4 Sanders, E. P., *The Historical Figure of Jesus*, p. 131.

5 Keener, C. S., *The Historical Jesus of the Gospels* (Grand Rapids MI: Wm. B. Eerdmans, 2012), p. 229.

6 Sanders, E. P., *The Historical Figure of Jesus*, pp. 212–18.

7 Sanders, E. P., *The Historical Figure of Jesus*, pp. 217–18, 220, 223.

8 Osborne, G. R., "Structure and Christology in Mark 1:21–45", in Green, J. B., Turner, M. (eds.), *Jesus of Nazareth Lord and Christ: Essays on the Historical Jesus And New Testament Christology* (Grand Rapids MI: Wm. B. Eerdmans, 1994), p. 163, highlights this area of Jesus' spiritual authority as described in the Gospels.

9 Wright, N. T., *Jesus and the Victory of God*, pp. 434–35.

10 To consider this in the context of interpretations concerning his later action in the Temple see Neville, D. J., *The Vehement Jesus: Grappling with Troubling Gospel Texts* (Eugene OR: Cascade Books, 2017), p. 155.

11 Wright, N. T. *Jesus and the Victory of God*, p. 435.

12 Regev, E., *The Temple in Early Christianity: Experiencing the Sacred* (New Haven, CT: Yale University Press, 2019), examines the relationship between early Christianity and the Temple.

13 Wright, N. T., *Jesus and the Victory of God*, p. 436.

14 Wright, N. T., *Jesus and the Victory of God*, p. 435.

15 And the furthest north we know of Jesus travelling on his preaching missions, with the possible exception of the vicinity of Tyre and Sidon (Matthew 15:21).

16 Luke adds that, at the time, his disciples did not understand what he meant (Luke 18:34).

17 Sanders, E. P., *The Historical Figure of Jesus*, pp. 268–69.

Chapter 12. Enter the Romans

1 BBC History, "Augustus (63 BC – AD 14)", 2014, *BBC*, https://www.bbc.co.uk/history/historic_figures/augustus.shtml (accessed April 2020).

2 BBC History, "Augustus (63 BC – AD 14)".

3 Horsley, R. A., "Jesus and Empire," in: Horsley, R. A. (ed.), *In The Shadow of Empire: Reclaiming the Bible as a History of Faithful Resistance* (Louisville KY: Westminster John Knox Press, 2008), p. 79.

4 Horsley, R. A., "Jesus and Empire", p. 81.

5 Philo, *Embassy to Gaius*, paragraphs 299 and 304.

6 Bond, H. K., *Pontius Pilate in History and Interpretation* (Cambridge: Cambridge University Press, 1998), p. 46.

7 Josephus, *The Jewish War*, 2.9.2 and *Antiquities of the Jews*, 18.3.1.

8 Josephus, *The Jewish War*, 2.9.4 and *Antiquities of the Jews*, 18.3.2.

9 Bond, H. K., *Pontius Pilate in History and Interpretation*, p. 89.

10 This was a tradition known to Matthew and Luke but apparently not to Mark.

11 Manning Jr., G., "Soldiers in the Gospels", *The Good Book Blog*, Talbot School of Theology, 2011, https://www.biola.edu/blogs/good-book-blog/2011/soldiers-in-the-gospels (accessed April 2020).

12 Horsley, R. A., "Jesus and Empire", pp. 23–24.

13 Green, J. B., "The Gospel of Luke", in: Fee, G. D., (ed.), *The New International Commentary on the New Testament* (Grand Rapids MI: Wm. B. Eerdmans, 1997), pp. 715–16. See also Horsley, R. A., *Jesus and Empire: The*

Kingdom of God and the New World Disorder (Minneapolis, MN: Fortress Press, 2002), p. 99.

14 Horsley, R. A., "Jesus and Empire", p. 90.

15 Wright, N. T., "God and Caesar, Then and Now", N. T. Wright, http://www.ntwrightpage.com/Wright_God_Caesar.pdf (accessed April 2020).

16 For a thought-provoking examination of this – and its implications for the twenty-first-century Christian church (explicitly in the USA), see Willems, K., "The Roman Empire During the Time of Jesus (Background of Luke's Gospel)", 8 April 2017, *Theology Curator*, https://theologycurator.com/roman-empire-during-time-jesus/#_ftn23 (accessed April 2020).

17 Rowland, C., *Radical Christianity* (Cambridge: Polity, 1988), p. 17.

18 Rowland, C., *Radical Christianity.*

19 Aslan, R., *Zealot: The Life and Times of Jesus of Nazareth* (London: Saqi, 2013), EBL ebooks online.

20 Aslan, R., *Zealot: The Life and Times of Jesus of Nazareth.*

21 Cline, A., "Profile and Biography of Judas Iscariot," 2019, *Learn Religions*, https://www.learnreligions.com/judas-iscariot-profile-and-biography-248814 (accessed April 2020).

22 Horsley, R. A., "Jesus and Empire", pp. 23–24.

23 Green, J. B., *The Gospel of Luke* (Grand Rapids MI: Wm. B. Eerdmans), pp. 122–23. See also McKnight, S., Modica, J. B. (eds.), "Introduction" in *Jesus Is Lord, Caesar Is Not: Evaluating Empire in New Testament Studies* (Downers Grove IL: Inter-Varsity Press, 2013), pp. 16–18.

24 McIntyre, G., *Imperial Cult* (Leiden: Brill, 2019), pp. 1–3.

25 Nystrom, D., "We have no King but Caesar: Roman Imperial Ideology and the Imperial Cult", in McKnight, S., Modica, J. B. (eds.), *Jesus Is Lord, Caesar Is Not*, pp. 33–35.

26 Heen, E. M., "Phil 2:6–11, And Resistance to Local Timocratic Rule", in Horsley, R. A. (ed.), *Paul and the Roman Imperial Order* (Harrisburg PA: TPI, 2004), p. 144.

27 Barclay, J. M. G., *Pauline Churches and Diaspora Jews* (Tübingen: Mohr Siebeck, 2011), p. 351.

28 Crossan, J. D., "Roman Imperial Theology", in Horsley, R. A. (ed.), *In The Shadow of Empire*, p. 66.

29 Nystrom, D., "We have no King but Caesar. Roman Imperial Ideology and the Imperial Cult", p. 33.

30 Wright, N. T., *Paul: Fresh Perspectives* (Minneapolis, MN: Fortress Press, 2005), pp. 64–65.

31 Crossan, J. D., "Roman Imperial Theology", p. 61.

32 Crossan, J. D., "Roman Imperial Theology", p. 61.

33 Walsh, B. J., *Colossians Remixed: Subverting the Empire* (Downers Grove IL: Inter-Varsity Press, 2004), pp. 69–70.

34 Cassidy, R. J., *Christians and Roman Rule in the New Testament: New Perspectives* (New York: Crossroad, 2001), p. 20.

35 Horsley, R. A., "Jesus and Empire", p. 82.

36 Hinkle Shore, M., *Was Jesus a threat to the Roman Empire? Enter the Bible*, Luther Seminary's Bible Q&A, Bible Question, 2013, http://www.enterthebible.org/blog.aspx?post=2496 (accessed April 2020).

37 Horsley, R. A., "Jesus and Empire", p. 88.

38 Horsley, R. A., "Jesus and Empire", p. 88.

Chapter 13. "Tell no one..." A secret messiah?

1 Wright, N. T., *Jesus and the Victory of God*, p. 479.

2 Dunn, J., *Christology in the Making* (London: SCM, 1989), p. 24.

3 Wright, N. T., *Jesus and the Victory of God*, p. 479.

4 Dunn, J., *Christology in the Making*, pp. 25–26.

5 The theological term "Christology" is used to describe Christian beliefs about Jesus. They are faith statements about his status, nature, and character.

6 Theissen, G., Merz, A., *The Historical Jesus* (London: SCM, 1998), p. 520.

7 Rowland, C., *Christian Origins* (London: SPCK, 1985), p. 174.

8 Rowland, C., *Christian Origins*, p. 174.

9 Wright, N. T., *Jesus and the Victory of God*, p. 166.

10 Or "to set Israel free". Both expressions imply a messianic hope consistent with Old Testament belief in a future God-sent ruler empowered to liberate Israel and bring in an age of restoration and peace.

11 Vermes, G., *Jesus the Jew* (London: SCM, 1973), p. 129.

12 Theissen, G., Merz, A., *The Historical Jesus*, p. 459.

13 Rowland, C., *Christian Origins*, p. 177.

14 Wright, N. T., *Jesus and the Victory of God*, p. 488.

15 Vermes, G., *Jesus the Jew*, p. 152.

16 Rowland, C., *Christian Origins*, p. 181.

17 Wright, N. T., *Jesus and the Victory of God*, p. 507.

18 Theissen, G., Merz, A., *The Historical Jesus*, p. 516.

19 Burkett. D., *The Son of Man Debate* (Cambridge: Cambridge University Press, 1999), p. 23.

20 Dunn, J., *Christology in the Making*, p. 95.

21 Burkett, D., *The Son of Man Debate*, p. 185.

22 Burkett, D., *The Son of Man Debate*, p. 185.

23 Vermes, G., *Jesus the Jew*, p. 123.

24 Theissen, G., Merz, A., *The Historical Jesus*, p. 563.

25 Dunn, J., *Christology in the Making*, p. 17.

26 Vermes, G., *Jesus the Jew*, p. 192.

27 Elwell, W. A. "Transfiguration", *Evangelical Dictionary of Theology*, 1997, Bible Study Tools, https://www.biblestudytools.com/dictionary/transfiguration/ (accessed April 2020).

28 Elwell, W. A. "Transfiguration".

29 Elwell, W. A. "Transfiguration".

30 Eisenstein, D., "Blasphemy", *Jewish Virtual Library*, A Project of AICE, https://www.jewishvirtuallibrary.org/blasphemy (accessed April 2020).

Chapter 14. "O Jerusalem..."

1 Olsen, T., "The Life & Times of Jesus of Nazareth: Did You Know?" *Christianity Today*, https://www.christianitytoday.com/history/issues/issue-59/life-times-of-jesus-of-nazareth-did-you-know.html (accessed May 2020).

2 Shanks, H., "Ancient Jerusalem: The Village, the Town, the City", *Biblical Archaeology*, 14 January 2020, https://www.biblicalarchaeology.org/daily/biblical-sites-places/jerusalem/ancient-jerusalem/ (accessed May 2020).

3 Pliny the Elder, *Natural History*, 5.70.

4 For an examination of Herod's building work at the Temple, see Netzer, E., *The Architecture of Herod, the Great Builder* (Grand Rapids MI: Baker Academic, 2008), Chapter 7, "The Rebuilding of the Second Temple and its Precinct" .

5 Grabbe, L. L., *An Introduction to Second Temple Judaism: History and Religion of the Jews in the Time of Nehemiah, the Maccabees, Hillel, and Jesus* (London: T&T Clark, 2010), pp. 40–41.

6 Josephus, *The Jewish War*, 2.44, *Antiquities of the Jews*, 15.268 and 17.254–55.

7 Chancey, M. A., "Jerusalem in the New Testament Period", *Bible Odyssey*, https://www.bibleodyssey.org/en/places/related-articles/jerusalem-in-the-new-testament-period (accessed May 2020).

8 Curtis, A., *Oxford Bible Atlas* (Oxford: Oxford University Press [4 ed.], 2007).

9 Vanelderen, B., "Praetorium", in Bromiley, G. W. (ed.), *The International Standard Bible Encyclopedia* (Grand Rapids MI: Wm. B. Eerdmans, 1995), p. 929.

10 For example Bible Gateway: https:/ www.biblegateway.com/quicksearch/?qs_version=NRSVA&quicksearch=Jerusalem&startnumber=1&begin=47&end=73 (accessed May 2020).

11 Paul, I., "How many times did Jesus visit Jerusalem?", *Psephizo*, 24 April 2014, https://www.psephizo.com/biblical-studies/how-many-times-did-jesus-visit-jerusalem/ (accessed May 2020).

12 For an examination of the question see Anderson, P. N., *The Riddles of the Fourth Gospel: An Introduction to John* (Minneapolis MN: Fortress Press, 2011), pp. 4–5.

13 Paul, I., "How many times did Jesus visit Jerusalem?".

14 Chaffey, T., "When Did Jesus Cleanse the Temple?", in Chaffey, T., Ham, K., Hodge, B. (eds.), *Demolishing Supposed Bible Contradictions Volume 2: Exploring Forty Alleged Contradictions* (Green Forest AR: Master Books, 2012), p. 130.

15 See Walker, P. W., *Jesus and the Holy City: New Testament Perspectives on Jerusalem* (Grand Rapids MI: Wm. B. Eerdmans, 1996), p. 163.

16 Barclay, W. (ed.), *The Gospel of John, Volume 2* (Louisville KN: Westminster John Knox Press, 1975), p. 126.

17 For a criticism of this way of approaching the evidence see Evans, C. A., *Jesus and His Contemporaries: Comparative Studies* (Leiden: Brill, 1995), p. 320.

18 Sanders, E. P., *Jesus and Judaism* (Philadelphia PA: Fortress Press, 1985), pp. 61–76.

19 For an examination of this apocalyptic view of Jesus' outlook see Ehrman, B. D., *Jesus: Apocalyptic Prophet of the New Millennium* (Oxford, Oxford University Press, 1999).

20 Evans, C. A., *Jesus and His Contemporaries: Comparative Studies*, p. 342. See generally pp. 342–44.

21 Horsley, R. A., *Jesus and the Spiral of Violence* (Minneapolis MN: Fortress Press, 1993), p. 287.

22 Horsely, R. A., Hanson, J. S., *Bandits, Prophets, and Messiahs: Popular*

Movements at the Time of Jesus (Harrisburg PA: Trinity Press, 1999), p. 234.

23 Wright, N. T., *Jesus and the Victory of God*, p. 317.

Chapter 15. From Palm Sunday to the Last Supper

1 According to the Gospel of John (though it may possibly have been the Friday immediately after Passover if the calendrical information in the synoptic gospels is preferred).

2 Humphreys, C. J., Waddington, W. G., "The Jewish Calendar, a Lunar Eclipse and the Date of Christ's Crucifixion," *Tyndale Bulletin* 43.2 (1992), pp. 331–51, https://legacy.tyndalehouse.com/tynbul/Library/TynBull_1992_43_2_06_Humphreys_DateChristsCrucifixion.pdf (accessed June 2020). See also Akin, J., "7 Clues Tell Us *Precisely* When Jesus Died (the Year, Month, Day, and Hour Revealed)", 10 April 2020, https://www.ncregister.com/blog/jimmy-akin/when-precisely-did-jesus-die-the-year-month-day-and-hour-revealed (accessed June 2020), which concludes with the same precise date.

3 For an accessible outline of the Jewish names of the week and their place within Jewish traditions see https://www.ivritalk.com/2018/12/12/hebrew-days-of-the-week/ (accessed June 2020).

4 A view exemplified in *Jesus Christ Superstar*, songwriters Andrew Lloyd Webber/Tim Rice, in the song "Heaven On Their Minds" lyrics © Universal Music Publishing Group, 1970.

5 A number of studies have been made of this document. One of these examinations of the so-called *Gospel of Judas* is: Ehrman, B., *The Lost Gospel of Judas Iscariot: A New Look at Betrayer and Betrayed* (Oxford: Oxford University Press, 2006).

6 Schweitzer, A., *The Quest of the Historical Jesus: A Critical Study of its Progress from Reimarus to Wrede* (London: SCM Press Ltd, 1954), pp. 368–69.

7 Licona, M. R., *Why are There Differences in the Gospels?: What We Can Learn from Ancient Biography* (Oxford: Oxford University Press, 2017), pp. 155–56.

8 A helpful overview of these possible explanations can be found in Licona, M. R., *Why are There Differences in the Gospels?*, pp. 162–163.

9 Morris, L., *1 Corinthians, Tyndale New Testament Commentaries* (Leicester: Inter-Varsity Press, 1985 [revised ed.]), p. 31.

10 For example: Cline, A., "Gospel Contradictions of the Last Supper", *Learn Religions*, 11 February 2020, learnreligions.com/last-supper-contradictions-in-the-gospel-250143 (accessed June 2020).

11 Menken, M. J. J., "John 6, 51c-58: Eucharist or Christology?", *Biblica*: vol.74 (Rome: Gregorian Biblical Bookshop, 1993), p. 24, suggests that John's wording at 6:51 ("the bread that I will give for the life of the world is my flesh") represents the words of Eucharistic institution. However, John was more interested in Christology than church practice.

12 Kodell, J., *The Eucharist in the New Testament*, Chapter 9, "The Eucharist of John" (Collegeville MN: Liturgical Press, 2017), asserts that Jesus' multiplication of the loaves, his teaching on the bread of life and his teaching on the vine, were all vehicles for Eucharistic teaching to a community familiar with the rite.

13 Morris, L., *The Gospel According to John, Revised Edition* (Grand Rapids MI: Wm. B. Eerdmans Publishing, 1995), p. 542.

Chapter 16. Messiah on trial...

1 Pruitt, S., "Why Jesus Was Betrayed by Judas Iscariot", *History*, 2020, https://www.history.com/news/why-judas-betrayed-jesus (accessed May 2020).

2 Notably: Klassen, W., *Judas: Betrayer Or Friend of Jesus?* (London: SCM Press, 1996).

3 For the overall interpretation see Klassen, W., *Judas: Betrayer Or Friend of Jesus?*

4 "The Passion, Judas", *BBC*, 2014, http://www.bbc.co.uk/thepassion/articles/judas.shtml (accessed May 2020).

5 Pruitt, S., "Why Jesus Was Betrayed by Judas Iscariot".

6 "How much might Judas' 30 pieces of silver be worth today?", *Catholicsay* https://catholicsay.com/how-much-might-judas-30-pieces-of-silver-be-worth-today/ (accessed May 2020).

7 Pruitt, S., "Why Jesus Was Betrayed by Judas Iscariot".

8 Pruitt, S., "Why Jesus Was Betrayed by Judas Iscariot".

9 Rowland, C. C., *Christian Origins: An Account of the Character and Setting of the Most Important Messianic Sect of Judaism* (London: SPCK, 1985), p. 166.

10 Itself written at a time of the parting of the ways with Judaism and the persecution of Jewish Christians by some members of the contemporary Jewish community.

11 Horsley, R. A., "The Death of Jesus", in Chilton, B., Evans, C. (eds.), *Studying the Historical Jesus* (Leiden: Brill, 1994), p. 395.

12 Wingo, E. L., *The Illegal Trial of Jesus* (Ontario: Chick Publications, 2011), p. 92.

13 *Sanhedrin*, 6.1.

14 Chandler, W. M., *The Trial of Jesus from a Lawyer's Standpoint*, Volume 1 (New York: The Empire Publishing Company, 2018), p. 183.

15 Chandler, W. M., *The Trial of Jesus from a Lawyer's Standpoint*, p. 184.

16 Theissen, G., Merz, A., *The Historical Jesus: A Comprehensive Guide* (Minneapolis MN: Fortress Press, 1998), p. 435.

17 Theissen, G., Merz, A., *The Historical Jesus*, p. 463.

18 Sanders, E. P., *The Historical Figure of Jesus* (London: Allen Lane, 1993), p. 271.

19 "Blasphemy", Jewish Virtual Library, A Project of AICE, Eisenstein, Dinim, 68, https://www.jewishvirtuallibrary.org/blasphemy (accessed May 2020).

20 Bornkamm in Horsley, R. A., "The Death of Jesus", p. 400.

21 Horsley, R. A., "The Death of Jesus", p. 415.

22 Sanders, E. P., *The Historical Figure of Jesus* (London: Allen Lane, 1993), p. 264.

23 Sanders, E. P., *The Historical Figure of Jesus*, p. 267.

24 Rowland, C. C., *Christian Origins*, p. 167.

25 Schneider, G., "The political charge against Jesus (Luke 23.3)", in Bammel, E., Moule, C. F. D. (eds.), *Jesus and the Politics of his Day* (Cambridge: Cambridge University Press, 1984), p. 403.

26 Hinkle Shore, M., "Was Jesus a threat to the Roman Empire?", *Enter the Bible*, Luther Seminary's Bible Q&A, Bible Question, 2013, http://www.enterthebible.org/blog.aspx?post=2496 (accessed May 2020).

27 Sanders, E. P., *The Historical Figure of Jesus*, p. 268.

28 Horsley, R. A., "The Death of Jesus", p. 402.

29 Grundmann, W., "The decision of the Supreme Court to put Jesus to death in its context: tradition and redaction in the Gospel of John", in Bammel, E., Moule, C. F. D (eds.), *Jesus and the Politics of his Day*, p. 296.

30 Van Voorst, R., *Jesus Outside the New Testament: An Introduction to the Ancient Evidence* (Grand Rapids MI: Wm. B. Eerdmans Publishing, 2000), pp. 29–39.

31 Horsley, R. A., "The Death of Jesus", pp. 396–99.

Chapter 17. The death of Jesus

1 Tzaferis, V., "Crucifixion—The Archaeological Evidence", *Biblical Archaeology*, http://www.biblicalarchaeology.org/daily/ biblical-topics/ crucifixion/a-tomb-in-jerusalem-reveals-the-history-of-crucifixion-and-roman-crucifixion-methods/ (accessed August 2020). See also Tzaferis, V., "Jewish Tombs at and near Giv'at ha-Mivtar, Jerusalem", *Israel Exploration Journal*, 20/1, 2, 1970, pp. 18–32; Haas, N., "Anthropological Observations on the Skeletal Remains from Giv'at ha-Mivtar", *Israel Exploration Journal*, 20/1, 2 (1970), pp. 38–59; and Naveh, J., "The Ossuary Inscriptions from Giv'at ha-Mivtar", *Israel Exploration Journal*, 20/1, 2, 1970, pp. 33–37. For a different hypothesis as to the position of Yehohanan on the cross see Yadin, Y., "Epigraphy and Crucifixion", *Israel Exploration Journal*, 23, 1973, pp. 18–22.

2 Zias, J., Sekeles, E., "The Crucified Man from Giv'at ha-Mivtar: A Reappraisal", *Israel Exploration Journal*, 35, 1985, pp. 22–27.

3 Evans, C., "The Family Buried Together Stays Together: On the Burial of the Executed in Family Tombs", in Evans, C. (ed.), *The World of Jesus and the Early Church: Identity and Interpretation in Early Communities of Faith* (Peabody MA: Hendrickson, 2011), p. 92.

4 Friedman, M., "In a stone box, the only trace of crucifixion", *The Times of Israel*, 26 March 2012, http://www.timesofisrael.com/in-a-stone-box-a-rare-trace-of-crucifixion/ (accessed August 2020).

5 Römer, F., *P. Corneli Taciti, Annalium Libri, XV–XVI*, Wiener Studien 6, Böhlaus, Vienna, 1976, pp. 65–67.

6 Holmén, T., Porter, S. E. (eds.), *Handbook for the Study of the Historical Jesus*, Volume 1 (Leiden: Brill, 2010), pp. 2155–159.

7 Van Voorst, R., *Jesus Outside the New Testament*, pp. 83–104, examines various interpretations, before concluding in favour of the authenticity of Josephus's account regarding Jesus' death, as found in *Antiquities of the Jews*, 18.3.3, 63–64 (as well as the other reference to "Jesus called Christ", in Josephus's account of the execution of James, found in *Antiquities of the Jews*, 20.9.1, 200).

8 Tombs, D., "Prisoner Abuse: From Abu Ghraib to The Passion of the Christ", in Hogan, L., Lehrke, D. (eds.), *Religion and the Politics of Peace and Conflict* (Eugene OR: Wipf and Stock, 2009), p. 191, note 61 on John 20:25.

9 Acts 12:7.

10 Van Voorst, R., *Jesus Outside the New Testament*, pp. 20–23. If so, this oblique comment constitutes the earliest surviving written reference to a Jesus-tradition (earlier even than the writing of the synoptic gospels).

11 Tasker, R. V. G., *Tyndale New Testament Commentaries, The Gospel according to St. Matthew* (Leicester: Inter-Varsity Press, 1961), p. 266.

12 Tasker, R. V. G., *Tyndale New Testament Commentaries, The Gospel according to St. Matthew*, p. 267.

13 Fenton, J. C., *The Pelican New Testament Commentaries, The Gospel of St. Matthew* (London: Cox & Wyman, 1963), p. 444

14 Fenton, J. C., *The Pelican New Testament Commentaries, The Gospel of St. Matthew*, p. 444.

15 Rutledge, F., *The Crucifixion: Understanding the Death of Jesus Christ* (Grand Rapids MI: Wm. B. Eerdmans, 2017), p. 41.

16 The original is in (crude) Greek letters: Αλεξαμενος ⊠εβετε θεον.

17 Holden, J. M., Geisler, N., *The Popular Handbook of Archaeology and the Bible* (Eugene OR: Harvest House, 2013), p. 309; see also Bauckham, R., *Jesus and the God of Israel: God Crucified and Other Essays on the New Testament's Christology of Divine Identity* (Milton Keynes: Paternoster, 2008).

18 Evans, C. A. (ed.), *The Historical Jesus, Volume 4* (London, New York: Routledge, 2004), p. 387

19 Van Voorst, R., *Jesus Outside the New Testament*, p. 63.

20 Chapman, D. W., "The Crucifixion in Paul", *Bible Odyssey*, https://www.bibleodyssey.org:443/people/related-articles/the-crucifixion-in-paul (accessed July 2020).

Chapter 18. "On the third day"

1 See *Anglicans Online*, 2017, http://www.anglicansonline.org/basics/nicene.html (accessed July 2020).

2 For an exploration of the socially radical significance of the women witnesses to the resurrection, as seen in the Gospel of Mark, see Witherington, B., *The Gospel of Mark: A Socio-Rhetorical Commentary* (Grand Rapids MI: Wm. B. Eerdmans, 2001), p. 401.

3 Warner, J., "How many women visited the tomb of Jesus?", *Cold Case Christianity*, 11 December 2017, https://coldcasechristianity.com/writings/how-many-women-visited-the-tomb-of-jesus/ (accessed July 2020).

4 Warner, J., "How many women visited the tomb of Jesus?"

5 Warner, J., "How many women visited the tomb of Jesus?". See also Taylor, J. E., *Introducing Apologetics: Cultivating Christian Commitment* (Grand Rapids MI: Baker Academic, 2006), p. 206, who makes a similar point.

6 Osborne, K., *The Resurrection of Jesus: New Considerations for Its Theological Interpretation* (Eugene OR: Wipf & Stock, 2004), p. 30.

7 An interesting exploration of Matthew's account being designed to counter an accusation encountered in Antioch c. 70 can be found in: Osborne, K., *The Resurrection of Jesus: New Considerations for Its Theological Interpretation*, pp. 52–53.

8 For an accessible overview of various alternative theories for the empty tomb, and their rejection in favour of the traditional Christian account see Taylor, J. E., *Introducing Apologetics: Cultivating Christian Commitment* (Grand Rapids MI: Baker Academic, 2006), pp. 206–08.

9 For a debate regarding the authenticity, or otherwise, of the final section of this Gospel (Mark 16:9–20) see Black, D. A. (ed.) et al, *Perspectives on the Ending of Mark: Four Views* (Nashville TN: B&H Publishing Group, 2008).

10 "Gospel Mysteries, The Ending of Mark", *Gospel Mysteries*, http://www.gospel-mysteries.net/ending-mark.html, (accessed July 2020).

11 Tabor, J., "The "Strange" Ending of the Gospel of Mark and Why It Makes All the Difference", *Biblical Archaeology Society*, 1 April 2018, https://www.biblicalarchaeology.org/daily/biblical-topics/new-testament/the-strange-ending-of-the-gospel-of-mark-and-why-it-makes-all-the-difference/ (accessed July 2020).

12 Dummelow, J. R., *A Commentary on the Holy Bible* (New York: MacMillan, 1927), pp. 732 –33.

13 Shanks, M. A., *Papias and the New Testament* (Eugene OR: Wipf & Stock, 2013), p. 153.

14 Juel, D. H., "A Disquieting Silence", in Roberts Gaventa, B., Miller, P. D. (eds.), *The Ending of Mark and the Ends of God: Essays in Memory of Donald Harrisville Juel* (Louisville KY: Westminster John Knox Press, 2005), p. 11.

15 Benson, J., *Commentary on the Old and New Testaments* (New York: T. Carlton & J. Porter, 1857), commenting on Luke 24:36–49.

16 Sanders, E. P., *The Historical Figure of Jesus* (London: Allen Lane, 1993), p. 277.

17 For a reflection on the dramatic effect of the Easter faith on early Christianity see Bond, H. K., *The Historical Jesus: A Guide for the Perplexed* (London: Bloomsbury, 2012), p. 174.

18 Dodd C. H., *The Apostolic Preaching and Its Developments* (London: Hodder, 1936), p. 20.

19 Dunn, J. D. G., *Unity and Diversity in the New Testament: An Enquiry into the Character of Earliest Christianity* (London: SCM, 1977), p. 17.

20 Peterson, D., *The Acts of the Apostles* (Grand Rapids MI: Wm. B. Eerdmans, 2009), p. 78.

21 Sanders, E. P., *The Historical Figure of Jesus*, p. 277.

22 Bond, H. K., *The Historical Jesus: A Guide for the Perplexed*, p. 174.

Index